THE

MIRACLE

Y·E·A·R

Also by Lanie Carter

Congratulations! You're Going to Be a Grandmother

THE
MIRACLE
Y·E·A·R

*An Expectant Parents' Guide
to the Miraculous Six Months
Before—and After—
the Birth of Their First Baby*

LANIE CARTER
with Lauren Simon Ostrow

POCKET BOOKS
New York   London   Toronto   Sydney   Tokyo   Singapore

This book is intended to inform and advise the reader of probable experiences and encounters as well as to suggest avenues of comfort during the pregnancy, birth, and first few months as a new mother. The author of this book is not a doctor and this book is not intended to replace the advice of a trained health professional. If you know of or suspect a health problem, you should contact a health professional. The author and publishers disclaim any liability arising directly or indirectly from the use of this book.

POCKET BOOKS, a division of Simon & Schuster
1230 Avenue of the Americas, New York, NY 10020

Carter, Lanie.
    The miracle year : an expectant parents' guide to the miraculous
six months before—and after—the birth of their first baby /
[Lanie Carter].
    p.   cm.
Includes bibliographical references.
ISBN 0-671-70433-8.
1. Pregnancy. 2. Childbirth. 3. Infants—Care. I. Title.
RG525.C357   1991
618.2′4—dc20   90-49929
                                                                     CIP

First Pocket Books hardcover printing April 1991

10 9 8 7 6 5 4 3 2 1

POCKET and colophon are registered trademarks of
Simon & Schuster

Printed in the U.S.A.

The authors gratefully acknowledge the permission to publish the following excerpts: on pp. 14–15, from *Infants and Mothers, Differences in Development* (revised edition), by T. Berry Brazelton, M.D., published by Delacorte Press/ Seymour Lawrence, a Division of Bantam, Doubleday, Dell Publishing Group, Inc.

Permission to quote Dr. Paul Pearsall from *The Power of the Family* is kindly granted by Doubleday, a Division of Bantam, Doubleday, Dell Publishing Group, Inc.

Permission to quote from *The New Parent Advisor*, copyright © 1990, is kindly granted by Whittle Communications L.P.

ACKNOWLEDGMENTS

A great many people helped us to complete this book. We would like to thank all of them. First, this book would not have been possible without the contributions of our two medical consultants: pediatrician Joseph Pennario, M.D., and obstetrician Allan Silver, M.D. Their expert input and meticulous review of the manuscript were invaluable. We also would like to thank our editor, Leslie Wells, and our agent, Sandra Dijkstra, and her staff for guiding us through the publication forest and for sharing our enthusiasm for the project. A very special thanks to the administration and staff of Scripps Memorial Hospital for their support of the professional grandmother program, and especially to Ginger Walborn, R.N.C., Charge Nurse, Labor and Delivery; Mary Ellen Manley, R.N., Charge Nurse, Nursery; Linda Prior, B.S.N., Lactation Specialist; Betsy Wilber, R.N.; Christine Harvey, R.N.; Lawrence Eisenhauer, M.D.;

Laura Nathanson, M.D.; Sarita Eastman, M.D.; Dierdre Elliot, M.D.; and Karen Lee, M.D. We also want to acknowledge Marianne Engle, Ph.D., and Audrey Teren Phillips, M.S., and all the parents who delivered at Scripps Memorial for sharing their feelings and concerns about the emotional challenges of parenthood. Thank you to Cindy Polger, Patti Gentes, Bill Keane, North County OB-GYN Medical Group, and the many obstetricians and pediatricians affiliated with Scripps Memorial who have been so supportive. Most of all, we thank our families for giving us the gift that lasts a lifetime.

—L.C. and L.S.O.

CONTENTS

PREFACE

I began working with Lanie Carter on *The Miracle Year* in April of 1989 when I was four months pregnant with my first child. Despite Lanie's insistence at the time that, as an expectant mother, I was about to embark upon the most miraculous year of my life, I did not feel that way.

Certainly I was thrilled to be pregnant and to have come through the critical first three months relatively unscathed. I relished my visits to the obstetrician when I heard my baby's heartbeat pounding its reassuring, primal rhythm on the Doppler stethoscope. Fantastic, yes; miracle, no. My belly grew bigger and our manuscript grew thicker throughout the summer. I was shocked by the weight of both; but neither was the blessed event I had anticipated.

When my daughter, Charlotte Rose, was born and placed in her father's arms for the very first time, the miracle began to take form. I could see bits and pieces of it like stars in a clear night sky, but I couldn't make out the constellation. As Charlotte grew, I saw it in her smile, sniffed it on the back of her neck, felt it in my husband's embrace as we lay with our daughter between us. It was not until Charlotte was six months old and our miracle year was over, however, that the brilliance of Lanie's promise revealed itself completely. When your miracle year comes full circle, you, too, will understand. It is impossible for me to fully describe the miracle of creation. In the meantime, you will need all the help you can get, because, although they are filled with excitement and wonder, the six months before birth and the first six months of your baby's life can sap your strength and your spirit.

During this year, you will need guideposts to show you the way. Extended families once served this purpose, as they do now for those of us lucky enough to live near our parents, aunts, uncles, and grandparents. Cloning Lanie Carter would be the next best thing, but we are limited by the bounds of modern science.

It is because all new parents need someone to hold their hands that we decided to write *The Miracle Year*. It is my hope that through *The Miracle Year*, each of you can take home a piece of Lanie as your own and that she can guide you through your pregnancy and the months following childbirth with wit, wisdom, and the nurturing spirit for which she is so loved. Lanie Carter is the world's most comforting security blanket.

—LAUREN SIMON OSTROW

INTRODUCTION

As an expectant parent, you have signed on for the most important job in the world. Not only will you be your child's chef, laundress, chauffeur, bather, dresser, baby-sitter, playmate, hand-holder, dishwasher, teacher, and protector, you will also be the standard on which the child models his or her life. Your baby will create himself or herself in your image.

Considering the immense responsibility that accompanies having and raising a baby, you might think that you could sign up for some sort of preparation course for it, such as those available for college exams. Yet there is no formal training for parenthood.

I have no plans to endow a University of Mommies and Daddies, but I do believe that you can educate yourselves and prepare yourselves for parenthood. I help young people do just that in my role as a "professional grandmother."

At Scripps Memorial Hospital in La Jolla, California, I teach young people before and after their babies are born about everything from buying baby equipment to finding the right pediatrician to preparing for the changes in their relationships that come with parenthood. I do not venture opinions on health and illness because I have no medical training. However, the questions that expectant and new parents ask me rarely require medical answers. They are questions young people would ask their own grandmothers. They are questions that some doctors are too busy to field. They are questions that new parents are embarrassed to ask anyone else for fear that their concerns are trivial or silly.

After thirteen years on the job, I have "grandmothered" more than 20,000 babies and have answered more than 100,000 calls for help on what has become a twenty-four-hour "warm line" for expectant and new parents. No call is the same, yet I cannot count how many times conversations with new moms and dads have turned from questions about their babies to underlying fears about their parenting skills. It is not uncommon for my telephone to ring around midnight and for a teary, high-pitched voice on the other end to whimper, "Lanie, I don't know what to do. My baby has a diaper rash, and he won't sleep." Even the worst diaper rash is not likely to cause this much woe. It is clear that something else is bothering this new mom. She needs help. She needs to be asked, "How are *you* feeling? What else is happening?" That is why she really called, and that is why I am there to answer.

I chose to address *The Miracle Year* in this book because it is the period from six months before birth through the first six months of life that truly is the center of the miracle of your new baby. It is during this time that you come to appreciate how a baby alters your life and how your future is and will be forever bound to your family.

It is not until after the first trimester of pregnancy (the first twelve weeks) that most women are awake past the dinner hour and have enough energy to consider the work and the joys of parenting. In the first trimester, pregnant women are lucky just to be able to enjoy the smell of fresh-brewed coffee or broiled fish without heading straight for the bathroom.

In addition, expectant mothers are adjusting to a rapid-fire injection of hormones into their once-stable endocrine systems.

The same hormones that prepare the body to sustain the fetus can wreak havoc on a woman's emotions and cause mood swings and various other roller-coasterlike behaviors.

The first trimester is also a tentative time, with as many as 20 percent of pregnancies ending in miscarriage by the twelfth week. For all of these reasons, most expectant couples are in no mood to talk about drooling and diaper rash. The year of the miracle has yet to begin.

Then, by about your thirteenth or fourteenth week, when the nausea and fatigue subside, your perspective begins to change. You start to "show" and rush to the nearest maternity shop. You notice other couples with infants. You are drawn to advertisements for nursery furniture and may visit your local baby store "just to look around." In all of these ways, you prepare yourself for becoming a parent.

As the weeks pass, you feel your baby kick, and you hear the heartbeat in the doctor's office. Your due date nears. You may enroll in childbirth classes where you learn what to expect and what decisions you must make concerning labor and delivery. You meet other young people like yourselves who are as anxious and excited to become parents as you are. You all want to know what it will feel like when your labor starts.

None of us is fully prepared for childbirth when it comes, but somehow we all get through it. You manage to survive the first few weeks at home, too, even though you fear that you will never sleep eight hours a night again. At the same time, as you get to know your baby, you feel awestruck sometimes by the depth of your love. During this time, your emotions run higher and lower than you have ever known.

Around the third month postpartum, you reach another milestone in your development as a parent. It comes more subtly and gradually than some of the others; it is when you finally believe that your baby is a real person and that you can be friends. You *like* your baby in addition to loving him or her.

Most couples seem to come into their own as new parents at about the six-month mark. While you still have questions and concerns, you are more secure in your ability to care for your baby. You probably have discovered infant play groups or friends with whom you feel comfortable sharing your concerns. By this time, you also are adept at talking with your pediatrician and feel comfortable relying on a combination of medical and instinctual judgments.

The Miracle Year is structured chronologically to guide you through the changes and milestones of this very special time in your lives. Each chapter begins with a section that is meant to help expectant and new parents make the emotional transition to parenthood smoothly and successfully. The remainder of each chapter discusses what to expect during that time of the miracle year, decisions that you may have to make, and ways of coping with problems that you may encounter. I will advise you on buying maternity clothes and estimating your baby budget. I will review options in childbirth and what to expect when you go into labor. I will tell you how to handle a colicky baby, how to prepare infant formula, and how to babyproof your home. I will hold your hand when you need it and encourage you to rely on your head and heart at the same time.

Twelve months from now, I hope that you will reflect upon your miracle year with great joy and pride in how far you will have come. Creating a family is indeed the most wondrous miracle on this earth. Remember these words when your pride and joy wakes you at 3:00 A.M. This baby is your hope for the future.

—LANIE CARTER

THE

MIRACLE

Y · E · A · R

Are You Ready for a Miracle?

Every month I stand before a new, apprehensive audience of young people expecting their first babies. Although I teach many parenting classes, "Getting Ready for Baby" is my favorite because it gives me the opportunity to pass along a great deal of useful advice at a very important time in the lives of these parents-to-be. Parenting education that begins before the baby is born is crucial to the long-term survival of the entire family.

One day I received a phone call from a woman who wanted to know if husbands were required to attend the class with their wives. No, I said.

"Do you have a husband?"

"Yes," the caller told me. "He just isn't excited about the baby, and he doesn't want to come."

After I talked with this woman for a while, it became clear that she and her husband were having a serious problem. There was no communication between them about the baby. They both were feeling isolated and angry.

"I really hope you can bring your husband to the class," I insisted. "I think that if he listens to what I have to say, it may make a difference."

Somehow she managed to convince her husband to make an appearance. I knew them the minute they walked in. He was hunched over and sour-faced, making it clear to everyone that he was not happy to be there.

I make no claim to performing miracles, but I have to admit that by the end of the evening, I sensed that he was coming around. A few days later, the woman called to thank me for changing her husband's attitude. Knowing that it was not I, but he, who made the change, I asked her what had happened. "After the class, he felt he was as important to the baby as I am," she said. "I guess I had shut him out a little bit, and he didn't know how to talk to me about it.

"Apparently he didn't have a good childhood, and was uncertain whether or not he would be a good dad. The class opened the lines of communication so amazingly. Now we have begun to pick out names for the baby, which he had not wanted to do before. We went shopping for nursery equipment, and we had a wonderful day for the first time since I got pregnant."

It comes as no surprise to me that this couple felt closer to each other and to their baby-to-be when they were able to talk with each other. Honest communication about your fears, hopes, and feelings about becoming a mommy or a daddy is essential to good parenting. If you can learn to improve your communication skills now, before your baby comes, you will be taking the first step toward building a healthy family.

Most of you will find that the second trimester is the most delightful time of your pregnancy. Many of the symptoms of the first twelve weeks are gone. You are no longer sick to your tummy. You find yourself staying awake past 7:00 P.M. "Going to bed" once again signifies something other than going to sleep.

Excitement about the pregnancy and the baby come naturally once the first trimester has passed, and you notice some pleasant indications of the new life inside you. Around your fourth month, you may find that you can no longer zip your jeans. You probably never expected to feel good about this, but having a baby changes your perspective in ways you never dreamed it could.

You may find yourself feeling more womanly as your breasts become full and round. (They may be sore, too.) If you have been flat-chested all your life, this may be the first time that you look voluptuous. Your partner may enjoy this. I hope you will enjoy it, too, while it lasts. Any visions you harbor of becoming another Jane Mansfield will be shattered once your belly sticks out farther than your breasts.

As your baby grows larger and stronger, you feel it moving inside you. When and how these movements start varies from woman to woman, so you probably will not feel the kicking at the same time that your neighbor or your sister did. Once it happens, though, you and your partner anticipate the blessing that has befallen you even more.

As all these physical changes take place, you may ask yourself if you are ready for the miracle of a new life. Indeed, pregnancy is a period of great emotional as well as physical change. This chapter addresses some of the changes that a baby will thrust upon you. I will suggest some ways of dealing with the changes. More important, however, I hope that this material will promote discussion with your partner and, through that discussion, that you improve your communication skills.

Getting Fat: Adjusting to Your Changing Body

Be prepared for your body to go through major changes during your second trimester as the fetus inside you grows from the size of a plum to become about as large as a honeydew melon in just twelve weeks.

During month four (weeks thirteen to seventeen), your baby grows steadily, weighing four ounces and measuring seven inches by the end of the month. The fetus fills your uterus, and from now on, the larger it grows the more your belly protrudes. Human-looking although tiny, your baby has begun to grow eyelashes and eyebrows as well as tiny tooth buds. It can swallow. In fact, the fetus swallows about a pint of amniotic fluid every day.

Also in the fourth month, you begin to "show," and you probably need to wear maternity clothes. Your breasts are full and heavy, and unless you tell your friends you are pregnant, they may wonder if you have been putting on weight. You may feel frustrated if you look fat instead of pregnant and because you cannot feel your baby moving around yet. This reaction is quite normal. The good news is that most of the nausea and fatigue are gone by now.

As exciting as this growth is—with all its promise of life to come—it also can be somewhat disconcerting to the woman who prides herself on her physical fitness. From long experience, I know that no matter what kind of exercise routine you force upon yourself, when you are pregnant, you gain fat and inches. Even your hair and nails "fatten up" and grow faster.

Average Weight Gain Distribution

Baby	6–10 lbs., avg.
Placenta	1–1.5 lbs.
Amniotic fluid	1–2 lbs.
Uterus	2 lbs.
Breasts	1–2 lbs.
Blood volume	3–4 lbs.
Fat, fluid	3–10 lbs.

Try not to be concerned about your weight gain, particularly if it occurs gradually over several months. Unlike when I was pregnant and some expectant moms were chastised by their doctors if they gained more than twenty pounds, most doctors today agree that gaining between twenty and thirty-five pounds is just fine.

What is important is that you gradually learn to become comfortable with your new image. The transition from beauty queen to Earth Mother may be difficult. You may feel that your weight gain is unattractive or that you want to limit what you eat. Your partner, too, may find your new shape less than sexually appealing. Terms of endearment such as "butterball" or "pumpkin-belly" quickly become annoying.

These feelings are quite common, and they may not go away until well after your baby is born. (In fact, until your uterus shrinks back to its normal size, you may still look pregnant.) Partners need to be aware of how expectant moms are feeling. Expectant moms also need to adjust. You cannot allow your or your partner's body consciousness to result in poor eating habits. Maintain a proper diet according to your doctor's instructions and exercise as you are able within the guidelines suggested by your obstetrician or childbirth educator, and try not to worry too much about the weight gain, which is, after all, natural.

Keeping fit inside and out is crucial to your baby's health. I know you plan on giving the baby the very best care once he or she is born. Why not do the same while the baby is still inside? It may surprise you to hear this, but I find that the women who complain the most about gaining weight while they are pregnant are the same ones who miss it the most after their babies are born. So often I find new moms in the hallway outside my office with their babies in their arms and their noses pressed against the nursery window. When they see me, they almost always admit: "I loved being pregnant. I miss it so much. I wish that I had appreciated it more. It goes by so quickly."

That is so true. When you are pregnant and catch a reflection of yourself in a store window, you may think you'd like to be the size eight of the mannequin inside. When you look back on your pregnancy, you may be surprised that you are saddened by your "emptiness."

What Is Good for You Is Good for Your Baby

It is really wonderful to see the awareness that many expectant moms have today about diet and exercise. It is something that those of us in my generation never considered.

Many, many books and magazine articles have been written concerning proper diet and exercise during pregnancy. Much of this information is useful, and your doctor can offer additional guidance. The following common-sense rules should get you off to a good start:

1. Do not smoke cigarettes, cigars, pipes, or any other toxic substances.

2. Do not drink alcohol, but drink a lot of fluids—at least eight glasses a day. Limit your consumption of coffee and drinks with caffeine and artificial flavors, coloring, and sweeteners.

3. Eat a well-balanced diet, with as much emphasis as you can on protein and calcium-rich products.

4. The best diet is one in which foods are eaten as closely as possible to their natural state—i.e., the less processed the foods are, the better. This helps you to avoid food additives and preservatives that are potentially harmful to the fetus.

5. Ask your doctor about supplementing your diet with prenatal vitamins.

6. Avoid all drugs, illegal and legal, as well as over-the-counter medicines unless prescribed by your doctor.

The following rules can be used as guidelines to your exercise routine:

1. Start slowly, particularly if you are not used to vigorous exercise. This approach gives your body time to adjust to a new routine and at the same time offers you the confidence that comes from small victories.

2. Although you should be able to continue your regular athletic routine if you do not have health problems, the best exercise for pregnancy is slow, steady, and frequent—at least three times a week. Walking and swimming are excellent choices because they improve heart and muscle fitness without jarring the body. If you are a runner, check with your doctor for his or her advice on continuing your regular running routine.

3. Do not become extremely fatigued. Remember that you are literally caring for two bodies now instead of one, and you tire more easily. Adjust your routine accordingly.

4. Avoid exercise that strains your abdomen, especially exercises done while lying on your back, such as sit-ups.

5. Your pulse rate should not go above 150 at any time. Temperature should not become elevated above 100.4.

One of the best pregnancy exercise routines for your body and your soul is to join an expectant mothers' fitness class at a local gym or community center. Many women who have taken these classes report that they enjoy them because they provide an opportunity to meet and talk to other women at various stages of pregnancy. Other pregnant women are excellent resources for kinship, advice, and support (as are other moms later on). They give women early in pregnancy a glimpse of what is to come and motivate each other toward physical and emotional well-being.

Many couples have shared with me how they had incorporated healthy diets and exercise into both of their lives when they were expecting a baby. Keeping fit can be a joint project that fosters increased awareness and improved communication. One expectant dad said that he and his wife loved to go on long walks. Her pregnancy gave them a built-in excuse to do it more often. "As we did this, we realized that we were doing something good for our baby as well as for ourselves," he said. "It gave us a perfect opportunity to talk quietly about the baby without interruptions by the telephone." Another dad-to-be said that he and his wife enjoyed grocery shopping together. They read the food labels together to determine which foods were most healthy for themselves and for the baby.

Your New Look in Fashion

Whether you exercise or not, by the time you enter your twelfth week of pregnancy, you probably need to wear maternity clothes. If your initial reaction to this news is to panic, hold off until after you visit your local maternity shop or department store. Maternity wear is very stylish and versatile these days. No longer are you destined to wear one of three versions of the old burlap sack from which women in my day were forced to choose.

Shopping for your maternity wardrobe is something that I encourage you to do with your partner. It is fun to imagine what you will look like as the months pass, and you can leave the store not only with a bag or two of clothes, but with some nice memories as well. This time is also a perfect opportunity to talk about your feelings about becoming parents.

By the time you need to consider a new wardrobe, I hope you will be proud of the way you look. Believe me, women today have it a lot easier than in my day, when the first purchase we made upon discovering our "little secret" was a maternity girdle. Nowadays pregnant women look wonderful in fitted leggings, leotards, even bathing suits. Maintain your sense of humor about the way you look. Take photos as you go, perhaps even once a month, to mark your progress. When you fit into your old clothes again, you will not believe that you ever looked or felt that big. Your children will love to look at your old pictures, too.

If your job requires that you wear a professional wardrobe,

buying a full line of maternity suits and dresses can be expensive. Even purchasing enough casual clothes for the next six months can run you several hundred dollars. If money is tight, ask your friends if they have any maternity clothes stored away. Since most women wear their maternity outfits for only a short time, the clothes often remain in good condition and can be shared with several friends before they wear out. Garage sales and used-clothing shops are also good sources for maternity outfits for the same reason. What you wear depends only on your life-style and budget.

A word on sizes: do not buy clothes that fit you early in your second trimester because they probably will not fit you later. No matter how out of shape you were in the past, during your initial visit to the maternity department everything seems too big. Even when you tie on one of those "pregnancy pillows" many motherhood shops provide, you look only about three months further along than you are during the fitting. So if you shop in your fourth month, anything that fits, even with the pillow, probably will be too small by your third trimester.

There are two items for your wardrobe that I recommend specifically to help you through your pregnancy: bras and shoes. Your breasts may already have become swollen and sore in your first trimester, but chances are that they will continue to change throughout your pregnancy and even after the baby is born. For this reason, you need larger bras than usual and should even consider buying one or two nursing bras during the end of your pregnancy if you plan to breast-feed. Most saleswomen are able to advise you on the proper size, but a general rule is to look for a nursing bra that is one cup size larger than your usual bra. The size around should stay the same. (If you choose not to nurse your baby, you can avoid having your breasts become engorged after you deliver by asking your obstetrician for an injection to suppress your milk production. After this shot, you will be able to fit into your regular bras within a week or so.)

Some women, when they buy their bras in the latter months of pregnancy, feel more comfortable not only increasing by one cup size but also increasing by a full size around as well (i.e., 36C to 38D). However, in my experience, new moms lose so much water weight after they deliver that the additional increase around is not needed. In fact, the larger bras may even be too loose despite the fact that your breasts are larger. If you have gained a lot of weight and feel the need to wear a larger bra, limit your initial purchase to two (one is usually in the wash). That way, if you do become thinner "overnight," you will not be stuck with several nursing bras that are too large.

As the rest of your body gets larger, your feet, too, will swell. Some women report that their feet actually grow up to a full size during the nine months. The swelling combined with the extra work you are asking your feet to do by carrying around an additional twenty-five to thirty-five pounds or more makes your feet tired and sore. The best method to help alleviate this problem is to employ a full-time masseuse. Failing that, purchase at least one pair of comfortable, flat shoes at least one-half size larger than you normally wear. Even if you wear these shoes only while you are pregnant, the comfort that they offer, especially in the last few months, will be worth the money you spend on them.

One final word on maternity wear: you probably will find as your pregnancy progresses that you have more vaginal discharge than usual. This is a normal side effect of the increased hormonal activity in your body and does not require any medical attention provided that it is not accompanied by any signs of infection or rupturing of membranes (heavy flow, bloody show). To help make you feel fresher, I suggest wearing mini-pads and cotton crotch underwear, which is breathable. Do not douche. (Some women may find the mini-pads irritating; if so, discontinue their use.)

It's Really Real: Don't Miss the Magic

One of the nicest parts about your second trimester is that you find yourself getting really excited about your baby. You may catch yourself "oohing" and "aahing" when you walk by a children's clothing store or pass a baby carriage on the street. You may stop to ask the mother or father how old the baby is, if it sleeps a lot, and if labor was hard. When you are pregnant, you invariably notice mothers and babies and other pregnant women (who all seem further along than you do).

Even a mundane trip to the market becomes special when you are aware of the budding life inside you. One woman I know told me that early in her fourth month she was standing in line in the supermarket when the checkout clerk asked if she needed any help with her groceries. "Oh yes," she blurted out, unconsciously patting her rounded tummy. "I can't carry my groceries. I'm pregnant!"

Not all expectant parents are ready to feel this way, however. "It doesn't seem real to me," some moms-to-be tell me. "I know that I have a baby inside me, yet I still can't believe it's going to be a real person." Feelings of unreality and distance from your baby wax and wane throughout your pregnancy and sometimes even after delivery. Do not be ashamed of them. They are perfectly normal. All you have to do is consider the enormity of the changes in your life at this time to realize that some apprehension and plain old strange feelings are to be expected. After all, you have only nine months to prepare to love and care for a person as yet unnamed, whom you have never seen. You may not know the baby's sex, and you certainly cannot be sure what he or she will look or act like. It is a job for which no one can prepare completely, so it is bound to make you feel a bit awkward.

Dads-to-be, in particular, may have a hard time becoming "connected" with their babies-to-be in the early months of pregnancy. For some, it takes hearing the fetal heartbeat or seeing the baby's image on an ultrasound monitor to make them feel close to their child. If either partner is getting off to a slow start, it may help to enroll in a parent education course like my "Getting Ready for Baby" class. Men often tell me that attending this class really made them feel more involved with their partner's pregnancy.

Sometimes "talking" to the baby through mommy's tummy is helpful, even if you feel silly doing it. One daddy-in-waiting told me, "Every night when I come home, I give my wife a hug and a kiss, and I say to her belly, 'Hi, baby. How are you, baby?' Sometimes I turn on music, and I wonder if the baby likes that sound or if he prefers something softer or louder. Sometimes my wife and I dance, and we wonder if the baby knows we're dancing."

Life can be full of many wonderful moments like these. Find things that make you happy. Build memories. Your first pregnancy—with all its wonder and newness—comes around only once in life. Sometimes other life events interfere with pregnancies, of course. A parent or grandparent may be ill, a spouse may have lost a job, or your boss cannot reassure you that your job will be there after the baby is born. The pregnancy itself may be unwanted or unexpected. That, too, can put stress on a relationship. I encourage you to be realistic about your expectations, particularly during times of crisis. Have fun when you can. You do not want this special time to pass unnoticed.

Your Obstetrician: A V.I.P.

As your body takes the shape of pregnancy, your relationship with your obstetrician takes on a new shape as well. During these nine months, he or she becomes a confidant, helpmate, someone with whom you can discuss the most intimate details of your pregnancy and of your baby's birth. In fact, the person who delivers your baby most likely will live on in your memory long after your recollection of the actual event fades away. Many new moms have remarked, some with tears in their eyes, that they cannot believe that someone whom they barely knew became so important to them so quickly. It is a relationship that is unique and special.

The first rule in building a good relationship with your OB is to learn to ask questions not only about your physical health but about your emotional concerns, too. If and when your obstetrician suggests certain tests, ask him or her about them. Find out about the procedure involved and why it is being ordered. For example, if your doctor is concerned about gestational diabetes, and you do not know anything about it, ask! Your doctor will be reassured by your concern, and he or she will be glad to tell you what to expect.

Do not be afraid to ask for a second explanation if you do not understand. Ask for additional reading material. Both of these methods will help make you a better informed patient. As I have said over and over in my child-care classes, "There is no such thing as a dumb question if you do not know the answer." Doctors feel this way, too!

Many questions arise during pregnancy when you experience sudden and unexplained mood swings. Usually these emotional highs and lows are pretty well resolved by your second trimester, but still there are times when women have great concerns about their baby's health, for example. Many expectant women worry about their babies being born too soon or in some odd fashion. These topics are not too "silly" to raise with your doctor. You need reassurance that your concerns are normal and healthy—and they usually are! If they are not, your doctor can suggest ways to resolve them.

When you are in the doctor's office, try to remember that most doctors work on very tight schedules and that sometimes unexpected surgery or other emergencies can pull them from their daily routines. Try to be efficient in your discussions with your obstetrician by keeping a written list of your questions and your concerns. If you keep a list handy throughout the month, then you will not become flustered during your appointment, and you will not miss anything for which you later find yourself telephoning.

Some people may feel intimidated by their doctors, especially if the doctors are very busy. Many times women have particular difficulty talking with OB-GYNs because they think that pregnancy is a sex-related topic. Of course, this fear is unfounded. (By the time you give birth, sex seems the farthest thing from pregnancy that you could imagine.)

Once in a while, I have an expectant mother call me to say, "Lanie, I'm just not comfortable with my doctor. I've been to see him four or five times, and I don't feel that he spends enough time with me or that he's interested in what I have to say. He always seems to be rushing." If you are feeling this way, you might consider changing doctors before you get too far along in your pregnancy. There is nothing more important than feeling comfortable with your OB at this time. Some communities have doctor referral services that can help you make the switch. Neighbors and friends who have had babies are also good sources to help you find a doctor who is right for you.

If possible, it is important for your partner to visit the obstetrician. These visits can help him feel a part of the experience and encourage him to ask questions. I like to suggest that couples plan their doctor visits near lunchtime so that they can share a special time together before or after the appointment. Some obstetricians have late office hours or Saturday appointments that help facilitate joint visits at convenient times for working couples.

Sometimes men want to join their pregnant partners in the examining room. If you are comfortable with this intimacy, then I see no reason to discourage it. The more tied in a man feels with pregnancy, the more likely it is that he will continue that healthy feeling after the baby is born. If, on the other hand, your partner prefers not to be in the examining room or prefers to turn away during the internal exam, that is fine as well. If he stands by your head, chances are that the drape across your tummy and legs will block his view anyway. The important thing is to talk about how you both feel about sharing this time together and set a pattern with which you both feel comfortable.

"Honey, I Felt a Kick" (Soon Dad Will, Too)

By the fourth month, your baby has grown to fill your uterus, and for that reason you begin to see your belly protrude around this time. If you have a sonogram early in your second trimester, you are able to see the image of your baby, which looks very much like a tiny version of yourself. The outlines of the head, spine, and limbs are clearly visible, and if you are lucky, you may even see your new little friend sucking his or her thumb. "Baby's first photo"—taken from the inside out—is shown with much excitement by expectant parents. One daddy-to-be brought such a photo to a softball game in which he and my son-in-law were playing. What a wonderful sight it was to see these grown men huddled over the photo, speculating what position the little guy might play in fifteen years!

It is about this time that your doctor begins listening to the baby's heartbeat during your regular monthly visits. For expectant parents, hearing your baby for the first time is very comforting. It makes the baby seem real and human, and is a source of reassurance, especially since you may not feel anything moving yet.

In the fifth month (weeks eighteen to twenty-two), your baby begins to develop muscles and continues to increase in size. He can curl his fingers and throw a pretty strong right jab (or left). By the end of the month, he may weigh up to a pound and measure up to a foot in length. As hard as it is to imagine, he is quite a hairy fellow (or gal). The lashes and brows grow full, and a fine, downlike fur covers the head and body.

During this month, you may feel your baby move. You may not be sure. The movement may be very light. Some women think they have indigestion. If you do not feel anything, do not panic. Every woman and every baby are different, and there are several reasons that fetal movement might seem delayed. For example, if the placenta is attached to the uterine wall just behind the belly button, it may mask tiny movements that would ordinarily be felt on the outside. As with hearing the heartbeat, feeling these pops and kicks can be terribly exciting, as well as greatly reassuring.

What does it feel like when the baby "kicks"? That is a big question for first-time parents. There probably are as many descriptions for what it feels like as there are pregnant women. Generally, however, in the beginning the "kicks" feel very soft and light, quick puffs of movement as if a butterfly barely touched you as it fluttered by. One expectant mother imagined the first movements she felt as tiny soap bubbles that floated around and "popped" as they bumped into the uterine wall. Sometimes the sensation is so quick and light that you may not even be sure you felt it at all.

Even if the feeling comes and goes in a flash and is at this point too light for anyone to feel from the outside, do not become discouraged. Enjoy every tiny movement when it comes and try to share how it feels with your partner. He may be feeling a little left out at this point, and your excitement may help. Besides, within a month or six weeks, the baby's kicks will become so much stronger and more distinct that the two of you can share them from inside and out. Just wait—that's when things get really exciting!

Being Afraid

Of all the concerns that pregnant women bring to their obstetricians during the second trimester, the most common are fears about the birth and about the health of the baby. If you find yourself being afraid, remember that these fears are quite normal and are part of the process of accepting the reality of parenthood.

In fact, as surprising as it may seem, renowned pediatrician and author Dr. T. Berry Brazelton writes in his book, *Infants and Mothers, (Revised Edition),* that he is "always concerned when a mother accepts her new role too easily."

"This conflict (about the reality of having a baby) in a new mother is a common one and is not to be criticized," Brazelton writes. "It goes back to her struggle with herself about giving up her independent role to be a mother. This is never as easy as it may seem in prospect. The balance a woman has achieved as a woman and a wife must be shaken. She must face a new role—that of having an unknown person entirely dependent on her. Any woman who cares how she meets this responsibility will wonder whether she will be equal to this new role."

What Are You Afraid Of?

Most pregnant woman have the same fears. Among them are:

- Fear of having an unhealthy baby
- Fear of not being a good parent
- Fear of financial obligations of a family
- Fear of labor pain
- Fear of hospitals
- Fear of the inability to handle a career and a family
- Fear of your body not returning to its prepregnant state
- Fear of changes in the parents' relationship

These fears may be shared by expectant dads. Some dads also may be afraid of being left out and unloved. Try talking to your partner about them. You may find he understands more than you might have thought.

While you do not always have enough control over your emotions to make your fears disappear—particularly at night, when fears crop up from your subconscious in the form of nightmares—you may be able to better handle your fears if you talk about them. Talking to your partner is a good place to start. Opening the lines of communication between partners is crucial to building solid family relationships.

In addition to your partner, seek the counsel of your doctor, clergyman, friends and family, even other mothers whom you might meet in prenatal exercise classes or elsewhere. Everyone has had bouts with fear—both real and irrational—and somebody else may be able to offer you just the perspective that you need.

Some of your fears, such as those surrounding your baby's health, may never go away completely. To this day, I worry about my children even though they are grown. I worry about my grandchildren and about the many babies that I see delivered each day at the hospital.

You will find that you love your child so much that you worry about every little part. At first, you worry whether the baby will be born healthy and with all its fingers and toes. Once the baby is born, you will worry if it cries too much or for too long—and you will worry when it does not cry at all! Then, as the baby grows, you will worry over the first cough, the first fever, immunizations, diarrhea, a fall from a jungle gym. The worries go on and on. All you can do is live each day accepting life's risks and doing the best you can to live your days to their fullest.

It would not be fair to suggest that fears never, ever become reality. Sometimes in our imperfect world babies are born ill. There is a very special woman I met a few years ago who at the time was waiting to adopt a baby. She and her husband had been trying to conceive a child for many years. When they decided to adopt, they prepared themselves by attending my "Getting Ready for Baby" class, and that is where we met.

Nearly a year passed until I saw this woman again. Our second meeting was at the hospital where, after more than eight years of trying, she gave birth to a baby of her own. Like her adopted baby, her newborn was a boy. He was as cute as a button. He also had Down's syndrome.

When I visited the new mother in her postpartum room after having seen the child, I have to say that she was no less excited about having a baby than any mother on the floor. When I asked about the Down's syndrome, she told me that she and her husband had known for five months that their child would be retarded. When they first found out from the amniocentesis, she said they were, of course, disappointed and saddened. But after having discussed it, they decided not to abort the child for whom they had waited so many years. He was God's answer to their prayers. They knew that they would love him despite his imperfections. It was at that moment that I realized God gave her and her husband that special baby because He knew the child would be in good hands.

Concern about your ability to be a good parent is another fear that may surface during your second trimester. It is hard to imagine now how you can give so unselfishly as mothers and fathers do. But the minute you fall in love with your baby—and it might not be in the first five minutes or even the first five days—everything else takes a back seat. Of course, knowing this does not automatically erase the insecurity about competence that most new parents feel. That takes time and practice. As one new mother explained, "As I touched my baby's soft skin and rubbed my hand over her little head and kissed each tiny finger, I knew that I would do everything in my power to be the best mother there could be. Any doubts that I had about what to do just disappeared. I knew that I would do whatever it took to keep her safe. My love for her was the only guide I needed."

Drive Me to the Nearest Bank

As if fears from within were not enough to cope with during your pregnancy, pressures may build between you and your partner with regards to money matters during this time. Until this time, you may have been wrapped up in the romantic side of baby-making. However, in your second trimester, when you start paying medical bills, inquiring about leaves of absence from work, and shopping for baby furniture, you realize that having a baby does not come cheaply. In fact, no matter how much you might guess it will cost to raise your child for the next eighteen years, it probably will cost more.

To help estimate your budget for the first year or so, I have developed the following checklist of expenses for a normal birth and a healthy child. This list should be useful in financial planning and in stimulating constructive discussions between you and your partner about this important matter.

Once you have determined your estimated baby budget and your anticipated income and expenses, the time is ripe to open discussions with your mate about the financial reality of having a baby. Try to be open and honest about your money problems and your priorities. If you are used to spending a large portion of your income on clothes or entertainment, these habits might need to be curtailed. The more you talk about how to reorder your priorities as a couple, the less likely it will be that money is a source of conflict after the baby is born.

"We never thought that our new life-style would be so much fun," reported the father of a four-month-old. "Because my wife wanted to take time off from work for the first six months, we decided to make it on one salary. We have learned how much fun it is to stay home. We partied and ate out all the time before our

little girl arrived. Now, fixing a salad together and ordering a
pizza is what we do for excitement. I guess you'd call it nesting,
and we love it."

Your Baby Budget

Expense	Estimated Cost	Estimated Coverage*
Medical Care		
Obstetrician's fee	_____	_____
Hospital room/board	_____	_____
(Includes medications, delivery room fee)		
Lab tests/diagnoses	_____	_____
(Usually billed separately from OB & hospital fees; tests are given regularly from early pregnancy through hospital stay; ask OB about ultrasound, amnio fees)		
Anesthesiologist's fee	_____	_____
Pediatrician/G.P.'s fee	_____	_____
Maternity Wardrobe	_____	_____
(Daytime and nighttime wear, bras and underwear, shoes, nursing garments)		
Childbirth/rearing Classes	_____	_____
(Also include postpartum classes for mom and baby)		
Baby Equipment	_____	_____
(See chapter 2 for details on nursery furniture, bath needs, car seats, etc.)		
Baby Clothes/Diapers	_____	_____
(Be sure to include diaper-related essentials)		
Baby Feeding Needs	_____	_____
(See chapter 2)		
Added Postpartum Help	_____	_____
(Optional)		
Day Care/Baby-sitting	_____	_____
Medications/Vitamins	_____	_____
Miscellaneous	_____	_____
(Dental care, increased insurance, family vacations, baby announcements, parent support group dues, extra telephone calls)		

*What you can reasonably expect to be picked up by your insurance company, and
expenses that you anticipate will be covered by baby gifts.

In considering your expenses, remember that a newborn takes up not only your
personal energy, but also energy in the form of gas and electricity, with the gas and
electric company in my community estimating that households with babies use 25
percent more electricity and 13 percent more gas. Figure these hidden expenses into
your budget.

Dads-to-be: The Other Half of the Parenthood Team

One of the reasons communication is so important during pregnancy is that expectant moms and dads usually differ greatly in the way that they feel about what is happening to them. The reasons for this difference are both biological and social.

Many women instinctively want to be mothers from early on in their lives. They practice doing so by caring for dolls, playing house, and watching their mothers cook. As girls, women are taught to develop certain aspects of their inborn nature that men are not. Girls are encouraged to be nurturing and to think of others' needs before their own. These lessons are reinforced in their modes of play. Girls are rewarded for intimacy and for sharing their feelings.

Most boys do not seem to share these instincts. Rather, they seem to be more aggressive and nonverbal from infancy. Unfortunately, society encourages them to remain that way. Boys' games do not reward nurturing skills nor emotional bonding.

Unlike women, most men had few role models of nurturing behavior until very recently. Think of the expectant fathers that one saw on television and in the movies in previous generations: pacing, cigar-toting worrywarts who cluttered the waiting rooms while their wives were off-camera giving birth. Most of our fathers did not go through natural childbirth classes. Most of them did not have paternity leaves. Most did not go to the doctor with their wives, nor were they privy to listening to their baby's heartbeat. How were their sons to learn anything different?

Life for dads and dads-to-be in this generation has changed more than at any other time in history. It warms my heart to see dads changing diapers and getting involved so genuinely with so much care and attention. Men today are working hard at being full partners to women in all stages of pregnancy and parenting. I encourage expectant and new mothers to be patient and encouraging while the expectant and new dads are finding their way.

Practicing tolerance about the fact that your partner does things differently than you do is an excellent skill to learn during pregnancy. Let him load the dishwasher without complaining that he is putting the forks in upside down. Do not challenge the way he folds the laundry; chances are that the clothes will not be irrevocably damaged. If you have a pet, both of you can learn to share the caretaking tasks, so you may be better able to divide your child-care tasks with equal security later on.

If both parents are adept at child care, they will be more flexible and able to react to modern-day pulls and tugs. For example, mom may need a little space to complete a pressing assignment for work, or dad may need a back rub after a difficult negotiation. Everybody's needs can be met if the responsibility for your child can be passed between you easily and equally and both partners are willing to give a little extra at times.

We Interrupt This Chapter with a Message for Dads

A good father can be the most important person in a child's life. You dads-to-be may be surprised to hear that, especially because, during the pregnancy, you may feel less than an equal partner in the childbearing process. Nothing could be further from the truth.

Think back to the impact—good or bad—that your dad had upon you. If he was a dominant and positive force in your life, chances are that he taught you about stability and loyalty. He might have been the disciplinarian. He might have been the parent with whom you had the most fun. He might have coached your Little League team. He might have helped you with your homework. Interaction with your dad helped shape who you are.

If you were raised in a single-parent household and did not know your father very well or at all, you can only imagine how much you missed. Your mother provided for you as best as she was able, but she could not be your dad. No one but your dad could fill his role.

I will discuss the role that dads play in the lives of newborn babies later on in this book. For now, I urge all the dads-to-be to work on two goals before the baby comes. First, get to know your baby's mom as well as possible. Strengthen your relationship by sharing your feelings about parenthood. Spend time together creating memories of these special days. The better you two get along, the more you can support each other through the transition to parenthood.

Second, take some time on your own to think about your dad. In what ways was he a good father? What do you plan to do with your child that mimics what he did with you? What would you like to do differently? This exercise is helpful in preparing you for your new role.

Sharing the Good News with Fido

As a teenager, I lived in a two-bedroom apartment in New York City with my mother and my mother's French poodle, which she affectionately called "Miss Perfect." Upon my decision to marry, my fiancé decided that the perfect engagement present would be a dog of my own. Enter an Irish setter puppy with the biggest feet you ever saw. Naturally, she bounded in and attacked the perfect poodle. That is how my first pet came into my life.

Of course, our new puppy's boundless enthusiasm made my new husband and I fall in love with our dog even more. We had fallen so much in love with her, in fact, that by the time I was about to deliver our first child, it was hard to imagine how we could love a baby as much. After all, our puppy *was* our baby!

Just as it is when you have an older child, it is a big transition to bring a baby home when you have a dog or a cat. Many times I get calls from grandparents who say that their son or daughter is expecting a baby and the parents-to-be have a cat that sleeps all over the house. "I even found the cat in the baby's crib," one grandmother lamented. Of course, the grandmother was appalled, and I can understand her reaction, but as I told her, as soon as the new baby is brought home, the parents are going to be so protective that the pet will not come near their precious bundle. Following these guidelines will help ease the transition.

1. The day after your baby is born, have dad bring home a receiving blanket or T-shirt worn by the baby so that your pet can sniff the baby's odor.

2. When you return from the hospital, have dad carry the baby so you have open arms to reassure your pet that it still holds a place in your heart.

3. Do not leave your pet alone with the baby. Cats, in particular, will want to sniff and rub against everything that is new. A newborn cannot protect itself. The story about cats sucking the breath out of babies is an old wives' tale, but cats still should stay out of the crib and bassinet at all times.

5. Pet cleanliness is important, particularly when your baby is old enough to crawl and share the floor with your pet. Keeping your pet clean includes worming it and making sure it does not have fleas or other pests riding on it. Cat owners: make sure the litter box is covered or kept out of reach, not only after the baby comes home but during pregnancy as well. Pregnant women should not clean the litter box. Cat feces can transmit toxoplasmosis, a prenatal disease that may cause serious harm or death to the fetus.

Grandparents: Your Child's Roots

"We couldn't wait to tell our parents the news!" I hear this reaction so often from parents-to-be. It is encouraging to know that young people still feel this way.

Many of you will find that during your pregnancy you want to reach out to your parents and your extended family. As new parents you may feel a new understanding and appreciation of your own parents.

Although your family may live far away, the anticipation and arrival of a newborn provide a perfect opportunity to get together. Spend time with the baby's grandparents-to-be during the pregnancy. Try to iron out past differences and work on improving communication. Even if your relationship with your parents and in-laws is good, it is helpful to discuss how you hope to share in your child's life and how you can work together toward a three-generational approach to the growing family.

If your mother or mother-in-law is planning to visit after the baby is born, talk to her beforehand about the ways in which she can be most helpful. *Congratulations! You're Going to Be a Grandmother* is the book that I have written for grandparents-to-be to help them appreciate the delicate role that they play in the life of a new baby and in the new family structure.

The Past Creates the Future

> I love you a bushel and a peck
> A bushel and a peck and . . .
> A hug around the neck

I started singing this rhyme to my grandchildren when they were about a year old. I would sit them on my lap looking toward me and sing "I love you," gently poking their little chests. When I would reach the part with the extra-long "and . . ." I would throw my arms out and squeeze them in a big bear hug. At about eighteen to twenty months, the children learned the song themselves. When I would sit them on my lap and start to sing "I love . . ." the smiles on their faces were just wonderful as they anticipated what was coming. By the time I got to the "and . . ." they would giggle, throw their arms around me, and cry "and . . . a hug around the neck."

In reaching out to your family and to the generations that came before you, there is nothing more fun than to recall the nursery rhymes, lullabies, and other family traditions of your childhood. You can find these memories in old books or records that your parents may have squirreled away or by looking at mementos of your childhood and using them to spark long-lost memories. Ask your parents about family traditions. If they don't live nearby, encourage them to make video or audio tapes of their favorite songs and stories to share with your child.

Grandparents' stories of their own growing years can expand a child's awareness of the continuity of a family. When a child understands where his grandparents stand in relation to mommy and daddy, he may better understand his own place in the family. Because they have listened to their grandparents' tales, your children's memories can stretch back for several generations.

Grandparents' stories do not help only the grandchild. Your parents and grandparents will appreciate the opportunity to talk about these special moments, too. They give people an opportunity to go back to their own childhoods. Through their grandchildren, their hopes go forward as they look into the future, when your child will be an adult and perhaps a parent himself.

Twenty-six Weeks and Counting

Whether you were prepared or not, the last thirteen weeks brought about tremendous changes in your body, mind, and heart. By the end of month six (weeks twenty-three to twenty-seven), the average-sized baby weighs as much as two pounds and is eleven to fourteen inches long. Although the fetus has developed increased muscle tone by now, it still looks quite birdlike because there is little fat under the skin. The baby can open its eyes at this time and look around. It can suck its thumb. Sometimes the sucking gives the baby hiccups, and you might be able to feel them.

With the baby getting larger and stronger, the kicks and punches become more easily distinguished. If you watch your belly, you may see your baby move near the surface like a restless sleeper under a taut sheet. These movements seem even stronger as the amniotic fluid surrounding the baby lessens, bringing your baby closer to the surface under your skin. According to some experts, a six-month-old fetus can hear its mother's voice and that of others close to her. The fetus may react to these voices and noises. The weeks to come will continue to amaze you as your baby nears delivery into the world and into your arms.

At this time, you may not yet believe that you are living through a year-long miracle. Most people feel this way as they prepare for and anticipate their first child. Instead of wondering if you are missing something, enjoy each and every day as you ready yourself for your baby's birth. Nine months from now, you will be happy that you have so many good memories of your pregnancy, and you undoubtedly will agree that starting a family is truly the greatest miracle you can share.

2

Buying for Baby: Old-fashioned Wisdom for Modern Couples

he first time that I heard of a coed baby shower was when one of my daughters announced that she was going to be given one in preparation for the birth of her first child. I was surprised at first because I could not imagine men sitting around sipping tea, eating sandwiches with the crusts cut off, and making small talk about baby nightgowns and crib mobiles. How old-fashioned my ideas were!

The shower, it turns out, was a great success in large part because of the men. They were so enthusiastic and happy to be included. Even the grandfathers, whom I am sure did not even know the term "baby shower" when they were fathers, were so intrigued by the new little garments and toys I almost could not believe it. They marveled over the way the snaps run up and down the legs of a stretch suit as if they had never seen or heard of such a thing before.

The younger men, too, were fascinated. One innocent husband admitted that he thought a bassinet was something you bathe a baby in. "No, that's where the baby sleeps," a more experienced uncle-to-be told him, and he launched into a five-minute lecture about bathtubs, water temperature, and baby shampoo. Later, when my daughter with her big tummy held up a front pack and declared, "This is how I'm going to wear our baby," another new father in the group stood up and demonstrated to my son-in-law how the pack is worn.

When the expectant couple went home that night, my daughter said that her husband insisted that they go shopping the very next day to buy the baby's dresser. "We have to put all his little clothes away," he had said.

The next evening they did go to the baby store to order the dresser. After shopping, they went to dinner, over which they discussed where the crib would be placed in the nursery. By the end of the evening, they had the entire room laid out on a paper napkin. This enthusiasm all started from the baby shower. Instead of my daughter being with her friends and her husband watching football or cleaning the yard, he was there, and he became involved.

The special time they spent together discussing the nursery helped to cement their relationship as best friends. When you think of best friends, you find that the sharing of special moments such as these is what binds you together. In the same way, parents are bound by a mutual respect for one another, by shared moments, and by a deep friendship that sustains them through difficult times. When you are pregnant, take time to treasure each other as individuals, distinct and separate from each other and from your baby-to-be. Look for the qualities in each other that made you fall in love. Appreciating each other and making each other feel good is the second step toward becoming good parents.

No matter how busy you are, nine months of waiting for anything is a long time. Waiting for your baby, because you probably are so excited about his or her arrival, is like enduring the day before school lets out for 280 days in a row . . . with the last day of class always just around the corner. Take heart, my friends, because God created shopping!

As you approach your final countdown, you will find that

there are oodles of projects and preparations that you can accomplish during this time to get ready for your baby. In fact, as you head into months five, six, and seven, you have reached the ideal time not only to begin shopping for baby equipment, but also to start thinking about suitable names and birth announcements, sewing curtains for the nursery, stenciling or painting wooden cubes for storage shelves, or building a cradle or a changing table. Bargain hunters can pass the time scouring the classified ads for garage and yard sales—always excellent places for good buys on baby clothes, furniture, and equipment.

No matter what you do, have fun! This is a very special time for expectant couples to share in joyous anticipation of the little miracle that will change their lives—and the state of relative calm in their homes—forever. Besides, a nursery that you are proud of is a nursery in which you will spend time. What could be a greater coming-home gift to your baby than for the three of you to have such a very special place to grow into a family?

Setting Up the Nursery: Baby's First Room

If you have the space in your home, it is nice for your baby to have his or her own room. However, for the first three to four months a nursery is not a prerequisite to good parenting. What is important is that you have a comfortable and reasonably quiet place for your baby to sleep, away from drafts and fluctuating temperatures. In addition to a protected sleeping area, you need safe places for diaper changes and baths. Again, the area should be draft-free and permit easy and comfortable access to washcloths, diapers, and your baby's rubber duckie.

When your baby reaches four months of age and has (we hope) established a regular nighttime sleeping pattern, I suggest that he or she become accustomed to sleeping in a separate room or in an area that is set apart from your common living space by a screen or room divider. By this time—after you have endured hours of crying in the darkness (perhaps "his and hers," as well as baby's)—the entire family will benefit from the privacy that the separation offers.

If, like most parents, you have a room or a section of a room that you plan on devoting expressly to your baby (although do not think for a minute that your baby's equipment will not dominate the entire house soon enough), setting up the nursery can be one of the most rewarding and fun projects that you and your partner tackle together in preparation for your new child.

Safety First, Convenience Second

From a safety standpoint, I have several recommendations for your baby's nursery. First, place the crib away from the window. When your baby is old enough to throw things, he or she might take great pleasure in heaving the heaviest toys out the window like a shot-putter practicing for Olympic competition. If the window happens to be closed at the time, your little one's enthusiastic efforts could shatter the glass into the crib. This potential hazard can be avoided by leaving about five feet between the crib and the window. In addition, a bassinet too close to a window may be bathed in direct sunlight, which is bright, warm, and can interfere with your baby's naptime. The area nearest the window also may be drafty and chilly at night. Second, wherever you place the crib, make sure you have good access to it, preferably on both sides. During an emergency or when your baby is ill, the last thing you want to do is squeeze into a tiny space or move a lot of clutter to grab your child from his or her bed.

In planning the nursery, consider how the various important pieces of furniture that you would like to use fit into the room. Make sure that the room layout allows you adequate space around the changing area for a diaper pail, trash can, and clothes hamper, as well as a place where you can store clean diapers (remember, they take up a lot of room) and other changing accessories. Since you will be spending many, many hours in the next two years standing beside the changing table swinging your little one by the ankles, carefully mapping out the most convenient places for your washcloths, diaper rash ointment, and nail clippers will save you lots of headaches and back strain later.

Pink or Blue, or Yellow or Purple or Red . . . ?

Decorating the nursery can be a lot of fun, especially with the cute wallpapers and border strips that are available in baby patterns today. In fact, most large wallpaper and paint outlets have so many patterns to choose from that deciding may take more than one trip to the store.

Wallpaper generally is more expensive than paint, but a room in which even one wall is painted and decorated with a border strip can really show off your baby furniture with a unique flair. Borders can be placed along the ceiling molding or at crib level so your baby can look at them. As your baby grows up, borders can be changed to update the look of the nursery.

Although pastel colors are still many parents' choice, primary colors such as red and yellow are in vogue as well. Newborns respond positively to bright, bold prints within a few months. Black-and-white geometric patterns also are popular, reflecting academic studies that have shown that black and white stimulates visual perception. If your nursery has a window, you can accessorize with curtains and/or blinds that not only look nice but also keep out the sunlight during naptime.

When I worked in a pediatric office, we had eight examining rooms: four with vinyl floors for boys, and four with carpet for girls. The distinction may not seem important to you before you have a baby, but you will find quickly enough how sensible it is to tread on linoleum if you have a boy—with his own personal fountain. Linoleum is practical because it is easy to keep clean. If your home is carpeted, you might consider investing in carpeting with a stain-resistant coating.

There is a lot of equipment needed for your baby—and a lot of equipment promoted by salespeople that you can do without! How do you decide? This chapter lists the items that you should consider buying in preparation for your baby's homecoming. I will make suggestions on how many of each you need and what features to look for when you go to the store. There are some additional pieces of equipment, such as a high chair, that you do not need right away. These things have not been included in this chapter. (See chapter 8 for this information.)

Whatever you do, remember to do it together. This is a great time to talk about the baby and about how you think he or she will change your family and yourselves. Life will change when the baby comes. If you really love one another, you can welcome that change with confidence and joy.

Now I Lay Me Down to Sleep

BASSINET OR CRADLE

When most of you dream about your baby's homecoming, you probably see an image of a pastel-colored nursery with a handsome crib lined with a handmade quilt and matching eyelet-trimmed pillows ready and waiting like a cushioned manger for your baby's arrival. Most baby stores promote this vision, prominently featuring their cribs (also their highest-priced items) beautifully crowned with arched canopies and lined with matching quilts, pillows, and dust ruffles. Some parents-to-be come home to a scene like this, but if you do not have your crib set up right away, do not feel that you have automatically failed Parenthood 101.

On the contrary, I prefer that newborns come home not to a crib initially but to a bassinet or cradle or some other small bed, and that they sleep there at least for the first three or four months of their lives. I have several reasons for recommending a bassinet or cradle rather than a crib as your baby's first bed.

Bassinets and cradles are small—usually less than three feet long and sixteen to eighteen inches wide—and tiny babies seem to prefer lying in the enclosed space rather than in a more open and unprotected environment. With its small mattress, a bassinet or cradle also offers an easier way in which to swaddle your baby and tuck him or her into tightly wrapped blankets, giving the baby additional comfort and security. All you need to do is watch a tiny baby "scrunch" its way into a corner of a crib to realize how much infants prefer small, "safe" spaces. (See chapter 5 for instructions on swaddling.)

Another reason I suggest using a bassinet is that most come equipped with wheels and can easily be rolled around the house and into whatever room you happen to be (or out of the room for naptime). Most cradles are not portable.

Second, especially if you are breast-feeding, it may be preferable to have your baby sleep in a bassinet or cradle next to your bed and not in a separate room, at least for the first three to four weeks of life. Your newborn will be awake and need to be fed about every two to three hours around the clock. It is a lot easier to reach into a cradle, grab the little screamer, and bring the baby under the covers with you than to don your robe, walk to the nursery, and find a comfortable place to sit four times each night.

Some parents disagree, of course, finding it more convenient and less bothersome to their routine for the newborn to sleep in a separate room from day one. Some parents do not sleep well with their babies in the master bedroom. One couple I know tried the arrangement but found that their cat already had dibs on the bedroom! With their baby in the nursery with the door closed, the cat could not bother the infant during the night. (Remember, cats are nocturnal.) Use your judgment and personal tastes to determine what works best for you.

WATERPROOF SHEETING

When you are making up your bassinet or cradle, of course, the mattress is placed on the bottom. On top of that you need a waterproof sheet to protect the mattress when your baby's diaper runneth over. One of the most popular types of sheets available today is called flannel waterproof sheeting. A soft-surface waterproofed flannel, it is an excellent product and can be purchased in prepackaged bassinet and cradle sizes in baby and department stores or by the yard in many fabric stores. (Note: waterproof sheeting also is available in crib size, twenty-seven inches by thirty-six inches.)

Because this sheeting is made with rubber, it usually smells strongly when you first remove it from the plastic package. For this reason, I suggest airing it out for a few days before you use it or washing it once before placing it in the bed. If you plan to use the bassinet for several months, you need two to four sheets of waterproof lining, which should be washed regularly.

SHEETS AND BLANKETS

The bassinet or cradle sheet is then placed over the waterproof sheeting. Since the sheets are used only for a few months, you may opt to bypass purchasing them in favor of using your flannel receiving blankets for the same purpose. Receiving blankets are the softest material against your baby's skin, and they are easily tucked under the bassinet or cradle mattress much as a flat sheet is prepared on a grown-up's bed. In either case, you need three to five sheets or blankets for the bed because they should be changed each time your baby wets or spits up on them. As with waterproof sheeting, launder the sheets and blankets in warm water, using detergent and a nonchlorine bleach.

A covering sheet is not used until your baby graduates to a full-size bed, so basically the setup described to this point is all you need. Your baby goes into it with one or two receiving blankets tucked around, depending on the climate. In addition to the flannel receiving blanket, I highly recommend a thermal blanket as well because this loosely knit fabric is breatheable, making it cool in the summer and warm in the winter. It needs only to be draped over your baby and tucked under the mattress, rather than used for complete swaddling. (See chapter 7 for more on your infant's sleeping routine.)

A full-size crib is made up the same way as a bassinet or cradle, except that I suggest adding an optional mattress pad between the mattress and the waterproof sheeting. The pad helps make the bed a little softer and keeps the cold of the plastic mattress from chilling your baby in the winter or causing the baby to sweat in the summer. In addition, to avoid having to change the crib sheet after every nap, place a receiving blanket or a clean cloth diaper under your baby's face when the baby sleeps. If the baby spits up, you can merely change the cloth and leave the sheet.

MOSES BASKET

One alternative to purchasing a cradle or bassinet is to use a Moses basket for the first few weeks of your baby's life. Portable and compact, these baskets, named for the ark of bulrushes where the biblical baby Moses lay, are useful outside of the house as well as at nighttime and serve double duty for families on the go.

A Moses basket is hard to resist for any expectant mother, in particular because the idea of placing a tiny baby in a handled basket lined with dainty prints and ruffles is almost too cute to bear. Unlike a portable bassinet, however, a Moses basket does not come with a stand, and I do not recommend using it at night or in chilly weather without placing it on a sturdy surface or purchasing an optional frame to raise it off the floor, where it may be drafty and cold.

CRIB

Whether you decide to begin with a crib, or postpone its use until your baby outgrows his or her bassinet or cradle at about four months of age, the crib is one of the most important pieces of baby equipment that you will purchase.

With the vast variety of colors, shapes, and styles available today, deciding which one to buy might make you feel like a kid in a candy store for the first time. Prices vary by hundreds of dollars, depending on the brand name, where you buy, and how fancy the design is. What you choose depends only upon your budget and personal tastes.

Regardless of what you spend, there are a few safety features to check for, particularly if you are buying a second-hand crib or are planning to use an antique model that was not built to comply with today's rigid safety standards.

- The spaces between the vertical slats should measure no more than two and three-eighths inches (three to four adult finger widths).
- Rail height should be at least twenty inches above the top of the mattress when the mattress is at its lowest point; the crib sides, when lowered, should fall at least four inches above the mattress.
- The release latch on the side rails should lock into place. Some cribs require two hands to release the crib sides, making it impossible for the baby to do so from inside the crib. Others have a foot-operated release latch.
- The guide rails on which the crib sides slide up and down should be sturdy and fit securely to the corner posts.
- Wood surfaces should be free of splinters and cracks, and should be painted with only lead-free enamel. Washable paint is preferable.
- Avoid cribs with exposed bolts, sharp edges, or raised corner posts that protrude more than five-eighths of an inch. One consumer group has demanded a recall on cribs with higher corner posts, claiming that they could snag a child's clothing, necklace, or pacifier cord and cause strangulation.
- Be sure no openings in the headboard or footboard are

large enough for your baby's head to become wedged in them.

If you are uncertain your selection meets these safety criteria, I suggest buying a new crib from a nationally known company because all of their products are tested and approved.

I cannot urge you enough to buy a crib that is sturdy and will withstand your shaking it rather vigorously, particularly if you are planning to have more than one child. If you are as fortunate as I have been, the crib will last through several two- and three-year-old temper tantrums, and then will be handed down to your grandchildren (who also will have two- and three-year-old tantrums).

MATTRESS

Purchasing a mattress for the crib is one time on your shopping spree where you can be guided by your salesperson. New types of mattresses are developed all the time and offer updated designs in coils and interior support systems that promise the best support for your growing baby.

In most cases, any of the major brands are fine and offer proper support with a combination of inner springs, foam-wrapped coils, and/or high-density foam. If the mattress is stuffed with animal hair, it may cause an allergic reaction, but if you cover the mattress with an airtight plastic, that problem should subside. Crib water mattresses also are available these days in a standard size to fit any crib. Infants and children do very well on them.

Although I urge you not to stint on the mattress, it also is not necessary to buy the most expensive mattress—unless you are planning to have twelve children. A more expensive mattress will not necessarily give your baby more support, it might just last longer.

One word of caution: make sure the mattress fits snugly into the crib frame. If it does not, make the necessary adjustments now before your baby arrives so no part of the baby's tiny body can become wedged between the mattress and the crib bars.

CRIB MATTRESS PAD

Much like a mattress pad you would buy for your own bed, the crib-size version adds comfort, keeps the chill off, and protects the crib mattress. Pads are available in baby specialty and department stores. As was suggested for the bassinet, be sure to top the pad with waterproof flannel sheeting before adding your top sheet.

CRIB SHEET

I recommend crib sheets made of knit cotton and/or polyester because they stretch tightly, stay on the mattress better, and are softer than nonstretch muslin or percale. You need to buy three to four sheets to start.

BUMPERS AND OTHER SOFTWARE

At this point in your shopping trip, when you have selected your crib and have begun looking at bedding, the salesperson who has been helping you may try to make a major sale by saying, "Okay, now you have your crib. Let me show you the software that goes with it." There are some wonderful quilts, pillows, bumper pads, wall hangings, and all kinds of the cutest things in matching fabrics available to line your baby's crib and walls these days. I am sure that major bedding manufacturers disagree, but I hate to have parents think that they must buy these items if they cannot afford them. Most of them are totally unnecessary.

A quilt is definitely a no-no. It looks pretty to put over your baby while you are watching him or her, but it is not a safe way to cover the baby at night. Quilts are heavy, and they are not breatheable like thermal blankets. If your baby scrunches down underneath a quilt, he or she may have trouble getting enough air. Despite my opinion, you will find that quilts are popular shower gifts, and they make beautiful wall hangings. Like quilts, pillows are unnecessary and can be dangerous. Children do not need pillows until much later.

If fancy linens do fit into your budget, I agree that they are cute accessories to buy, but please do not let anybody tell you that this is the way it should be as far as decorating is concerned.

Your baby does not need these things; the choice is up to you. If you purchase crib bumper pads, make sure that they are secured by at least six ties so they do not fall into the crib. And remember to remove all decorative pillows, quilts, etc. when your baby is sleeping unsupervised.

"This Is Your Fourth Outfit in Three Hours!"

DRESSER

Of course, your baby needs someplace for clothes, but a special dresser is not a necessity as long as you have drawer space available for his or her first tiny garments. The amount of storage space you need will depend on how much you have to store, but generally one small-to-medium-size dresser will suffice. I say small-to-medium because although you might wonder how much space tiny clothes can take up, infants today often receive so many clothes as gifts that the parents may look like poor relatives in comparison. A pint-size dresser may look cute, but you will find it impractical as you accumulate new clothes.

If your dresser holds your baby's clothes, but has no room for anything else, wooden cubes make excellent storage shelves, and they can be painted or stenciled in any color to match the nursery decor. Whether you choose a dresser or wooden cubes or both, check for lead-free paint that is not chipping or cracking.

CHANGING TABLE/SURFACE

In addition to a dresser, you need a changing surface. Some dressers, if they are deep enough, convert to changing surfaces, or you can buy a portable, plastic changing surface that you can place on top of your baby's dresser. Some new parents living in cramped quarters find that changing their baby on the kitchen or bathroom counters works, too.

The most important thing to consider when deciding where and how to arrange your baby's changing area is that the changing surface should be high enough so that you are not bending over uncomfortably each time you have to change a diaper. For this reason, I strongly advise you not to plan on changing your baby on your own bed, which requires you to bend down for several minutes at a time, sometimes up to fourteen times a day. If more new mothers avoided doing this, obstetricians would see fewer cases of postpartum women suffering from backaches. By the same token, some shorter women find that the four-drawer dressers that are sold as convertible changing tables are too tall for them to use comfortably. Test changing tables in the stores before choosing one that is right for you and your mate (obviously, you have to compromise if one of you is tall and the other short).

In considering the purchase of a changing table or a dresser with a convertible changing top, look for a surface that is flat and firm and topped with a loose mattress pad or a piece of foam rubber covered with moistureproof fabric. I also prefer a top that is enclosed by small railings, which might someday keep your baby from rolling off. Safety straps serve the same purpose. Some styles come with utility shelves underneath, which I find quite useful since you can have everything at your fingertips during what is sometimes an anxiety-provoking time (remember little boys and their big fountains). Finally, all toiletries used for changing should be placed within your reach and out of your baby's reach; and never, ever, should your child be left unattended, even if he or she is strapped onto the table.

DIAPER PAIL

If you are using a diaper service, a diaper pail, liner, and deodorizer may be provided. If not, do not rent one, as it is cheaper in the long run to buy. Look for one that has a snug top that snaps on and is made of a sturdy but lightweight plastic.

HAMPER

A clothes hamper is very important because, to keep your baby clean and smelling sweet, you will need to change him or her often. Place the hamper near the changing area and diaper pail.

TRASH BASKET

Buy one large enough to hold at least eight disposable diapers, cotton balls, wipes, etc. To complement the nursery decor, the trash basket may be stenciled or decorated with appliqués to match your paint or wallpaper.

DIAPER STACKER

A diaper holder or stacker is not a necessity, but these adorable cloth creations often come in fabric to match bedding and can be a convenient way to store clean (but bulky) diapers, especially if you do not have enough shelf space in your baby's changing area. Diaper stackers can be hung on the end of the crib or changing table.

When Every Day Is Christmas

MOBILES

Black-and-white mobiles are all the rage these days because of reports that infants are stimulated by bold patterns and designs in black and white. A simple "happy face" drawn with black marker on a white paper plate seems to do the trick as well.

Babies react well to bold, bright colors, particularly if the shapes are simple and are placed close to their range of vision (initially eight to twelve inches) above the crib, changing table, or bathing area. Look for mobiles on which the hanging objects are facing down toward the baby; these styles are more interesting for an infant to watch than the kind that are hung to be best seen by parents.

TOYS

Newborns love human features and simple drawings of smiling faces. Similarly, they often are keen on seeing their own face. Nonbreakable mirrors are available in many styles to hang inside the crib and near the changing and bath areas.

After a few months, as motor skills are refined, you may want to add lightweight rattles and perhaps a "crib gym" so your baby will have something to pull on and kick at while lying in bed.

Remember, too, that it is never too early to interact with your baby by reading and singing (babies do not care if you sing off-key) and dancing. A few good books and audio or video tapes may help you recall your favorite nursery rhymes and lullabies. Audio and video tapes are available in most toy stores to help you learn all the old favorites, and some new tunes as well.

Finally, everybody loves stuffed animals, and your baby

probably will receive many of them during the first year. Babies love to look at faces, and stuffed animals are no exception. They also make great teaching tools to help you interact with your baby by adding a third party to your "conversations."

SWING
Expectant parents are always surprised when I tell them that of all the baby toys and equipment they will buy, the most useful in saving their sanity from the time their baby is three weeks old is an infant swing.

A swing seems like a pretty sophisticated purchase for an expectant couple to consider. "What in the world will our tiny baby do with a swing?" you might ask. But trust me, if you do not buy another thing for playtime, a swing is a must.

Basically a swing is an infant seat molded to baby's shape that is suspended from a metal frame, and it rocks your baby back and forth in a front-back motion. The front-back motion is something babies love far better than the side-to-side motion.

In almost all cases, babies have discovered that the dinner hour is the time for screaming. The only way of calming them is in the swing. They do not want to be held or fed or rocked or burped; they want to be swung. When they are swinging, you and your partner can eat. It is a good trade-off.

Swings come in two basic styles. The first is a hand-operated, wind-up version that swings for ten to twenty minutes before stopping. Be careful not to overwind. The other style is battery operated, which I find more convenient, although it is more expensive. The batteries operate for quite a long time. In fact, you could probably go away for a weekend and come back and the swing would still be swinging.

In either case, look for a swing that is mounted on strong posts with a wide stance to prevent tipping, has a seat of soft sturdy material, and comes with safety straps. Some swings convert to portable infant seats; please note that they are not meant for use in the car.

A footnote: about 5 percent of babies, according to my observations, do not love swings, but the 95 percent that do make up for the others. Babies who do not like swinging do not seem to calm down while riding in the car either. If your baby is not thrilled with a swing, try placing a phone book underneath your baby to weigh down the swing. The added weight slows the swinging, and your baby may like it better.

I learned another way to getting full use of a swing from one of the daddies whose wife delivered at our hospital. He told me that sometimes when the swing stops and you have to rewind it, the winding mechanism clicks and the noise wakes up the baby. In some models, if you pull the swing back and then wind it, the clicking noise stops and your baby will stay sleeping— sometimes.

Babies can be swung as early as three weeks of age, but they seem to outgrow their swings by about four months. For that reason, swings are a good item to purchase at garage sales, because no baby seems to wear them out.

Maybe the Bank Will Extend the Loan

LAMPS
Any moderate light source will do in your baby's room, although adorable baby lamps are hard to resist. Some parents say that they prefer wall dimmer switches or rheostats, which are particularly useful at night.

ROCKING CHAIR
Please, mothers, remember your own needs when setting up the nursery. A comfortable rocker or chair for feeding and relaxing with your baby is a must.

NIGHT LIGHT
Night lights are not necessary, but often are nice to have for nighttime feedings and changings.

MONITOR
The first night or two home from the hospital, every burp and strange noise your baby makes will jolt you out of bed, so a nursery monitor may seem appealing. Mothers are so tuned in to their baby's every move and noise that a monitor probably is not necessary after that time unless your baby is well out of earshot or if you live in a two-story home. Nevertheless, moni-

tors are popular, if only to give parents extra peace of mind. The choice is yours.

SMOKE ALARM

Although you do not need a smoke detector in the nursery, it is a good idea to have one in a hallway or other area between the most likely fire hazard (the stove, or where parents smoke) and the entrance to the nursery. Mounted on the ceiling or high on a wall, the smoke detector should be checked regularly and its batteries changed twice yearly for maximum security. (See chapter 7 for more safety tips.)

SHEEPSKIN

Wool has been used in incubators of neonatal wards for years to soothe and comfort babies, and it has become increasingly popular in homes, too. According to industry sources, wool has a unique fiber structure that absorbs moisture vapor but repels liquids, insulates against heat and cold, and resists flames. In addition, recent technology has made some wool products machine washable and dryable.

Sheepskins for babies come in a variety of sizes and styles, some washable and some not. While this is not a necessary piece of equipment, it can be comforting for fussy or colicky babies. Check with your local baby stores and/or your pediatrician for their advice on what kind to buy.

Making Your Decisions

With all of these purchases to consider, remember that you do not have to buy everything on your first trip to the store. In fact, I highly recommend that instead of making a decision on the spot, you go home and think about what you really need and can afford. Check other stores for prices on the same items. You can buy the exact same equipment at different stores for different prices. Not only can comparison shopping and talking over your decision be a lot of fun (and a great way to share in the anticipation of the baby with your spouse), it may also save you money.

While you are still thinking about the crib and other major

purchases is a good time to ask your parents if there are any baby items of yours that they might have put away after you outgrew them. I am fond of recalling that very special day when I searched the attic and found a box of baby clothing that I kept over the years for my first grandchild. Each one of us might have one garment like that. Even if you do not, think of the wonderful memories that the question will bring back to your mother just by your asking.

Most grandparents-to-be really enjoy their children's pregnancies, and yours can be an excellent time for sharing and building bonds with your family. If your parents want to buy your baby something and if they can visit you sometime in the last few months before the baby comes, it makes the experience so much nicer to go shopping together. I cannot emphasize enough how important it is to make your pregnancy a period in which family relationships are strengthened, both with your spouse and with the baby's grandparents. Shopping time can provide a wonderful opportunity to rekindle these shared experiences.

Diaper Matters

I hope you are sitting down when you read this because what I am about to tell you may be something of a shock. You know babies wear diapers, but do you have any idea how many diapers you are going to be changing from the time you take your newborn home from the hospital until the time he or she is potty-trained about two and a half years later? You may not welcome this information, but I will tell you anyway. You are going to be changing somewhere between five thousand and six thousand diapers—three thousand for mom and three thousand for dad.

When you are doing six thousand of anything, you probably want a good idea of what to expect. These are your options: to save money, you can buy cloth diapers and wash them at home. You might say, "That would be great, but I do not have a washer or dryer." The truth is that with the money you save by doing your own diapers, you can afford to buy a brand-new washer and dryer. To figure your cost, add up the purchase of at least four dozen diapers (prefolded gauze are the best), plus the cost of gas, electricity, water, and laundry soap.

Another option is a diaper service. There are services throughout the country. Most markets are pretty competitive, so the cost difference generally is a matter of pennies between one and another. If you are using a diaper service, your first delivery will be a batch of eighty to ninety diapers, which are expected to last about seven days. The following week, the serviceman will bring you ninety fresh diapers and take away the soiled ones. The first delivery usually includes a lined diaper pail with a deodorant bar in the top. Diaper service is a great convenience for parents who prefer cloth diapers, and some companies offer a combination service so you can purchase your disposables from them as well. Call the diaper service during your third trimester for details.

A third option is to go with disposable diapers full-time, which is the choice of many parents. There are many disposable brands on the market, and most work very well. They are very absorbent, so your baby's bottom probably will not chafe when he or she wets. In some ways, today's superabsorbent diapers may be too good. I remember one mother calling me in despair saying she checked her baby's diaper regularly and that he had not had a wet diaper in two days. The diaper might feel dry, I told her, but change it anyway; and when she did, she found that the diaper weighed about two pounds, it was so full of urine. She had not felt the moisture because it had soaked into the diaper below the lining.

If you plan to use disposables, you can shop for them as early as your third trimester. Watch for coupons in the newspaper; using them is a great way to save money. Despite the many commercials, I find that there is not much difference among the major brands. The approximate cost of disposables or diaper service is about double the cost of doing your diapers at home, depending on where you live.

Very often I am asked which type of diaper is best for a baby. Being a typical grandmother, I used to believe that good parents would use cloth on their little one's bottom. In fact, at one time I was so righteous that I refused to use disposables at all. The first time my daughter asked me to baby-sit, she and her husband arrived at my house with the baby and a box of paper diapers. Naturally, I was horrified, and I said so. After all too much shouting, my daughter turned around and left, taking her baby and the disposables with her.

After that incident, stubborn as I am, I set out to find all the terrible rashes disposables caused, to prove that my daughter was wrong. But, to be honest, I couldn't find anything. Many parents have expressed concern that disposable diapers are filling up our landfills and are harmful to our environment. You may want to consider this issue when making your decision.

But babies really don't care what's on their bottoms so long as they are changed frequently. With both cloth and paper diapers, it is important to change diapers often. Diaper rash almost always occurs because baby is not changed frequently enough. Any diaper that fits well enough so that bowel movements do not squirt out all over the place is a good diaper.

Regardless of your personal choice, I do suggest buying at least a dozen of your own cloth diapers because they make wonderful burp cloths and bibs. Also, if you run out of whichever type you are using, you always will have these on hand for emergencies.

CLOTH DIAPERS

If you use cloth diapers, plan to buy four or five dozen to begin with. Prefolded gauze are the most popular. Reduce to one dozen if you are using a diaper service.

DIAPER PINS

If using cloth diapers, you need four sets of rustproof, stainless steel pins with double-locking heads.

DIAPER LINERS

If you are planning to wash your own cloth diapers, you may want to use paper diaper liners. These rectangular liners are placed inside the diaper to "catch" your baby's bowel movements. The liners are lifted out and thrown away so you do not have to scrape the bowel movement from the cloth or "dunk" the whole diaper in the toilet to rinse it.

In addition to liners, there is a product available today called a diaper doubler, which is similar to a feminine napkin. It can be used inside a cloth or paper diaper for extra absorbency.

WATERPROOF PANTS

Waterproof pants are necessary over cloth diapers to prevent urine and bowel movement from leaking onto baby's legs and clothes and onto mommy's and daddy's laps. Four to six pants (size small) will give you a good start; remember babies grow fast! The pants are washable and dryable and may be used over and over. Waterproof pants are a particularly important part of your baby's wardrobe at night, although the pants may lead to diaper rash or chafing if the moisture locked against your baby's tender skin is left there too long. When using waterproof pants, change your baby often. If a rash does occur, leave the pants off as much as possible, exposing the rash to the air, double-diapering, or using diaper doublers without pants until the rash clears.

DIAPER WRAPS
A new alternative to waterproof pants, diaper wraps are manufactured to be more breatheable and therefore are touted to cause less diaper rash than the pants. They also have Velcro closures, so you do not have to bother with diaper pins. On the downside, however, until they are improved, diaper wraps are not as waterproof as rubber pants, and therefore I do not advise using them at night without plastic pants over them. They also may be quite expensive.

DISPOSABLE DIAPERS
If you use disposables, you need about ten per day and should buy a few weeks' supply to start. Begin with the newborn size, which fits babies up to fourteen pounds. Disposables are also very convenient for babies on the go, even if they are in cloth at home.

PREMOISTENED WIPES
Some pediatricians suggest that these chemically treated cleaning sheets not be used on very young babies except for travel. Others remain unconcerned. Please check with your doctor.

How Can These Tiny Clothes Take Up So Much Room?

Over the years, I have found most newborns are happiest in clothes that are not too cluttered with lace and ruffles around the neck and wrist and that give them room to maneuver as much as possible. For a time, just after the government came out with warnings about clothing made out of flammable material, mothers showed a strong preference for infant wear made from synthetic fabric. (Polyesters can be made flame-resistant and can be treated with flame-retardant chemicals.) That concern has died down recently, and cottons are back in vogue. Cotton is very absorbent and feels good against the skin, but it absorbs stains especially well, too. Formula is the worst offender, so if you like cotton and are bottle-feeding, get in the habit of using a bib. On all garments, check for scratchy labels and seams sewn with plastic thread that will irritate your baby's tender skin. (See chapter 6 for a stain-removal chart.)

UNDERSHIRTS

Undershirts come in two styles: the kind that go over the head, and those that snap across the chest. Most parents, and I agree, prefer the snap-on kind for newborns because they are easier to put on. Babies are not too thrilled about having things pulled over their heads. Plan to buy at least four if you have a washer/dryer and six if you do not. Purchase 100 percent cotton or stretch cotton/nylon. Some parents opt to skip the three-month size and start with the six-month size, which is only slightly large for the average newborn.

NIGHTGOWNS

For sleepwear, I prefer nightgowns to stretch suits because nightgowns are easier to lift up in a jiffy for your baby's 1:00 A.M. changing. And his 3:00 A.M. changing. And his 5:00 A.M. changing. . . . You get the picture. Most nightgowns have a drawstring, which is nice in cold climates so that you can secure the gown at the bottom. Drawstrings can be somewhat of a pain in the neck, however, as they entangle the rest of the clothes while spinning in the dryer. I recommend removing the drawstring before laundering. Plan to buy three or four nightgowns if you wash daily, four to six if you do not.

STRETCH SUITS

Stretch suits are just what they sound like—one-piece, stretchy garments made of cotton and/or synthetic, with ten to fourteen snaps or a zipper down the inside seam and/or in front. They are great for your baby to wear most of the time, unless the weather is very warm. However, I do not advise buying many stretch suits for your newborn right away. These are the type of garments that people love to buy as baby gifts because they are so tiny and cute. Wait a few weeks after your baby arrives to buy more than one or two.

SWEATERS

Depending on the climate, two or three cotton and/or wool sweaters will do for a newborn.

BUNTING/PRAM SUIT

Whether you purchase a warmer outer garment for your baby depends on the season and the climate in which you live. A good guide might be to look at how other mothers have dressed their babies in the local park or shopping mall.

SOCKS/BOOTIES

I prefer socks to booties because booties fall off easily, and most of the time your little ones do not need anything heavier than cotton socks on their feet. When purchasing socks, look for the athletic type, with an elasticized ankle; these stay on better than those without elastic. However, what new parent can resist tiny Weeboks or Mary Janes?

HAT

A hat with a visor is a must if your newborn is in the sun at all, particularly in the summer months or in warmer climates. Premature babies and small newborns wear little caps in the nursery because a lot of heat is lost through the skull. If your baby weighs more than seven pounds, however, he or she probably does not need a hat for warmth unless you are going outside in winter temperatures.

RECEIVING BLANKETS

If you have already visited a maternity ward, you saw many tiny newborns wrapped up like pink and blue burritos in the nursery. The swaddling clothes that the nurses use to wrap infants are called receiving blankets. They are used not only for swaddling but for 1,001 other things, such as sheeting for your baby's bassinet. I also advocate using flannel receiving blankets as baby bath towels because of their softness and absorbency. Receiving blankets come in cute pastel patterns or can be made easily from flannel purchased in the fabric store.

The other type of receiving blanket you will need is a thermal blanket, which you will use to cover rather than to swaddle your baby. Because they are breatheable, thermal blankets are the best type of blanket to use to control your baby's temperature, and they are unlikely to limit your baby's ability to take in air if he or she crawls underneath it. I suggest buying four to six flannel and two to three thermal receiving blankets to begin with. Double the number of flannel if you plan to use them for sheets and towels, too.

LAP PADS

Lap pads are small squares of waterproof sheeting that are handy for feeding and burping—and for under baby's bottom on the changing table. They come in handy when grandma or grandpa need extra protection from spills and accidents when your baby is on their lap. Keep at least three or four on hand.

BIBS

Bibs are most important after your baby is eating solid foods, but I have found that small bibs help keep your baby clean during bottle- and breast-feeding as well. Two to four should be enough.

LAUNDRY DETERGENT

You undoubtedly will marvel when you find that your tiny baby can produce a daily load of laundry more than twice his size. There is really no alternative to washing clothes every day or every other day, so if you have any choice at all, try to move your washer/dryer, if you have one, to an easy-to-reach spot in the house. There are several mild detergents on the market to use for your baby's clothing, and any one that contains borax should do the job without leaving any harmful chemical residue on baby's clothes.

In some states, the law requires that baby's sleepwear be made of flame-resistant polyester fabric, which means that the material burns slowly and when removed from flame is either self-extinguishing or easy to extinguish. To retain flame resistance, manufacturers recommend washing these garments in detergent before using them. Washing with soap products may reduce the flame-resistant quality.

Places to Shop

Most of the large baby furniture stores carry baby clothing, but I have found over the years that I have done better both price-wise and selection-wise by shopping for baby layettes at the major department stores. Most have large infant departments, many name brands, and excellent salespeople who are used to dealing with expectant parents.

When it comes to buying your baby's layette, I would highly recommend not buying huge amounts of any of the items I have discussed. That bundle that looks so tiny when you bring it home from the hospital will have outgrown everything by the time you turn around.

Once you start accumulating these wonderful clothes during your pregnancy, your excitement about your baby wearing them in the very near future starts to build. At least once a day, you look at the clothes with total disbelief that these are going to be worn by your child. It is an overwhelming feeling to think that you really are going to have a baby, and these are your baby's first outfits. Enjoy these feelings. Take pictures. Create memories. I promise that you will cherish them for years to come.

When you start getting ready to put your little garments into your baby's dresser, it is fun to use the wrapping paper you have received at baby showers to line the dresser drawers. You might even write the name of the person who gave you the gift right on the paper. Even years later as you open your baby's drawer, the paper will bring back very warm and tender memories.

"It Seems All We Ever Do Is Feed Him"

Chances are that, if you are like most women, you will not be well versed in the subtleties of breast-feeding versus bottle-feeding until you reach your third trimester. For this reason, it might be a good idea to refrain from purchasing items used for

feeding until after you have made a decision as to which alternative you prefer. You also may find that you change your mind
about what method of feeding is best for your baby once you try
it. However, should you wish to take care of your shopping needs
early, the followng items are required for baby feeding.

BOTTLES (DISPOSABLE/REGULAR)

Bottles come in all sorts of fancy shapes and sizes these days,
some of which feature high-tech handles to facilitate baby's
holding them. Others are made of specially treated plastic that
senses when the bottle's contents are too hot. I prefer the plain,
clear plastic bottles that you can buy in any grocery store. I
have not found these to be lacking in any way. Nor have the
parents I know told me that bottles with disposable inserts are
any better or worse (i.e., cause more or less ingestion of air into
your baby's stomach) than those without.

If you you plan to bottle-feed, purchase about eight large
(eight ounce) bottles and two smaller (four ounce) ones for juice
or water. If you plan to use the disposable bottles, two extra
rolls of disposable inserts are optional. It is best if you decide
before you buy what brand of bottle you want to use because
the caps and rings of some brands do not fit with others. The
disposable bottles, although excellent for travel, are an entirely
different size than the regular bottles. For this reason, buying
sets (bottles/nipples/caps and rings) is a good idea.

NIPPLES

As with bottles, my observation is that most nipples (regular,
orthodontic) are the same, despite what nipple manufacturers
want you to believe. Nevertheless, chances are that you will not
need to buy any extra nipples, as all bottles come with nipples.
The only important feature to check for in making your purchase
is that the nipple is made specifically for the liquid you desire.
Nipples with small holes are meant for use with formula, milk,
or water, and nipples with slits or larger holes are made for
juices.

STERILIZER

Check with your pediatrician to be certain that he or she agrees,
but from my experience sterilizing bottles is no longer consid-

ered a necessary part of the feeding process. Washing bottles and silicone nipples in a dishwasher cleans them well enough to avoid all potential health problems. (Latex nipples will become gummy if they are exposed to the heat of the dishwasher drying cycle.) They also can be washed in the sink with hot, sudsy water and rinsed well.

BOTTLE/NIPPLE BRUSHES
You need one bottle brush and one nipple brush for sink cleaning.

BOTTLE WARMER
As with sterilizers, bottle warmers are no longer considered the necessity that they were in my day, and babies have shown no ill effects from drinking cold milk or formula. However, I still prefer warmers over feeding your infant milk directly from the refrigerator. Electric or battery-operated warmers are nice to have because they are convenient to use by your bedside at night.

INFANT FORMULA
Most pediatricians have a favorite brand. Check with your doctor or with your hospital nursery for their recommendation.

NURSING PADS
These disposable pads are worn inside your bra and are recommended for mothers who choose to breast-feed and find that they leak milk between feedings. Also, when you are feeding on one side, the other side may leak, and pads or wads of toilet tissue are really the only way to keep your bra and outer clothes dry.

SWEDISH MILK CUP
One option or addition to breast pads is a plastic, dome-shaped cup that you wear in your bra called a Swedish milk cup, which collects breast milk if it leaks during feedings. If the cup is sterile and the milk is transferred to a bottle and refrigerated immediately, it may be used for a later feeding. Swedish milk cups are recommended to ease the pain of engorgement, help

make engorged nipples erect, and remedy inverted nipples during pregnancy. A lactation specialist can be consulted if you aren't sure if purchasing these is appropriate for you.

BREAST PUMP

Breast pumps, used for extracting milk for bottle feedings, come in hand-operated and electric or battery-operated types. If you plan on pumping a lot of milk—for example, when you return to work—a battery-operated pump may be most efficient. Otherwise, both types seem to be comparable. (See chapters 5 through 7 for more information on nursing.)

NURSING BRAS

Nursing bras offer extra support and are better than regular bras for breast-feeding mothers because they have a built-in flap that allows you to feed your baby without taking off your bra. (See chapter 1 for information on what size to buy.) Plan to buy at least three if you expect to nurse for several months.

PACIFIERS

When my children were born, and for many years afterward, pacifiers were a no-no and were said to cause malformations of the mouth, buck teeth, infections, and other nasty problems. Today, although some pediatricians still maintain the old thinking, most doctors agree that pacifiers are completely healthy for your baby. In fact, some pediatricians argue that if the baby does not use a pacifier, he or she is likely to begin sucking the thumb, and thumb sucking can result in jaw problems later in life.

Sucking a pacifier is your baby's way of gratifying the natural sucking instinct, which needs some extra practice in between feedings, particularly if your baby is on a bottle. By the time your baby is three or four months old and has mastered the art of sucking, the extra practice will not be needed and the baby is likely to begin spitting out the pacifier. This is the perfect time to wean the baby from it completely. As to the type of pacifier you choose, most parents seem to have a preference, and your pediatrician probably is up on what brand is best.

Everything for Bath Time, Including the Kitchen Sink

BATHTUB
When I had my children, many mothers opted not to buy a separate baby bathtub, instead bathing their babies in the kitchen sink. Today, however, sinks often are smaller and/or divided, and can no longer serve double duty like they used to.

Some parents may consider using their own adult-size tub for their baby's bath, but I do not recommend doing this. It is not only hard on your back and knees with all the bending over that is required, but unless you have apelike arms, it is very hard to get a snug grip on your baby while you are leaning over the tub side.

In looking for a baby bathtub, consider beginning with the large tub rather than the very small infant size. Not only does the baby outgrow the tiny one very quickly, but the larger one is really more fun to splash around in once your baby is used to the water. The tub should be placed at waist level if possible and on a firm surface.

If you are worried about your baby slipping and sliding, you can buy a sponge bath insert or place a towel on the bottom of the tub on which your baby can recline in cushioned comfort. However, even with the insert, infants always need to be supported in the tub until they can sit up on their own at about six months.

WASHCLOTHS
I agree with the advice of most of the pediatricians I know that newborn bottoms really are best served if they are wiped and cleaned with warm water and mild soap rather than disposable wipes. For this reason, I am a big fan of washcloths kept by your changing area, and you need a lot of them to wash your baby's bottom at every changing.

If there is no bowel movement, you can wring out the washcloths and reuse them once or twice before laundering, but you still should plan on having at least six on hand to get you through the day. To save money, you can make your own washcloths by cutting small squares from terry cloth purchased at a fabric store.

If you run out of washcloths, the second-best method for cleaning up baby's bottom, other than using a disposable wipe, is to use a soft, white paper towel. (The dye in the colored designs may be irritating to baby's skin.)

If your changing area is not close to a sink, try keeping a squirt bottle filled with water nearby to moisten the washcloth or paper towel for more effective and gentle cleaning.

TOWELS

As a new parent, you probably will receive several towel sets for your infant, so I would advise against buying any right away. In fact, if you want, flannel receiving blankets can be substituted for terry cloth towels.

The best feature of baby bath towels is their hoods. I say this not because the hoods are important to your baby's care but because babies look so cute wearing them after their baths. Some of the most precious snapshots I have seen are of new babies wrapped all cozily in their bath towels. You can almost smell their sweet odor. So if you are a camera nut, invest in a hooded towel.

SOAP

Any mild, nondeodorant bar will do for bathing and hair washing. Baby shampoo is optional.

BATH ACCESSORIES

Probably almost as scary as walking into the baby equipment store for the very first time is standing in the supermarket aisle under the sign that reads BABY NEEDS. Obviously, you think if the sign reads BABY NEEDS then your baby needs these things: oils and lotions and powders and shampoos and soaps, rubber pants and pacifiers, bottle cleaners and bottle tops . . . hundreds of items. It can be overwhelming.

To make life easier, let me say that when most hospitals send you home they will give you a rectal thermometer and a bulb syringe. The rest of the "baby needs" found in most stores basically are not necessary.

Among the items that you *do* need:

- Rubbing alcohol, for umbilical cord care.
- Cotton swabs or cotton balls.
- A&D ointment.
- Petroleum jelly.
- Safety nail scissors.
- Squirt bottle.
- Enema syringe (check with pediatrician).
- Acetaminophen (check with pediatrician).

In the hospital in which I work, some of these things and similar hygiene items are provided in a small washbasin in every mother's postpartum room. If your hospital does the same, please take all of the items home—you'll probably pay for them whether you use them or not. Take the plastic washbasin, too; it makes an excellent tray to keep by your changing table for soiled washcloths, wet clothes, and other changing paraphernalia.

To Grandmother's House We Go

CAR SEAT

Absolutely the most important item you buy for your infant is the car seat. Car accidents are the number-one cause of injuries and death in young children in this country today. Car seats are mandated by law in all fifty states, as well they should be.

When I think back to when my children were tiny, of course, there were no car seats. I can remember vividly how my right arm would fly out to the passenger side of the car and catch my children each time we came to a sudden stop. That was our only safety device for many, many years. It is frightening to think how many children could have suffered major injuries while riding in the car.

Today, car seats come in two different styles. The first is the infant seat, which takes the baby from the newborn stage to about six to eight months of age. The other one, which is a larger car seat, can be used from infancy until your baby is a toddler.

At first, it seems to make more sense to buy only the larger car seat, but trust me, the smaller car seat is not something you should pass up. There are several reasons for this suggestion. First, with any luck you will have a quiet baby that hardly ever will cry, but chances are that some days will not be as good as others. There will be times when your baby is so tired or so fussy that the only thing that you can do is take him or her for a ride in the car. For some magical reason, once a baby is in that car seat and the car starts going, he or she will fall asleep. If you have your baby in the larger car seat, when you get to where you are going you have to pick the child up out of the car seat, and there you are stuck with that screaming baby again. If you have the smaller car seat, which is very light, you can pick up the whole thing without waking the baby. It really is worth every single penny. The first time that happens, you will thank me.

Second, the smaller car seat doubles as an infant seat, which is a recliner in which your baby can sleep and watch the world go by when you are unable to hold him. The seat sits at a slight angle and can be used at home or out.

When trying to find the right car seat for your baby, check to make sure the model you like has a wide, stable base that attaches securely to your car with at least one seat belt. Look for a nonskid bottom surface and easy-to-use safety straps. All of the commercial car seats available have to have passed national safety standards, so there isn't any one that is safer for your baby than any other. (See Resource List for a toll-free number to check on car seat recalls.) You can go to a very expensive car seat with a plush lining in it, or you can get something less expensive, depending on your budget and how the seat appeals to you aesthetically. An infant car seat is something that can be bought at garage sales or borrowed from friends, but make sure if you do this that you have all instructions and pieces.

When you get home from the store with your car seat, open the box, read the instructions, and take the seat to the car. Borrow someone's baby or use a stuffed toy, but make sure you know how to buckle the car seat into the car and buckle the harness straps over your baby's head. Dads especially need to know this because the day they come to the hospital to pick up their wife and newborn baby, the car seat should be in place. Most hospital nurses are not permitted to put babies in the car seat, so that has to be done by dad. The safest place for baby to ride is in the middle of the back seat, facing backward. That is how all newborns should ride until they have adequate head and shoulder control (at around six months of age).

A reminder about using your car seat in the summertime: buckles can get very hot, especially when the car is closed up in the hot sun. It is a good idea to throw a receiving blanket over the buckles to keep them from absorbing the heat.

STROLLER/CARRIAGE

Because I lived in a major city when my first child was born and I had many friends who had babies in the city, I was lucky enough to receive a beautiful English pram when my eldest daughter was born. As I strolled my firstborn down Fifth Avenue, I was very proud to be pushing her in this carriage. Today life-styles have changed drastically and very few parents need to have prams unless they live in a large city and that is the only place they are going to be out walking. Because of their mobility, strollers are much more popular with parents today than carriages. Strollers fold easily, lay back flat for infants, and sit up to accommodate older children.

Strollers are made by many different companies throughout the world, and some are more aesthetically appealing than others. Look for features such as a wide wheel base to prevent tipping over, large double wheels that swivel and lock, and brakes that lock tightly (preferably on all four wheels). Look for a large shopping basket over the rear axle, a reclining seat that does not cause the stroller to tip, sun visors that move forward and back, and a firmly attached safety belt. Check that the stroller is not too heavy for you to lift with one hand and that it is easy to collapse and to steer.

Try out the stroller in the store with the help of a salesperson. Find out how easy it is to fold and put into the car. Another important feature is a reversible handle that will allow you to look into the stroller when your baby is small and lying down. When the baby is older and tired of looking at mommy and daddy and wants to see the rest of the world, the handle flips into another position and baby is facing outward. The handle should be expandable for tall parents. If you are tall, you will be bending over with a normal handle height. Test the strollers in the store to make sure you are not kicking the wheels; this, too, can be annoying during a time that is meant for relaxing and enjoyment.

You might be considering buying an umbrella stroller because they are so lightweight and less expensive than the regular strollers. I suggest that, if you can afford it, you wait to buy one of these until your baby can sit up. Most umbrella strollers do not recline all the way back as regular strollers do, and newborns can get really scrunched up trying to sit up in these strollers before their little bodies have adequate muscle tone to do so.

The running stroller is quite popular here in California. It is a large canvas slinglike seat mounted onto three large rubber wheels. Obviously it is very sturdy, and the rubber wheels cushion your baby's ride as you push him along at a speedy clip while you jog. As with the umbrella stroller, the portable running stroller works well with an older baby who can sit up on his own. Check with your pediatrician.

STROLLER LINER

A stroller liner is a washable, padded, cloth insert that is optional for use inside the stroller. A washable sheepskin works well for extra comfort and padding as well as protection for the stroller itself.

FRONT PACK

A front pack or sling in which to carry your baby like a papoose is not an absolute necessity, but it is convenient for shopping and doing other things for which you need two hands. Using a front pack permits your baby to be close to you without your having to hold him or her, and babies thrive on that physical contact.

Before buying a front pack, it is a good idea to borrow one from a friend either for the four to six months that you will use it or at least to test it out with a ten-pound baby fitted inside it. Some carriers will fit your shape and muscle tone better than others, and if you can find the best one before you buy, you will not get home with a carrier that you never wear because it is so uncomfortable.

Features to look for in carriers: washable durable material, sturdy heavy-duty straps, safety buckles, snug fit, good head support for baby, even weight distribution, easy to take on and off (particularly important when you want to place your sleeping baby into the crib without waking), cushioned waist and shoulder straps, and properly sized leg and arm holes. Do not buy a back pack right away. This type of carrier is useful only after your baby can sit up on his or her own (at about six months of age).

DIAPER BAG

Look for a diaper bag that includes a changing pad and plenty of outside pockets to hold various pieces of baby equipment that you need to grab fast. If you use the kind of bag that snaps onto the stroller handle (with Velcro or metal snaps), be sure that it does not cause the stroller to tip over. Another option is to purchase a mesh bag similar to a French shopping bag that does snap onto the stroller handle and in which you can put a small diaper bag or purse. (See chapter 7 for how to pack a diaper bag.)

THERMOS

To keep bottles cold, you may want to purchase a lightweight Styrofoam thermos container or insulated bottle bag. It keeps a bottle cold for several hours in moderate temperatures and helps prevent spoilage for a time.

Baby Announcements

Not everyone buys baby announcements, but if you plan to do so, I promise you a very rewarding experience if you go with your partner. Just thinking about the baby announcements raises all sorts of exciting prospects—most important, will you have a boy or a girl? Announcements can be as simple as a note or a postcard or as elaborate as the cards that tell the world every detail of your baby's birth, complete with professional photographs. I often have walked into a postpartum room to find a new mother writing her announcements or addressing the envelopes. This is always a special time for her.

LANIE CARTER'S LAYETTE CHART
Basic Clothing for the Newborn

ITEM	HOW MANY		COMMENTS
	Have Washer/ Dryer	*No Washer/ Dryer*	
Diapers (cloth)	4 doz.	4–5 doz.	Prefolded gauze most popular. Reduce to 1 doz. of your own if using diaper service.
Diaper pins	4 sets		For cloth only; look for double-locking heads.
Diaper liners	1 box		A paper-towellike protective liner; for use with cloth diapers only. Prevents stains and "dunking" to remove bowel movement.
Waterproof pants	4	6	For use with cloth diapers, especially at night. Watch for chafing, rashes; change often.
Diaper wraps	4	6	An expensive alternative to waterproof pants; limit to daytime use, substituting waterproof pants at night; Velcro closures easy to use.
Diapers (disposable)	2 boxes		Excellent for use away from home. If using all the time, plan on 80/ week. A box for outings is handy even when using cloth diapers.
Undershirts	2–4	4–6	Snap-side easier on infants; cotton or stretch cotton/nylon. Pullover style better for older infants. Some parents opt to skip 3-mo. size and start with 6-mo. size (4–6 shirts).

ITEM	HOW MANY		COMMENTS
	Have Washer/ Dryer	*No Washer/ Dryer*	
Nightgowns	2–4	4–6	Remove drawstrings for easier laundering. Preferable to kimonos.
Stretch suits	3–4	4–5	Typical baby gift; buy fewer until after shower and baby gifts arrive.
Sweaters	2	3	Depends on the climate.
Bunting or pram suit	1	1	Depends on the climate.
Socks	4	6	Best choice for footwear. Look for elastic tops to hold them up.
Hat		1	Use as protection from sun, cool air.
Receiving blankets	4	6	Flannel, knit, or thermal types. Flannel also make excellent sheets for bassinet or cradle and towels for baby's bath. Double amount you plan to buy if multipurpose use.
Lap pads	2	4	Use on lap when feeding, burping.

Clothing Size Chart:

Preemie	Birth to 6 lbs.
3 mos. or small or layette	Birth to 13 lbs.
6 mos. or medium	14–18 lbs.
12 mos. or large	19–22 lbs.
18 mos.	23–26 lbs.
24 mos.	27–29 lbs.

Feeding Needs for Newborn

ITEM	HOW MANY	COMMENTS
Bibs	2–4	Small ones fine until baby is eating solids.
Pacifiers	2	Check with your pediatrician.
Bottle-Feeding Disposable bottle kit	1	Buy nipple brush, too.
Disposable bottles or 8-oz. bottles	2 8	Glass or plastic. Standard supermarket type preferred.
Nipples	3	Any type should be okay.
4-oz. bottles	2	For juice or water. Often provided by hospital, so hold off on buying until after baby is home.
Sterilizer		Check with your pediatrician.
Bottle brush	1	With stiff bristle.
Nipple brush	1	With stiff bristle.
Bottle warmer	1	Not necessary, but nice for use at night.
Infant formula		Check with your pediatrician.
Breast-Feeding Nursing pads	1 box	To be worn inside bra.
8-oz. bottles	2	For emergencies, supplements.
4-oz. bottles	2	For emergencies, supplements. Often provided by hospital so do not buy before baby comes.
Bottle brush	1	With stiff bristle.

ITEM	HOW MANY	COMMENTS
Breast pump	1	For expressing milk.
Swedish milk cup	1 set	Helps reform inverted nipples; catches "drippings"; eases nipple soreness.

Nursery Needs for Newborn

ITEM	COMMENTS
Bassinet or cradle	Bassinet highly recommended because it is mobile, cozy environment for newborn.
Bassinet/cradle mattress	Use flannel waterproof sheeting to protect mattress.
Waterproof flannel sheeting	Used between baby and mattress. Plan to buy 2–4 sheets for each bed.
Bassinet/cradle sheets	Receiving blankets tucked over waterproof pads do nicely instead of fitted sheets on bassinet. If buying sheets, plan on 3–5 fitted sheets.
Blankets	40 x 60 thermal receiving blanket is the best choice for proper temperature control; breatheable.
Crib	Many parents opt to place baby directly in crib, which is fine as long as bumper guards are used. Bassinet/cradle babies move to crib at three to four months.
Crib mattress	Very important purchase; buy good quality.
Crib mattress pad	Cushions baby; protects mattress.
Waterproof flannel sheeting	Plan to buy 2–4 sheets sized to mattress dimensions.
Crib sheets	3–5 fitted sheets; knit cotton or cotton/polyester seems to hug mattress best.
Crib bumpers	Necessary with newborn; matching accessories such as quilt, pillows should be removed at night or when baby is unsupervised.
Blankets	40 x 60 thermal receiving blanket best choice.

ITEM	COMMENTS
Dresser or clothing chest	Any type with no-lead paint will suffice.
Changing surface	Changing table not necessary; but check height of surface for comfort.
Diaper pail	May be provided by service. Also available are pail liners, scented deodorizers.
Clothes hamper	Keep handy near changing area.
Swing	For hours of entertainment, buy early.
Nursery lamp	A typical gift.
Rocking chair	A comfortable feeding chair of any type is highly recommended. Rocker pad nice to have.
Diaper stacker	Convenient; a typical gift.
Night light	A safety feature for night feeding.
Wall decor	Personal choice; bright colors and black/white provide good sensory stimulation. Infants love mirrors (nonbreakable) near crib, bath.
Nursery monitor	Optional, mostly for parents' peace of mind.
Nursery smoke alarm	Personal choice.
Mobiles	A convenient distraction for baby if hung over changing, bathing, and sleeping areas.
Toys, stuffed animals	Typical gifts.
Sheepskin	Natural wool proven to calm newborns as well as cushion them on variety of surfaces.

Bath Needs for Newborn

Item	Comments
Bathtub	Rigid plastic recommended.
Washcloths	At least 6, but the more the better as these are useful not only for washing but also to wipe bottom at diaper changing.
Towels	1–2, hooded or not, the larger the better. Can use receiving blankets or terry cloth sheets as well.

Cotton swabs/balls	1 large box. Sterile cotton, not polyester.
Safety scissors	With rounded edges, for clipping nails.
Rectal thermometer	Good idea to have two since they break easily. Digital or glass is fine.
Nasal aspirator	Often provided by hospital.
Enema syringe	Check with your pediatrician.
Baby soap	Check with your pediatrician.
Rubbing alcohol	For umbilical cord care.
A&D ointment	Check with your pediatrician.
Premoistened wipes	Not recommended for newborns except while away from home.
Acetaminophen (liquid or suppository)	Check with your pediatrician.
Safety latches, etc.	Not necessary until baby is crawling.
Squirt bottle	For use when running water is not available.

Travel Needs for Newborn

ITEM	COMMENTS
Car seat (infant type)	Required by law; must be in car before baby is discharged; can double as infant carrier. Washable cover is convenient, as is padded infant head support.
Bassinet/crib (portable)	Buy early if you plan to use instead of regular bassinet.
Stroller or carriage	Look for one that reclines fully, has reversible handle.
Stroller/carriage liner	Cushions baby; buy one that is washable.
Front pack	Useful, especially for shopping; frees hands. Back pack cannot be used until 6 mos.
Diaper bag	Don't leave home without it.

By the Way, Don't Panic

I am sure that after reading this long, long list of the items that you want to consider buying for your newborn, you are undoubtedly a bit overwhelmed. Yes, a baby needs a lot of equipment. No, a baby does not come cheap (although there are ways to minimize your costs). Yes, your baby's things will take up a lot of room in your house. And no, you cannot keep the baby in the yard.

Please remember, however, that your baby will not thrive on how many fancy nightgowns he or she has or on whether the stroller is lined with the softest sheepskin. Your baby will thrive on your love. So whether you dress your baby in imported lace or in hand-me-downs, it does not matter. Provide for your baby as you see fit and as you are able within your means. Most of all, provide for the baby's emotional needs, and he or she will bring you joy every day of your life.

3

❖

A Time for Decisions

Not long ago a new father came to see me because he was concerned about his wife's relationship with their one-year-old son. His wife, he said, was a good mother. She spent time with their boy and cared for him with attentiveness and a sincere commitment to his well-being. She carried out her husband's philosophy of child-rearing perfectly.

Unfortunately, she was not good at making decisions. For example, she never disciplined their baby on her own. She was unable to choose a day-care program. She followed her pediatrician's advice on feeding, but would not offer the baby anything that the doctor had not suggested.

When we discussed the situation further, the father revealed that his wife was an only child raised by parents who believed in strict discipline. They had made all of their daughter's decisions for her from the time she was a child until she graduated college. They told her what to wear each day, what foods to eat, and what courses to take. When she married, her husband admitted, his wife relied on him to make many of the decisions that affected their lives.

After hearing this story, I tried to reassure this concerned husband and father that his son probably would not be harmed by his wife's unusual characteristic as long as the parents acted as a team. Even though daddy makes all the decisions, it is advised that mommy appears to be in complete agreement. Parents who act jointly are most effective.

Nevertheless, I could not help feeling sorry for this new mom whose parents had not allowed her to learn to make decisions for herself. From the time we are children, most of us build up our decision-making skills by trial and error, making small decisions to begin with and bigger ones as we get older. Our parents help us distinguish right from wrong. In this way, we gain confidence in our choices.

As parents, you gain confidence in your decision-making skills gradually, as well. With a newborn, the decisions are small ones: to breast-feed and/or bottle-feed, whether to take a long trip with the baby, how long to let the baby cry. These are really "baby" decisions. As your child gets older, the decisions become more consequential: How do you discipline your child? What educational path do you believe is best? The decisions that you make get bigger and bigger, and with each step your ability to make these decisions improves. Learning to make decisions that serve the family is step three on the stairway to parenthood.

Although physically difficult, the final months of your pregnancy may be the most spiritually and emotionally uplifting for you and your partner. In the seventh month (weeks twenty-eight to thirty-two), many fetuses turn upside down in preparation for birth as they "walk" around and around the uterus like astronauts in space. At this time, your baby's feet touch its forehead as it performs these somersaults. It is getting very cramped in there!

You may be able to distinguish you baby's body parts, such as a round bottom or a foot or knee sticking you in the ribs. The hand may feel like a fluttering movement, but when the whole body takes a dive, it is not hard to imagine the baby swimming inside you. Most women are still relatively free of side effects of pregnancy at this time.

In month eight (weeks thirty-three to thirty-seven), your baby is close to the size that it will be when born, and the internal organs are well developed. During the remainder of the baby's stay inside you, it continues to gain insulating fatty tissue under the skin (about two pounds) and the lungs become better equipped to breathe the air. Also at this time, your baby acquires antibodies to diseases that you have had or for which you have been immunized. Movements have become more forceful, as if your baby is calling to be let out. This is most distinctive when you are at rest; at night, for example. By the end of the month, however, do not be surprised if your baby's movements are more restrained; he or she is just too big to move around as much as before! You, too, may start to feel too big to move around and may begin to experience some late-pregnancy discomforts, depending on how big you are.

You and your partner share your third trimester getting ready for the baby by shopping for the layette, preparing the nursery, and deciding on names. These times, too, are special ones as you wait on the threshold of parenthood.

You will make many important decisions about your lifestyle and your baby as your due date approaches. As with other major decisions, I encourage you to work these out as a team and to use the next few months to discuss the areas in which you have different opinions.

Throughout this book, I return again and again to the importance of sharing in the experiences of pregnancy, childbirth, and parenting with your partner. It is as important to do so with big decisions, such as what to name the baby, as with small decisions, such as whether to paint or wallpaper the nursery. It is important because sharing your thoughts and working out compromises helps you grow stronger as a couple—and, with your baby, as a family.

Learning to make decisions together also helps you to learn to rely on your own judgment. That reliance bolsters your confidence as a parent. This chapter examines some of the decisions that you and your partner have to make before the baby arrives. I encourage you to read it together and to use it as a catalyst for discussion.

The ABC's of Parenthood Education

In preparing for your baby, you have many choices of prenatal education ranging from childbirth classes to exercise classes for pregnant women and new moms. Because I am a fan of education as preparation for having a baby, I encourage active participation in these classes. Not only may you feel more confident as a result, but you may benefit from the contact with other couples and individuals going through a similar life change. Community-based support is essential in the absence of strong family ties.

First among the classes that I highly recommend is a childbirth class, in which you learn what to expect during labor and delivery, your options for pain relief, and how to cope with the birthing process by using various relaxation techniques. These classes may be offered by your doctor's office, local hospital, and/or women's health center. You may find these classes most helpful if you take them early in your third trimester, when the prospect of your baby is becoming increasingly real. Learning what to expect is a good way of calming any irrational fears you may have, too. After the class, you will know what you can do to make the birth a positive and memorable experience for both of you.

Second, I suggest a class in breast-feeding if you are thinking about nursing your baby. For many women, breast-feeding is more difficult and frustrating than they had imagined. By attending a class you learn what to expect, and you are better prepared to handle any difficulties that may arise. Lactation classes are available in many communities through the local hospital or women's health center.

If you are not already worried that having a baby means more studying than you ever did in school, you should consider enrolling in a class in infant CPR and emergency care taught by someone certified by the Red Cross, the American Heart Association, or the American Academy of Pediatrics. Emergency care may not be a topic that you want to think about when you are pregnant or after the birth. Keep in mind, however, that injuries are the number-one killer and cause of disability in children. According to the groups mentioned above, one out of every three deaths among children in the United States results from an injury, and one out of every five children in this country each year will have an injury serious enough to require hospital emergency room treatment. Those statistics alone are good enough reason for every parent to enroll. (See chapter 8 for safety information.)

Options for Your Special Delivery

In the 1990s, childbirth options are blossoming, making the decision about how you want to deliver your baby a confusing one. When all is said and done, you will deliver your baby basically the same way as it has been done for centuries. Only the specifics of childbirth are different.

In my opinion, expectant mothers should deliver their babies in a hospital. A hospital is by far the safest place to have a baby for the mother, who may need the support of medical experts as well as medication, and for the baby, who may need specialized medical care *in utero* or during and after the birth. Many hospitals let dad stay overnight, too. This is a plus for brand-new dads who are in no condition to hit the road while still in the lingering postpartum state of euphoric exhaustion.

If you think that a hospital environment is too far removed from that which nature intended, remember that most hospital administrators have learned from the experiences of women who have delivered in settings more intimate than the traditional delivery room. This knowledge has led many hospitals to offer a wide array of birthing options that, while still medically safe, offer a personal touch to giving birth. Also, a hospital is a comforting place for you to be if you are handling an infant for the very first time and are feeling a little clumsy and unsure of your parenting skills. You may want to discuss the following options with your partner before making a decision.

Nurse/Midwife

Some hospitals have programs in which certified nurse/midwives are permitted to aid in delivery. Arrangements for delivery with a midwife need to be made well in advance of your third trimester, as midwives are expected to participate in your prenatal care as well as labor and delivery. Your midwife remains in charge as long as the birth progresses normally. If you or your baby is in distress, a doctor is called in.

(If you prefer a nurse/midwife, you may want to investigate the option of delivering in a birthing center, which is a low-cost alternative to a hospital for mothers who are at low risk for complications. If you encounter unexpected problems with delivery, you will be transferred to a nearby hospital or treated by backup M.D.s.)

In-Hospital Alternative Birthing Center (ABC)

The rules and regulations of what is commonly referred to as an "ABC room" differ in each hospital. Generally, this alternative offers a birthing environment for women who do not want or expect medical intervention. The ABC room is decorated to resemble a bedroom in one's home, and family members and friends are permitted to attend the birth. With the emphasis of this setting on low-risk, natural childbirth, you are not permitted any sophisticated pain relief such as regional anesthesia, which requires that you and your baby be monitored with machines. You are discharged within twelve to twenty-four hours of a normal delivery, oftentimes lowering your cost of giving birth in a hospital. The ABC room, because it is the closest thing hospitals offer to home birth, may be a good alternative for you if you have had extensive prenatal childbirth education and you feel very comfortable with birthing techniques.

Labor-Delivery-Recovery Room (LDR)

Traditionally, women labor in one room, are moved to another room for delivery, and then go to a third room (usually shared with other women) for postpartum recovery. With the LDR option, you are not moved, but instead go through the stages of normal birth in the same bed in the same room (unless you require a cesarean section). Becoming increasingly popular, the LDR option combines the best aspects of a private, homelike birthing experience with the benefits of professional hospital care. However, LDR rooms, if they are available, differ greatly from hospital to hospital. Some rooms have windows, for example, while others feel quite closetlike. Some doctors have no objection to the rooms, while others find them less sanitary than the traditional delivery room option. The best way to decide if this option is for you is to discuss it with your obstetrician and to visit the LDR room in your local hospital.

Labor-Delivery-Recovery-Postpartum Room (LDRP)

In the 1990s, we are seeing another option called the LDRP room, which permits all the stages of childbirth—including your postpartum stay—in the same room. This option seems to make a lot of sense and may make life easier for parents and staff because it will simulate the best aspects of home birth with the safety pluses of giving birth in a hospital setting.

Standard Birthing Routine

If you opt for the traditional labor and delivery routine, you begin in a labor room, in which you spend the majority of your time while in labor. These rooms are decorated like standard hospital rooms with additional monitoring equipment. Some rooms may have televisions, cassette (or compact disc) players, reclining chairs for the coaches, and private bathrooms. In the traditional setting, you are moved to a delivery room right before the baby is ready to come out or when doctors determine that you need intervention, such as when the baby is to be delivered by cesarean section. Immediately following the birth, you are moved to a common recovery room where you stay for several hours while you rest and stabilize. You check into your postpartum room at that time and remain there for the rest of your stay.

In choosing from the above options, it is necessary to factor in several other decisions for the type of childbirth that you want to have. These choices vary depending upon the wishes of your physician and the sophistication of the hospital you will be using. All of the options should be reviewed with the appropriate doctors and/or hospital personnel well in advance of your labor day so that you understand the pros and cons of each.

The types of pain relief available to women in labor are of primary concern to many moms-to-be whom I meet in my prenatal classes. This is a topic, of course, that you should discuss with your obstetrician. Basically, you have a choice of five different types of pain relief medication, each of which has different effects on you and your baby. While you may want to go through labor and delivery without any medication, I advise you to familiarize yourself with each of these options, just in case you change your mind.

The medication offered to most women in the earliest stages of labor is a narcotic, such as Demerol, which does not make you unaware of your contractions but relaxes you and offers some mild pain relief. Use of narcotics can cause nausea and mild breathing difficulties in mother and baby.

Also available during early labor is a local anesthetic injected into the cervix called a paracervical block. A more risky option because of potential negative effects on your baby, a paracervical block stops all sensations caused by the dilatation (also called dilation) of the cervix.

A third option for pain relief is called an epidural, which is an injection into the lower back. The degree of numbness varies depending upon the type and amount of medication in the epidural. You may experience a tingling, numbing sensation from the waist down or become completely numb so that you cannot move your legs. Although the epidural has been proven to be quite effective in relieving pain, and it is safe for you and your baby if administered properly, it requires monitoring to assure that the medication has no ill effects. An epidural may slow the progress of labor, amd for that reason, it may not be given until you are dilated close to 4 cm. Women who opt for this type of pain relief may require the drug pitocin to augment their contractions. Your doctor may opt to use forceps or a vacuum extractor for delivery.

A fourth type of pain relief is the spinal anesthetic, which is injected directly into the spinal canal and causes total numbness from the waist down. It is typically reserved for forcep vaginal deliveries and Cesareans. A spinal is given just prior to delivery.

Finally, a pudendal block is an injection of anesthetic into the vagina or vulvar area to relieve pain associated with delivery and episiotomy. Your baby is not harmed by this last-minute shot of medication, the effect of which is similar to novocaine administered by a dentist.

From my point of view, new mothers are happiest when they have remained flexible and have explored all the options for medical intervention prior to the onset of labor. Too often

OPTIONS IN PAIN RELIEF

Pain Relief Medication	How It Is Administered	Effectiveness	Possible Side Effects on Mother	Effect on Progress of Labor	Possible Side Effects on Fetus	Remarks
Narcotic (Demerol)	Intravenous or intramuscular.	Mild analgesic, sedation, euphoria.	Shallow breathing, nausea.	None in proper dosage; may slow labor if given too early.	May cause shallow breathing, poor crying at birth.	Side effects can be reversed.
Paracervical block	Injection into cervix.	Blocks pain of cervical dilation.	Systemic reaction including convulsions if given in blood vessel.	None.	5–30% depression in fetal heartrate, neonatal depression.	Risky because of side effects.
Epidural block	Injection into space just outside spinal canal; catheter may be left in place to inject more anesthetic.	Greatly reduces pain or makes it disappear completely; mother usually can feel contractions and move legs.	Possible drop in blood pressure. Block may occur above the waist and affect breathing.	May slow labor, make pushing less effective, and prolong second stage; increased need for forceps delivery.	None, unless severe and sustained drop in mother's blood pressure.	Requires close monitoring of mother and baby.
Spinal block	Injection into spinal canal.	Complete numbness from waist down.	Same as epidural.	Stops labor.	Same as epidural.	Used for forceps deliveries, cesareans.
Pudendal block	Injection into vagina and vulvar area.	Reduces pain by blocking nerves in perineum.	None unless inadvertently given in blood vessel.	None.	Same as epidural.	Used during episiotomy.

How Long Do You Have to Wait for the Medication?

CENTIMETERS OF DILATION OF CERVIX

PAIN RELIEF MEDICATION	1	2	3	4	5	6	7	8	9	10	Delivery	or	Cesarean
Narcotic			XXXXXXXXXXXXXXXXXXXXXXXXXXXXXX										
Paracervical block			XXXXXXXXXXXXXXX										
Epidural block				XXXXXXXXXXXXXXXXXXXXXXXXXXXXXXXXXXXXXXXXXXXXXXXXXXXXXXXX									
Spinal block													XXXXXX
Pudendal block											XXXXXX		

(See chapter 5 for details on the progress of labor.)

women are programmed to believe that they have to go through labor completely naturally. Others who are quite apprehensive about the ordeal may think that they want to be "put out" entirely. The truth is that pain and discomfort are different for each woman. There is no way to predict what any one experience will be like. You do not know exactly how you will feel until you are there. The bottom line is that it is a shame to miss the enjoyment of childbirth because you are paying so much attention to your discomfort. If you can take medication that makes you more comfortable and you are more aware of what is going on, it is certainly a big bonus.

Along with choosing the if, when, and what of pain medication, there are other procedures associated with labor that you may want to discuss with your obstetrician. Each of these affects your labor experience, and you and your partner may find that you have strong feelings about them.

Amniotomy

Performed when your membrane does not break spontaneously, an amniotomy (the intentional rupture of the membrane that holds the amniotic fluid) may be used to speed up labor and/or to permit the insertion of an internal fetal monitor. It also may allow your physician to see if there is meconium (a substance in the baby's bowel) in the amniotic fluid. If so, the meconium may be a sign of fetal distress.

Fetal Monitoring

Done externally or internally, fetal monitoring is used to make sure your baby's heartbeat is steady and strong. I find it reassuring to nervous couples, but it can cause worry unnecessarily if the monitoring device comes loose and the monitor stops working properly.

Enema

Some hospitals use the enema as a routine procedure on laboring women to empty the bowel. Check with your doctor.

Episiotomy

OBs tend to decide at delivery whether an episiotomy (the cutting of the thin skin between the vagina and the anus to make a larger opening through which the baby may pass) is necessary based on the size of the vagina and the size of the baby. Done under local anesthetic (pudendal block) so it does not hurt, an episiotomy is a very common procedure. Recovery can be painful, however, with local burning, stinging, and itching. If you prefer not to have an episiotomy, ask your doctor if he can perform perineal massage during labor, which may stretch the skin enough to avoid both an episiotomy and tearing.

Prep

The shaving of pubic and perineal areas was once a routine procedure performed to keep the area sanitary and prevent infection. Recent studies have proven otherwise. Check with your doctor.

Cutting the Cord

When fathers first were permitted to participate in the birth by cutting the cord, some were afraid to do so because they thought they might cut in the wrong place, or that their hands might shake when they held the scissors. Then, when fathers realized that they were adept at performing this honorable task, a sort of envy developed between dads whose OBs permitted them to cut the cord and those whose OBs did not. Now, permission to cut the cord is routinely granted as dads have become integral members of the delivery room team.

Some husbands find cutting and clamping their baby's umbilical cord an exciting and emotional part of the birthing process. Others do not. This is a good topic to discuss between yourselves and with your obstetrician in anticipation of your labor and delivery. (If you have a cesarean, your partner may not be permitted to cut the cord because doing so would interfere with the surgical field, which must remain sterile. Some pediatricians allow dads to "trim" the cord after the baby has been placed in the warming bed.)

If you find discussion of labor pains and other less-than-pretty details about labor and delivery somewhat unnerving, you are not alone. Many women (and men) come to me panic-stricken about childbirth. If you are afraid of losing your composure during labor, all I can say is, don't be. Nurses and doctors are so used to guiding women through long and difficult labors that nothing that you do will startle them. They are there with all of their knowledge and experience to make your delivery a safe, comfortable one.

Fear of childbirth is particularly acute in couples who arrive at the hospital in labor several weeks before their due date. They have not had time to become impatient with the pregnancies. Women who go into labor closer to their due date or after it find that their fears about the birth seem to have dissipated. If I were not in the hospital as much as I am, I might think—as perhaps you do—that couples come onto the maternity floor with the mom-to-be shaking and the dad-to-be sweating and panicked. That is not what happens at all. Instead, one has the feeling that they are thinking, "Okay, we've been waiting, and this is the time, and we're here, thank God."

I recall one woman who was so fed up with her huge stomach, lack of sleep, and the constant phone calls asking "Well . . . ?" that she told me, "I would rather have sat on an egg for a year." By the time you get into the labor room, you will find that you may not be apprehensive about it, either. You just want it to happen. I assure you, it will. Nature has a way of allowing its fruits the perfect amount of time to ripen.

Your Baby's Doctor: A Beacon in the Night

Choosing a pediatrician or general practitioner (G.P.) for your child is an extremely important decision. He or she not only cares for your newborn in the first few hours of life, but sets the tone for the way in which you raise the child for years to come.

Pediatricians influence young parents in many ways. In the beginning, they offer suggestions on feeding, appropriate weight gain, sleeping routines, and when and how to respond to your infant's cries. A little later, they guide you through immunizations and the many important aspects of your child's growth and development.

For these reasons, I strongly advise interviewing several

pediatricians to find one with whom your personal philosophies about children are compatible. A "live-and-let-live" doctor may not be right for a parent who believes in strict discipline. Likewise, a parent who finds it healthy to have his infant sleep with mommy and daddy may feel ill at ease with a doctor who advocates early separation between parents and babies during nighttime sleep.

Most pediatricians and G.P.s are happy to meet with expectant couples in a prenatal interview (free or for a small fee). At this time, ask the doctor to describe his or her approaches to common problems. Ask about office hours, fees, and if doctors or nurses return phone calls at night. Other issues to consider are the proximity of the office to your home (you may be visiting quite often in the first two months), whether the office has a separate waiting area for sick children (generally in larger practices), hospital affiliations, feelings about infant feeding and sleeping arrangements, and the doctor's education. Finally, look for a doctor with whom you feel personally comfortable. I hope you will find one you like and one with whom you can trust your most precious possession: your child.

The Circumcision Decision

Unless it is done for religious reasons, a circumcision (the cutting and removal of the foreskin on the penis) generally is performed by your obstetrician or pediatrician the day after your baby boy is born. The procedure begins when the baby is carefully restrained on a plastic circumcision board. Restraining him in this manner is necessary to keep him secure and still during the surgery. Based on my observations, unwrapping the baby and placing him on this board is the most nerve-wracking part of the whole operation. All babies scream when their arms and legs are outstretched, especially when they are naked. Usually a nurse tries to soothe the baby with a pacifier or by rubbing its head.

In the meantime, the doctor places a clamp on the penis to temporarily stop the blood flow. He may inject the area with a little novocaine to make sure there is no feeling in the penis. Then, in a few seconds, the surgery is done. Many times it happens so fast that the baby does not even cry. Following the surgery, a medicated gauze pad is applied to soak up any bleeding that may occur. Generally the wound bleeds very little. Most babies settle down and do not seem to have any discomfort.

While your baby boy likely will sleep after his circumcision, you probably will be upset for a while. Many times I have gone into a new mom's postpartum room to find her in tears following her son's circumcision. This reaction is perfectly normal. You will feel better in a few days.

Until recently, circumcision was performed almost routinely on all boys born in American hospitals. Today more parents are playing a role in the decision as to whether or not to have their baby boy circumcised. I advise that as you think about circumcision, you take into consideration the psychological as well as the medical implications of your decision. When a father is circumcised, he usually wants his son to be circumcised so that the son will be better able to relate to his father as a role model. The same reasoning applies when parents want their son to look like the other boys at school. A helpful source for an expert opinion on this controversial issue is your pediatrician.

How Do You Want to Feed Your Baby?

Most expectant parents do not realize that the decision to breast-feed or bottle-feed has a tremendous influence on your earliest interaction with your baby and on your first experience as a parent. Some women, for example, nurse their babies because it fulfills an instinctual desire in them. Nursing is something only a mother and baby can share. It creates a special bond between a mother and her child. For men who help with feeding, using a bottle is a great way to establish a strong bond with their infant right from the start. Fathers who feed their infants often find that the experience gives them quiet times with their babies that they otherwise would not have shared.

Whatever option you choose, it is wise not to merely accept what is popular at any given time but to consider the pros and cons of all your options to determine the feeding method that fits best into your life-style. There are several options from which to choose.

You Can Breast-feed Exclusively

This choice places the entire feeding burden on the mother, who is apt to be feeding her infant every two to three hours around the clock for the first few weeks. Each feeding takes about thirty to forty minutes. Breast-feeding takes a lot of time, commitment, and patience and does little to help the new dad feel an integral part of the new family. It does, however, provide the baby with the very best and most natural milk, offering the exact nourishment he or she needs as well as antibodies that help protect from disease. Breast-feeding also may be extremely rewarding to the new mother, and it saves money.

Certainly all infants benefit from sucking on the breast in the first few days of life because they receive the mother's premilk, called colostrum. Colostrum is a thick yellowish substance present in the breasts from early in pregnancy. High in protein and calories, it is easily digested and contains immune factors that help protect the baby from some infections (antibodies in breast milk do the same thing). Colostrom helps clear the digestive tract of meconium. Babies start to receive colostrum as soon as they start feeding and until the mother's milk comes in (at about the third or fourth day postpartum).

If you want your baby to get the colostrum but plan not to breast-feed, you will have to go through several days of rather painful, engorged breasts when your milk comes in. You can avoid engorgement by asking your obstetrician to administer a hormone to stop your milk production; however, if you do so, you cannot breast-feed at all.

If you are thinking about breast-feeding, you may be concerned about weaning. The average mom breast-feeds for about four to six months, if her schedule permits. Others give it up eight weeks postpartum when they return to work, and others persist for a year and then wean directly to a cup. (See chapter 8 for information on weaning.)

You Can Breast-feed and Supplement with Expressed Breast Milk in a Bottle

This option takes advantage of nature's milk, while offering some relief to the mom if dad takes over some of the feedings. To accomplish this, mom must pump enough breast milk for one, two, or more feedings per day. (See chapter 7 for how to express milk.) If you choose to supplement with breast milk regularly, you may find it helpful to buy a breast pump. You also need several four-ounce bottles, which you probably can get in the hospital. (Every time baby is fed in the hospital, the nurses will bring you a bottle of sterilized water or 5 percent glucose water to supplement the colostrum. These bottles are great to take home, come complete with nipple, and are ideal for supplements.)

You Can Bottle-feed Exclusively

Bottle-feeding can begin at any time, whether you start out breast-feeding or not. A relatively worry-free alternative to nursing, bottle-feeding offers parents a great deal more flexibility. It is easy to see if your baby is getting enough fluid because with a bottle you can measure exactly how much the baby is drinking. Some parents find that knowing how much their baby is eating is reassuring and less frustrating than breast-feeding. Bottle-feeding is, of course, not as convenient as breast-feeding, requiring careful preparation and storage of formula.

You Can Breast-feed, and Supplement with Formula in a Bottle

Again, this choice takes advantage of the positive aspects of breast-feeding while giving the mother some freedom to return to a relatively normal life-style and allowing relief from the daily chore of pumping her breasts. Formula-fed babies usually sleep more soundly because, I believe, formula "sticks to their ribs" better than breast milk. For that reason, formula is a nice alternative for nighttime feedings. (See discussions of feeding in chapters 5, 6, and 7 for more detailed information.)

Most important, I think parents should work together with the pediatrician to find the feeding method that is most comfortable for them. Remember, you do not have to choose between the breast and the bottle. There are a number of ways in which you can get the best of both worlds. As long as you provide your baby lots of love and affection, whether the baby drinks breast milk or formula or both, he or she will be getting all the nourishment a baby needs.

Hi Ho, Hi Ho, It's Off from Work You Go . . .

In the 1990s, it is safe to say that most American women are working outside the home. When you become pregnant, whether or not it is by choice, when to stop working—and for how long—may pose a dilemma. Your decision depends on several factors: your health, your employer's maternity leave policies, and your financial situation. I encourage you to talk about each of these issues with your partner.

Health Issues

In the vast majority of normal pregnancies, doctors are not concerned about your working until the very end of your pregnancy unless your workplace poses particular health hazards, such as inhalation of dangerous fumes, or your job requires heavy lifting that might strain your abdominal muscles. Of course, this is a question that you should discuss with your obstetrician.

Employer's Policies

Maternity leave policies vary greatly under state law, and it is up to you to discuss the specifics of your situation with your company's personnel adviser or whatever individual regulates employment policies. Inquire from your employer or from the local labor office about disability and other benefits to which you are entitled when you stop working.

Finances

Previously, I discussed finances and the importance of working out a financial plan for your pregnancy and early child care. The outcome of this discussion should be factored into your decision about employment.

It is nice to give yourself a week or two off work before your due date, if your leave does not cut into your time off after the baby is born.

Breakfast in Bed

The time that you have to yourself after you stop working can be used to take care of tasks that need to be completed before your own "labor day." Start by making a trip to the local pharmacy to pick up last-minute toiletries or other items you may need in the hospital and for the first few weeks at home. Stocking up on supplies such as toothpaste, sanitary napkins, nursing pads, soap, toilet paper, paper towels, vitamins, laundry detergent, and pain relief medication, for example, saves you from having to go out or having to ask someone to get you these items after you come home.

Some families cook and freeze meals ahead of time. Others stock up on nonperishable groceries as well, so that they do not have to concern themselves with a great deal of shopping until they have settled into their new routine. A few extra pairs of underwear and socks for dad is helpful, too; you will find that family laundry takes a back seat to baby laundry almost forever.

While you are out, make sure that your car has a full tank of gas for the trip to the hospital. The baby's car seat should be in the car, too. I also recommend having a pillow or two in the car to help ease the rough ride while you are having contractions. An old towel may come in handy if your "water" breaks before you reach the hospital.

Another task you can accomplish during the final weeks (and one that helps pass the time in glorious anticipation of the days ahead) is to make a list of people to whom you wish to send baby announcements. Gather names and telephone numbers of people you may want to call from the hospital. You will find both of these lists invaluable when you and your partner are so eager to share the news that you do not even remember your own phone number.

In your quiet time, you can occupy yourself by "practicing" for labor, spending time with relatives and friends, making things for your baby (needlepoint, embroidery, and sewing projects seem to come out of the closet at this time as if reaffirming your maternal instincts), sleeping, and reading. It may be a long time before you have the peace and quiet to enjoy these special, serene moments again.

Finally, don't forget that these are the final days that you and your partner can spend alone together. I urge you to do whatever you can to enjoy each other's company. Plan a romantic dinner for two. Go to a movie. (A double feature would kill more time, but it is hard to sit still that long.) Take turns serving each other breakfast in bed. I have said this so many times that the message should be loud and clear: the stronger the link between the two of you, the better parents you will be.

The Child-Care Decision

When your baby is born, it is hard to imagine turning over his or her care to a stranger. It is even difficult to think of leaving the baby with a grandparent, although there aren't many grandparents willing to take on full-time child care. Nevertheless, many women do not have the option of staying at home full-time. Others choose not to do so, having found a great deal of personal fulfillment in their careers. With two working parents, day care becomes an important decision.

From what I have observed, children who are enrolled in high-quality day-care programs from as early as six weeks old do just fine. Good care given by someone other than the parents is not harmful in any way. In fact, I have noticed that children who learn their social skills in large groups tend to be more independent and outgoing than children whose days are spent primarily at home with mommy. When my generation stayed home as full-time moms, we tended to spoil our children because we were totally available to them. Consequently, our children were never given the opportunity to be on their own and to meet their own needs.

Before you consider the practical question of how to find competent care for your child, understand that for many women—and men—leaving a child in someone else's arms is very difficult at first. This difficulty arises for two reasons. The first is an instinctive desire to protect your child and a belief that you are the best person to care for him or her. All things being equal, your instinct is probably right, particularly because you love the baby more than anyone else.

Ironically, at the same time as you think no one is as good a caretaker as you are, you also may harbor an unconscious fear that the person you find to care for your baby *is* as competent and capable as you are. New mothers often find that they do not yet feel confident about their own parenting skills before they have to relinquish their caretaker role to another person. When day care starts too soon, the mother may feel jealous and resentful.

Even if you resolve all the emotional issues concerning child care, finding the right situation for your baby can be frustrating and confusing. Basically, day care comes in four varieties:

Day-Care Centers

Like major colleges, day-care centers may be hard to get into, with a six-month to one-year waiting list quite common. If you plan on returning to work immediately, it is not unreasonable to register your child in a day-care center the moment you find you are pregnant. Some employers provide day-care centers. Check with your personnel office to enroll or ask about the possibility of one starting.

Private Day Care in Someone's Home

These facilities vary greatly, and the only way to really know what you are getting is to visit the home in person. You can call the state licensing bureau for a list of people who provide in-home care in your zip code area. Then plan to visit at least three to five homes to find one you feel good about.

Private Day Care in Your Home

The most important aspect of finding someone to come into your home is to devise an airtight screening process, including checking several references. To find interested sitters, ask friends and neighbors for people they recommend. Ask at your place of employment or your church. Some parents report success advertising in local newspapers. You can go through an agency, which may be expensive, but that way you can be certain the applicants have been screened and are bonded. Finally, do not be too quick to turn qualified people away; it is useful to have alternate sitters in case your main caregiver is ill or is unavailable on a work day.

Co-op Baby-sitting

If you are in a position to watch other people's children part-time, you may be able to find other mothers to share in co-op baby-sitting. Mothers' support groups are an excellent place to find other interested parties.

Finding Child Care

This is a list of questions that you may find helpful in finding good day care:

1. What experience do you have working with children? How old are the children with whom you have worked?
2. Why do you like working with infants? What sorts of things do you like to do with children? Do you consider it part of your job to help them learn?
3. How do you go about setting limits and providing discipline?
4. What will a typical day be like for my baby when he or she is in your care?
5. What will you do if my child becomes sick?

Things to Look For:

1. Are children assigned a primary caregiver?
2. Does the caregiver cuddle, play with, and talk to the infants as she cares for them?
3. Does the caregiver try to stimulate the infant by pointing out things of interest and offering different objects to taste, touch, and smell?
4. Does the caregiver seem warm and patient? Does she seem to have a sense of humor?
5. Does the caregiver pay attention to each infant? Does she treat the infant as a special person?
6. Does the caregiver take time to comfort an infant who cries or is unhappy?

Credentials to Check:

1. Does it have a license? When was it last inspected?
2. Is it reasonably clean and spacious?
3. Is there developmental equipment for each age group?
4. Is the diaper-changing area away from the food area? Are hand-washing facilities nearby?
5. Is drinking water readily available?
6. Are there working smoke detectors?
7. Are radiators and heaters away from children?
8. Is there an outdoor play area? Does it have a soft surface under playground equipment?

(Adapted from *New Parent Adviser*)

"Will my baby still love me?" is the question all new parents ask when they place their infants in day care. I have known many babies and many parents throughout the years, and I have to assure you that children always know their parents and are eager to see them. Even if they are cared for by another person five days a week, do not worry that they will forget you or not like you when you pick them up. To your baby, nobody looks or smells as wonderful as you do. No other grown-up holds your baby with as much love.

Working It Out Together

How many times have you watched the scene in old movies or television shows when someone shouts, "The baby's coming! Someone start boiling water!"? So many first-time parents come to me with these thoughts spinning around in their heads. I will tell you what I tell them: Don't worry. Most first babies take twelve to eighteen hours to deliver. From the time contractions begin on a regular basis, this gives you plenty of time to make your way to a qualified medical facility.

That said, I encourage you to be prepared, just in case you go into labor earlier than you expect. First, make sure your car's gas tank is full. Second, know the best route and one alternative route to the hospital. Third, learn where the hospital entrance is and whether it is open at night. Some hospitals close their main doors after 9:00 P.M., and admissions are made through the emergency room. Fourth, complete your hospital admission papers in advance. Dads-to-be do not want to be in the admitting office when their partners are in labor.

In preparation for childbirth, I encourage you to tour the hospital in which you plan to deliver. Any time you can visit a hospital for a reason other than illness, you will feel more comfortable there. Many hospitals have organized tours. If not, visit the maternity floor on your own. Visiting hours usually are in the afternoon and evening.

When I meet expectant couples during their tours of the maternity floor, I am reminded of Hansel and Gretel standing in the forest. They hold hands and look into each other's eyes. Their faces lack confidence, but not love. In a sense, we all are Hansels and Gretels as we anticipate the birth of our children.

We are living a new life, playing new roles. We have all our life's experiences behind us making us who we are, but we have nothing like childbirth or parenting in our repertoires.

When expectant and new moms and dads look to one another for help and support, each may find that the person in whom they are confiding shares the same apprehension as they do. What can you do about it? First, talk about it. It is always comforting to know that someone else feels the way that you do. Even if you and your partner cannot make the apprehension disappear, you can make each other feel better just by being there.

Second, you and your partner need to find a way to be sympathetic to the other's experience of pregnancy and parenting. Men cannot be mommies, and women cannot be daddies, but we all can imagine what it is like to wear the other's shoes. In so doing, we learn to be more solicitous of our partner's feelings.

There is no better time to lessen the gap between our experiences than during the last month of pregnancy, when men and women really have no idea what the other is going through. For men, I am told, the last month is a very isolating and frustrating time. Men anxiously await the birth, but they feel helpless in making it happen. They cannot really understand what pregnancy feels like. They feel left out. They feel powerless and impatient, and on top of everything, they miss being the sole focus of your nurturing.

Women can help men through this time by doing several things.

- Place your partner's hand on your belly whenever the baby kicks. Ask him to push the baby very gently into a more comfortable position. This does not hurt the baby, but it makes "daddy" feel involved.
- Encourage your partner to pass the time by going to a concert or playing tennis with a friend. Unlike women, who can fill their days thinking about the baby, men may need a break from the pregnancy, yet they feel guilty taking the initiative. They will be grateful for your suggestion.
- When you talk to your partner, accentuate the positive rather than how bad you feel. He would rather focus on

life after the baby than to hear about your aches and pains, particularly if he feels helpless in curing them.
• Romance him, even if you do not feel like it. He probably feels worse about your aches and pains than you do. A little extra love does wonders.

The obstetricians with whom I work say that physical aches and pains are the most common concerns of pregnant women nearing the end of the third trimester. Most of the complaints are part of the normal course of pregnancy. Nevertheless, women need their partners to nurture them anyway. Here are my suggestions for men.

• Help your partner feel comfortable at night by bringing her extra pillows or a heating pad for her sore back. Massage her legs and feet after a long day, and loosen the sheets at the foot of the bed so her calves do not cramp. Moms need mothering, too.
• If she feels light-headed or her heart pounds after climbing the stairs, help her into a chair and bring her some juice. Offer to do the housecleaning or cooking or order a pizza.
• Respect her modesty if she has hemorrhoids, constipation, diarrhea, or vaginal pain. Ask if you can get her a cold compress, then let her be alone, unless she calls.
• Romance her, even if you're not as attracted to her as you normally are. She probably feels worse about her aches and pains than you do. A little extra love does wonders.

On Your Mark . . .

Now that you have made it through nine months of preparing for this child, you are finally ready to sit around and wait for the big day. When I say sit around, I literally mean "a round." By this time, you are certain to feel as big as a house, and probably do not feel like doing much more than resting and relaxing in anticipation of the hard work and long days ahead of you.

By month nine (weeks thirty-eight to forty +), in preparation for birth, your baby has dropped low down in your pelvis and the head has engaged in the space between your pelvic bones. Not all babies position themselves in this way prior to labor, but when they do, it is a good indication that delivery will proceed normally. Your baby gains about two more pounds and two and a half inches during the final weeks inside you, averaging seven and a half to eight and a half pounds and twenty inches at birth.

When your baby's head engages in your pelvis, you may have difficulty sitting, as if you were carrying a ball between your legs. Depending on where the baby is positioned in regard to your nerves, you may feel sharp sensations or pressure in your vaginal area. Other aches and pains common in the ninth month are: swelling and water retention, lethargy, backache, leaking from the breasts, irregular bowels, indigestion, difficulty sleeping, and frequent urination.

There will be days when you may feel as if you cannot sit still, and although you should resist the urge to do heavy chores, this is a good time to make sure that everything is in order for the birth and for your hospital stay. When I had my children, I found that packing my suitcase for the hospital was one of the highlights of my pregnancy. Packing my new robe and gown and the baby's going-home outfit was so exciting! After so many months, I would finally be meeting the little person with whom I would share my life forever.

Chances are you have a new robe or slippers that you have been saving. Of course, you have your baby's little clothes. Use the few moments that it takes to pack your suitcase to reflect and say good-bye to this pregnancy. As happy as you are to see it end, you will miss that feeling in the next few months.

Women bring all sorts of special things with them to the hospital. I have two lists of my own. The first contains suggestions for things that you need while in labor. The second includes items to have on hand later on. If you carry the items in separate bags, you have to bring only the bag of labor essentials with you when you first enter the hospital. All the other items can be brought from your car later.

Essentials for Your Labor, Delivery, and Recovery

- Socks, to keep your feet warm.
- Cassette tapes (with music and blank) and a tape re-

corder. (Some hospitals provide a tape player or radio for listening to music, but you may want to bring your own tape recorder as well to tape your baby's first cries and your own reactions to the birth.)

- A pen and paper, for recording your thoughts and for game-playing during labor.
- Focal point (a good-luck charm or amulet on a chain works nicely), on which to concentrate during hard contractions.
- Lollipops, hard candy, or Popsicles, if they are allowed, to moisten dry mouth during labor.
- Tennis ball or rolling pin. Ask your partner to use it for back massage.
- Camera, video camera, flash, film, all of which are allowed in many labor, delivery, and recovery rooms.
- Shopping bag, for holding your street clothes, and those of your coach while he is wearing sterile hospital scrubs.
- List of phone numbers of people to call with the happy news.
- Telephone credit card or a pocketful of silver for the pay phone.
- Labor guide, with breathing instructions, stages of labor.
- Chapstick or petroleum jelly for dry lips.
- Lotion or powder for massage during labor.
- Hair clips or bands, to keep long hair from your face.
- Toothbrush, toothpaste, and/or breath spray, for mom and coach.
- Coach's snack.
- Champagne. Ask a nurse to chill it for you.
- Eyeglasses, contact lenses, and cases, if applicable.
- Hairbrush.
- Watch, with a second hand to time contractions, in case the labor room does not have a clock.
- Insurance ID card.

Essentials for Your Postpartum Stay

- Toiletries.
- Bathrobe.
- Slippers or thongs, for hallways and showers.
- Several nightgowns, which get spills on them daily. Cot-

ton is best since it won't slide getting in and out of bed. Remember to choose a nursing gown or button-down style if you plan to nurse.
- Socks.
- Nursing bras.
- Underwear.
- Going-home outfit for you.
- Going-home outfit for baby, including a diaper, undershirt, nightgown or stretch suit, sweater or bunting in cold weather, and a receiving blanket for swaddling.
- Pacifiers, if you plan to use them. They should be sterilized at home by boiling in water for one minute.
- Baby announcements, if they are preprinted.
- Telephone numbers and address book.
- Magazines or books, although you may not have time to read them. Some women feel comforted by baby books so they can read up on what's happening to them. This is particularly true, I find, for women who have unplanned cesareans; they often want to read that chapter that they didn't bother to look at before.
- Hair dryer. Some hospitals prohibit electrical appliances. Check first.
- Needlepoint or crafts, although you probably won't have time to do them.
- Baby's car seat.

Do not bring anything of value with you to the hospital, including money, expensive jewelry, or any other nonreplaceable treasures. First, you will not need most of these things anyway. Second, because you will change rooms at least once and probably several times during labor and delivery, it is quite easy for these items to be misplaced or stolen. If you must have that special locket or bracelet, ask for someone to bring it to you in the postpartum room. Do not bring any medications or vitamins.

Get Set . . .

Like a high school senior awaiting graduation or a football player practicing for the Super Bowl, for months you have been preparing for one exciting day. The only difference is that when you are pregnant, you do not know when the big day will come. Let me assure you right here in black and white: your time will come, and your baby will be born. No one in the history of time has stayed pregnant forever.

How do you know when you are ready to make that mad dash to the hospital? Most obstetricians tell their patients to look for two signs of labor: the rupture of the amniotic membrane (with or without contractions) and regular contractions that are five to ten minutes apart for about an hour.

When your membrane ruptures (or your "water" breaks), it does not hurt, but you may be surprised or embarrassed by the constant and often quite heavy flow of amniotic fluid from your vagina. You cannot stop the flow voluntarily as you can with urine. Sanitary napkins (you may need several) and/or a towel are your best bet for keeping relatively dry as you dress and make your way to the car. Although you may want to wash up, do not bathe because of the risk of infection. You may shower.

Before you call the doctor, check that the amniotic fluid is odorless and clear or straw-colored rather than dark green or brown. If the color is dark, it is called "meconium staining" and may mean that your baby has had his first bowel movement. If this is the case, the meconium could be a sign of fetal distress. Your doctor will want to know this when you speak to him.

If your water breaks before contractions begin, call the obstetrician anyway. Most doctors prefer that you go directly to the hospital after phoning them. After your water breaks, you have an increased risk of infection since there is no longer a protective seal around the baby.

Many women begin to feel light contractions before their water breaks, so they do not have as clear a sign of the start of labor. The contractions that signal the start of true labor may begin as lower back pains that radiate to the front like the ebb and flow of cramps and tightening of the muscles in your back, tummy, and legs. These are different from the Braxton-Hicks contractions that you might have felt during your pregnancy. Real contractions gradually become more frequent and intense as time passes. Unlike prelabor contractions, true contractions do not subside if you lie down, walk around, or shift your position.

Many women lose the mucus plug that fills the opening of

the cervix some time during the last month. As the cervix changes prior to labor, the plug may come loose. This usually is accompanied by a light amount of bleeding. The blood is very mucousy and dark. If you have any discharge when actual labor begins, it will be bloody or very pink. If you are not sure whether you are really in labor, the safest course of action is to check with your doctor. Believe me, you would not be the first to call with a false alarm.

Go!

Every day seems like forever until your obstetrician confirms that you are actually in labor and you are given the okay to head to the hospital. From the moment you knew that you were going to have a baby, the final trip to the hospital has loomed in the back of your mind. Every time you have driven by it, you think, "That is the hospital and town in which my child will be born." It is a place that is fixed forever with your child, even as that child becomes an adult—it is on the birth certificate, the passport, and reams of forms for schools and jobs.

As you head out your door for the last time before you are parents, talk to each other about your feelings and reassure one another of your love. As you drive to the hospital, share with each other one story about something that happened during the pregnancy to make you laugh. Recalling pleasant memories and creating new ones brings you to the hospital with happiness in your heart.

Remember, too, that you do not have to put on a serious face just because you are about to have a baby. Being together during this momentous occasion can be a lot of fun. A friend of mine always marvels at how at ease she and her husband felt on their way to the hospital—they even took out the garbage on the way! If you feel happy or silly or just revved up with excitement, go with your feelings. Fear and gravity are not required emotions if you feel good. What is in your heart is what matters on this birthday of your parenthood. I wish you the very best as you take part in your own personal miracle.

4

❖

A Miracle in a Small Package

O n the wall of my office in the maternity waiting room, I have pinned hundreds of baby pictures sent to me by couples that I have helped start on the path to parenthood. My photo wall is special because it is a daily reminder of the lives that I have touched and those that have touched mine. It also is a wonderful conversation piece for the many expectant grandparents who wear out the carpeting as they pace back and forth, waiting for their grandchild to be born.

As I wait with these hopeful grandparents, I am reminded of the day when I wore down the carpet in the very same room waiting for my first grandchild to be born. My first concern that day was for my daughter. It was so hard for me to stand helpless in the face of her hurting, even though I knew that the hurt would bring joy. I was sad, too, because my husband, Bill, had passed away two years before. I wished he could have shared that moment with me.

As I thought about Bill, I remembered the birth of our four children, undoubtedly a common thought that grandparents have when their daughters are in labor. We reflect upon the cycle of life and upon the experiences that are part of the chain of generations.

When the magical moment arrives and you hold your newly born child in your arms, you may find yourself thinking about the generation that lies before you. In your baby's face, you see more than merely a reflection of you and your partner. Your baby is a part of his anxious grandma on hand in the waiting room and his grandpa sitting impatiently by the phone awaiting the good news. Through you, this baby is connected to history.

As you come to understand where your child fits into the past and the future, I hope that you appreciate the important role that grandparents will play in his or her life. Grandparents touch a child in ways that a parent cannot. They show a child where he or she is in the plan of things. They give the child a sense of permanence and stability.

In an age marked by family mobility and changing family life-styles, a child needs to learn about his or her roots. The grandparents are those roots. Strengthening your ties with your family is the fourth step that you can take to helping your child grow up in a stable and nurturing world.

"You cannot see the forest for the trees." I cannot count how often this old English proverb comes to mind when I meet young couples about to have their first baby. All of your attention from the moment you found out that you were pregnant has focused on this singular moment in time: the birth of your baby.

I would not dream of downplaying this great event. However, before you take your final step across the hospital threshold, I encourage you to wrap your experience in a bit of context. With what you are about to do, you are creating a family. You are creating a generation. You are creating a human being with potential to change the course of history. You are creating a person who will share responsibility for the future of the world.

Your imminent labor and delivery will probably blind you temporarily to the big picture. See it now. Feel it in your partner's sweaty palm holding yours. Smell it in the fresh air just outside the hospital door. Take it with you in your heart. It is the miracle.

At the Hospital

Once in the hospital, expect to be escorted to the maternity unit. You may be asked to sit in a wheelchair; this procedure is normal. Because you called your obstetrician before leaving home, he or she has reserved a labor room for you. You may have expressed your preference for a regular labor room or a modified birthing room, if such an option is available.

If your labor is not too far along when you arrive in the maternity unit, perhaps you can take some photos. Ask the admitting clerk or a nurse to snap a quick shot of the "three" of you—a "before" portrait that can be taken again in the very same spot "after" your baby is born.

Once you are in your room, you are greeted by your labor nurse, who will ask you to change into a hospital gown. You won't look glamorous, but at least the gown goes in someone else's laundry. Ask your labor partner to place your street clothes in the shopping bag you brought with you so nothing is lost. Your jewelry and other personal items, if you brought them, should be placed in the bag as well. (Some hospitals provide safety-deposit boxes; ask your nurse.)

When you have finished changing your clothes, your nurse returns to review your medical history and discuss your labor thus far. She checks your temperature and blood pressure. She attaches your hospital identification bracelet to your wrist. She also asks you to sign some routine hospital consent forms for possible, unanticipated surgery and anesthesia, and for your baby's circumcision (if applicable) and nursery photograph.

In many hospitals, routine labor procedure requires that you be hooked up to a machine that monitors your contractions and the fetal heartbeat immediately upon your arrival into your labor room. The monitor has a foam belt that is strapped around your abdomen. It has wires from the monitoring unit on the belt to a machine that records the contractions and the heartbeat on a video screen and a continuous strip of paper. The readout looks like the graph of a lie detector that you might see on television. Unlike some professionals who are critical of the monitor, I like it because the constant rhythm of the baby's heart going *beep, beep, beep* is calming to couples in the throes of labor.

With the help of the monitor, your labor nurse can see how

your labor is progressing. Some women are surprised to discover that their obstetrician does not stay in the labor room with them. Rather, it is the labor nurse who is with you most of the time. She advises your doctor upon your arrival and periodically as your contractions become stronger and more frequent. The doctor checks you now and again until you are in the last stage of labor or earlier if the nurse calls him or her to handle a problem or to prescribe a painkiller.

Most women expecting their first child progress through the stages of labor very slowly, the average time from the start of contractions through delivery being fourteen hours. While a long labor may seem scary, the slow process allows you to build your confidence as you find that you can—and do—pass through each stage with flying colors.

Depending upon how well you feel, your hours of early labor can be a wonderful time to talk with your partner about why you decided to become parents (too late to change your mind now!) or about what you are looking forward to as your baby grows. Perhaps you want to take more photographs, especially if you have no other record of your ninth month. If you have a cassette player in your room, you may want to listen to that special song or singer that reminds you of when you were dating. Reading poetry to each other is another way to express intimacy. Regardless of what you choose to do, try to do something fun to make the time pass. You remember the fun long after you forget the pain.

Someone to Watch Over You

If there is one person other than you and your partner who can make your birthing experience special, it is your labor nurse. Generally, couples have one nurse who stays with them throughout labor and delivery. Sometimes during long labors when there is a shift change, a second nurse comes on duty. The shifts overlap by about one half hour so the early nurse can report to the late nurse exactly how and what you are doing.

The nurses who work in labor and delivery fulfill many roles. First, of course, they have the medical expertise to care for you. They assess the strength and frequency of your contractions and the degree to which the cervix has opened, and they keep your doctor apprised. They can help you determine whether you are ready for pain relief medication, and they can administer it in some forms. The labor nurses also are responsible for recording everything that happens during labor in reams of "nurse's notes."

In addition to being a medical aide, your labor nurse can be like a therapist. She usually is in tune with your feelings and can relieve some of the apprehension that you and your partner may be feeling. If a father-to-be seems to be particularly nervous, for example, the nurse may suggest that he get his partner some ice chips or take a coffee break. This diversion may make him feel better.

Labor nurses are well known for helping couples maintain their senses of humor, which is particularly important during labor, when moms-to-be are subjected to such great invasions of privacy. Couples in labor should know that their nurse is their friend. Sometimes it may seem that she just goes in and out of your room to check your blood pressure or do an internal exam, but that is not so. Labor nurses are constantly watching the progress of their patients from the nurses' station. Often I overhear them saying things like, "Mrs. Pollack just had a good contraction. She's making so much progress, and the baby's heart looks great. I think she'll deliver soon." That supportive attitude and the ability and knowledge to back it up make the labor nurse the backbone of the childbirth team.

What Happens Next

One way that your nurse estimates the progress of your labor is to do regular internal examinations to feel how far your cervix has opened up and how far the baby's head (or other presenting part) has descended into the pelvis. Internal exams may be uncomfortable, but they usually are quick and tolerable. If you need help coping with the discomfort, the breathing patterns that you learned in your childbirth classes may come in handy. Make certain that you tell your labor partner what you are feeling so that he can comfort you and remind you to relax. He is not likely to know how you feel unless you tell him.

If you ask your nurse, she can describe the progress of your labor using two terms: "effacement" and "dilatation" (also called dilation). Effacement, described in percentages, is the softening and thinning of the cervix. For example, your nurse may tell you that you are 50 percent effaced, which means that the cervix has thinned to one half of its original thickness. Chances are that if you carry your baby to full term, your cervix will have begun to efface before labor starts. Your obstetrician may note its progress to you during one of your final prenatal office visits.

Dilation is the opening up of the cervix, and it usually proceeds along with effacement as part of the labor process. The nurse records your dilation in centimeters, ranging from one, which means the cervix is open only slightly, to 10, when you have reached the end of the first stage of labor and are ready to push your baby out. Both effacement and dilation are caused by contractions of the uterus.

In addition to measuring changes in your cervix, the nurse monitors the baby's descent into the pelvis. She describes this by stating that the baby is at a certain "station." When the baby remains floating above the pelvis, he is said to be at a minus four station. As the head moves lower down, it is said to have "engaged" in the pelvis. As the head descends farther, it is measured in plus stations such as plus one or plus two. When the baby is at plus four, he or she is on the perineum and is ready to be born.

During labor, you grow more and more eager for your cervix to open and for your baby to be born. However, labor does not always progress at a steady pace. Contractions may strengthen and weaken. Babies may engage in the pelvis and then dislodge. Your cervix may begin to dilate and then stop, temporarily or for an extended period of time.

There is, of course, disappointment when labor slows or ceases. Remember, though, that if your baby's heartbeat is strong and steady, that is all that matters in the big picture. One woman I visited in her postpartum room remarked that her baby had just reached his one-day-old birthday. "Only twenty-four hours ago, I was so disappointed because he was taking so long to be born," she said. "But looking back on it, it is so unimportant. Yet yesterday I felt it was the most important thing in the world." Truly, your baby is the most important thing in the world. If you remember that, even a lengthy labor will not upset you.

Depending on what your doctor orders in the way of routine care, your labor nurse may start an intravenous (IV) drip in your hand or arm. She may "prep" or shave your vaginal area, if ordered by your doctor. She may tell you that you are forbidden to eat or drink because once labor starts digestion stops, and you have an increased possibility of vomiting. (You may be allowed to suck on ice chips or Popsicles.) If you need an enema, your nurse can help you with this.

If your water has broken early in labor, you may be directed by your doctor or nurse to remain in your labor bed. The reason for this restriction is to avoid having the baby's umbilical cord rush out of the cervix along with the flow of amniotic fluid. If this happens, the cord can be crushed and reduce blood flow to the baby. (If the flow of amniotic fluid is so heavy that you keep wetting the bedclothes, you may want to ask your labor nurse for a towel or absorbent paper pad to absorb the flow. At least then you will not feel as if you are sitting in a puddle.)

Whether you are ordered to stay in bed or you choose to do so, you may have to urinate in a bedpan. Because the bedpan needs to be brought to you and emptied each time you feel pressure on your bladder (quite often, as you know from your pregnancy), you may feel helpless and humiliated. Acknowledging this possibility may help make you feel better if it actually happens.

I wish that I could stand at each and every hospital door to hand out antimodesty pills to expectant mothers as they check in to have their babies. Very few of your private parts remain private once you have donned the famous open-back hospital gown that has a great way of flapping in the breeze. No matter whether it is light or dark outside, once inside the hospital you are being poked in one end or the other. In postpartum care, the song remains the same as the nurses monitor your bowel movements and examine your sanitary pads to see how much bleeding you are doing. All these procedures have to be done, and we all get through it. The best way to survive it is not to worry about it.

Is It Going to Hurt?

As your contractions become stronger and more frequent, they force your cervix to open and permit your baby's head to drop down into the pelvis. If any one question comes up over and over again among pregnant women, it is about whether and how much the contractions will hurt. Each woman, of course, experiences pain differently, so nothing can describe what it feels like for everybody.

For some women, the discomfort resembles that which accompanies menstruation, with on-again, off-again cramping in the abdomen. For others, the pain is sharper, more localized. It may be a squeezing sensation that is interspersed with a relaxation of the muscles. If the baby is lying in a posterior position with its head pressing on the spine, labor may be felt most severely in the lower back or rectum and relatively little around the midsection.

Labor pains change as your labor progresses. At first you may not even be able to identify every contraction. Later, they may come like waves that begin with mild achiness or backache, crest a little later with a rush of tightness and pain, and then subside with a gradual relaxation of the uterine muscles. As you get closer to delivery, the "waves" come more closely together so that the individual contractions may once again be indistinguishable.

One of the skills that your nurse possesses is the ability to help you find labor positions that are most comfortable for you. Sometimes, labor pains are eased if you are lying on your side. Other times, being propped up with pillows seems to do the trick. Of course if labor becomes too painful, your nurses can provide you with medication.

Your Special Moment Is Almost Here

Once your cervix has dilated to close to ten centimeters, you are said to have reached the transition stage of labor. This is the most difficult time of labor for most women unless they have had some pain relief medication. It is during transition that contractions are very frequent and strong, coming one after the other with rhythmic intensity. They demand your constant attention.

Until your cervix is fully dilated, you are told by the nurses and by your labor coach not to succumb to the urge to push. Bearing down and forcing your baby's head against an incompletely dilated cervix can cause the area to swell, which would make the opening smaller rather than larger. Premature pushing also may cause the cervix to tear.

Because transition is a hard part of labor, women often ask how long it lasts. For the lucky ones, it is quite brief, perhaps a few minutes or so, although I promise it will seem like an eternity. Unfortunately, most first-time mothers go through transition for an hour or more.

During transition, you may get hot and cold flashes, perspire excessively, or feel nauseous. You may vomit or shake, and your teeth may chatter as you try to control an overwhelming urge to bear down. Try not to be ashamed or frightened by these uncontrollable urges; they happen frequently and are a natural part of labor.

As soon as your nurse or doctor determines that your cervix is fully dilated, you are told that you can start pushing. The doctor directs your pushing so that you bear down with each contraction. As you probably have seen on television or in your childbirth classes, pushing is hard work, but most women say that the physical effort is meaningless. I hear on a regular basis from new mothers that nothing—neither pain, nor medication, nor fatigue—mattered. "All I wanted was to hear his first cry."

Should your cervix fail to open up enough, if the baby is breech or does not descend into the birth canal, or should you or your baby go into distress, you may be a candidate for a cesarean section. Fifteen to 20 percent of first-time parents have unplanned cesareans.

If your doctor determines that a cesarean section is necessary, you are visited by the anesthesiologist while you are in your labor room. Most sections are performed today using regional anesthesia (epidural or spinal) that numbs the lower half of your body. Depending on your nerve structure, you may feel pressure or vague sensations on your skin during the operation, but you should feel no pain.

An anesthesiologist administers the pain medication either in your labor room or in the operating room, where the cesarean is performed. The operating room may seem particularly cold and bright compared to the more relaxed, semihomey labor room. Try not to be disturbed by this; the delivery room must be this way in order to be sterile.

Before the operation begins, a catheter will be inserted. Your abdomen is scrubbed with a sterilizing solution. A drape is placed around the sterile area, demarcating the surgical field.

The drape is in front of your face so that you cannot view the procedure, but it may be lowered later on so that you can watch as your baby is born. Your arms may be strapped to the table before the cesarean begins. While this may be frightening, it is necessary to prevent you from reaching into the surgical field.

As with a vaginal delivery, most hospitals today permit husbands or labor coaches to be on hand in the delivery room during a cesarean section; however, they may be asked to remain outside the room until after the surgical field has been set up. If this is the case, do not hesitate to talk to the labor nurse or the anesthesiologist if you have any questions or if you are just scared and need someone to comfort you. Both people have dealt with this rather strange and surreal situation many times before, and chances are that they will be invaluable in helping to calm you.

Sometimes parents are disappointed when they are told that the expectant mom must undergo a cesarean, especially if they have prepared for a vaginal delivery by attending childbirth classes. Almost always their disappointment dims right after the birth.

The Miracle

In the delivery room, the clock is meaningless until the baby is born. Time is measured only by the length and frequency of your contractions. When the baby's head begins to crown, you judge the passing of time by the head as it inches its way into view with each push.

To help your baby along, your obstetrician cups your baby's head gently in his hands. He guides the head on its final passage through the birth canal. One more push. Your baby's face appears!

With the torso still inside you, your baby's mouth and nose are suctioned to get rid of any mucus that could interfere with breathing. The head is turned slightly to one side so that the shoulders can slide out. One more push. Then, as if the world has come to a standstill, time seems to stop. Your baby is born. You listen for—and then hear—the very first cry.

The labor nurse checks the clock and announces the exact time of your baby's birth, a time that remains fixed in your mind forever. In the same second, the obstetrician tells you "It's a boy!" or "It's a girl!" When you hear his or her voice, you cannot help but cry.

If you delivered vaginally, your baby is placed on your tummy even before the cord is cut. Your baby might continue to cry or might settle down, once again comforted by the only body and soul that he or she has ever known. (If you have a cesarean, you cannot hold your baby on your belly, but your doctor may hold the baby up for you to see. Depending on your doctor's decision, you may be permitted to hold the baby for a moment or so before he or she is taken to the nursery.)

Even with the medical team in the room, these first few moments with your baby are a very personal time. Mommy and daddy look at each other, so proud and so full of love. Newborns usually are quite alert in the delivery room, making this an excellent time for you to make eye contact with your baby. Although the baby's vision is blurry, he or she can look up into your adoring eyes.

As the miracle unfolds, the delivery room takes on a magical aura. For the first time, you are able to touch this human being that you have been feeling inside of you. You reach out to your baby, you feel the baby's skin against yours, and you caress the tiny, wet head with trembling hands. Dad counts ten fingers and ten toes. Solemnly, he caresses his baby's hands and puts his pinky finger in his baby's palm. A reflex causes baby to grip the finger tightly. Daddy accepts this as a symbol of love.

New dads have their proudest moments in the delivery room. The expressions on their faces as they watch their children come into the world are beyond words. There they stand gazing down at their newborns as if nothing were as wonderful or as miraculous. Indeed, nothing is. New mothers always say how surprised and proud they are of their partners in the delivery room. Men surprise themselves, too, when they find that they are composed and unafraid.

One new dad said that the obstetrician handed him his baby almost immediately after it was delivered by cesarean section and its cord was clamped and cut. "I guess he didn't know that I never held a baby before," the dad said. "If he had known, he probably wouldn't have let me hold the little guy for fear I would drop him. But, guess what? I didn't drop him! In fact, I could not believe how natural it felt to hold my baby in my arms."

Chances are you will surprise each other with how well you

act and feel during the birthing process. As I said before, you probably will find that you enjoy yourselves, that you are proud of yourselves and each other, and that you look back on the experience with powerful and joyous memories. I hope that you feel this way, because never again, my children, are you closer to God and to the miracle he just performed.

Baby's Very First . . . Everything!

Some women nurse their newborns while still on the delivery table, while others prefer to wait until they are in the recovery or postpartum rooms. I advise making your decision if and when to nurse based on what your baby seems to need at the time. If the baby is crying, he or she may be comforted by being put to the breast, and usually will latch on easily. A more sleepy newborn may not be as successful at trying a new experience. If you have a cesarean, your baby may not accompany you into recovery, and nursing may have to wait until you are settled in your postpartum room.

After your initial few moments with your baby, the umbilical cord is clamped and cut, either by the doctor or by dad. Then the baby is carried to a warmer where the nurse or pediatrician checks the heartbeat to make sure it is regular and strong; the lungs, to make sure they are clear; and the skin, for robust color. The baby's condition is rated on a scale of one to ten, using a measurement called an Apgar score. The rating is done at one minute and again at five minutes after the baby is born.

Most babies are rated in the range of seven or above, with the only perfect tens going to pediatricians' or obstetricians' children. Even babies who receive low scores at birth usually test in the nine or ten range when they are retested five minutes later. As long as your doctor tells you that your baby is all right, do not worry what number it was given. There are many "fives" who make it to Harvard.

While you are moved to the recovery room, your baby is taken to the nursery, where it is measured and weighed (and you wonder why we are so diet-conscious!). The nurses put ointment in the baby's eyes to prevent infection. Vitamin K is administered by injection in the baby's thigh to compensate for

Apgar Score

Heart rate:	0 — Absent
	1 — Under 100 beats/min.
	2 — 100 beats/min. or more
Breathing:	0 — Absent
	1 — Slow or irregular
	2 — Regular
Skin color:	0 — Blue
	1 — Body pink, extremities blue
	2 — Pink all over
Muscle tone:	0 — Limp
	1 — Some movements
	2 — Active movements
Reflex response:	0 — Absent
	1 — Grimace only
	2 — Cry

a natural deficiency at birth. If your baby is large, he or she may receive a dextrose test to see if there is a need for a sugar water supplement.

There is one more test, for a rare metabolic disease called PKU, that is done on the day your baby goes home. The PKU test involves taking a sample of blood from your baby's heel. Because the sample usually is taken just before your baby is discharged, you may notice a tiny pinprick on the heel for several days after you go home. This almost unnoticeable spot is perfectly normal and nothing to be concerned about.

After the initial tests are completed and your baby's temperature is stable, the baby is given its first bath. Many hospitals permit the baby's dad to join the baby in the nursery. I love to watch brand-new dads around their babies for the first time. They are so shy and gentle. Sometimes new dads are afraid to touch their babies right away. If I see this happening in the nursery, I always take the dad's hand and say to him, "Feel how soft your baby's foot is. Isn't it just like velvet?" Then, like magic, the dad touches his baby's foot and then the leg and the chest . . . It is a wonderful sight to see.

The nurses in the admission nursery in our hospital try their best to involve the dads right away with their newborns. They have the father record his baby's time of birth, height, and weight on a pink or blue slip of paper that eventually becomes part of the baby's album. They also might suggest that dad hold his baby's little hand to comfort the baby when it receives the vitamin K shot. Fathers seem to really enjoy this important experience. I think their babies like it, too. What could be as comforting as feeling your dad's big, strong hand wrapped around your own as you doze off for your very first nap?

Mom's Recovery

Mom's recovery may take a variety of paths, depending upon many factors: the duration and difficulty of your labor, your physical condition, the amount and type of medication you took, whether you had a vaginal or cesarean delivery, and so on.

Your recovery begins in what is logically called the recovery room in the hospital, in which you stay with other new moms for a few hours until your body stabilizes from the birthing experience. (Women in LDR rooms recover in the same room and bed in which they delivered.) With a vaginal delivery, the recovery period is relatively brief and may only last as long as it takes for your anesthesia to wear off. You are pressed, prodded, and poked to make sure that your uterus is not filling with blood. Your belly is massaged to promote uterine contractions. You are washed and "dressed" in clean sanitary pads. The procedure is not that different from that which is done to your baby in the nursery; it, too, is bathed and diapered! If you had a cesarean, you stay in recovery until the effects of surgery have worn off. You continue to wear your IV and bladder catheter until your doctor orders them discontinued, probably the following day. If you had morphine in your epidural or spinal IV, you may not need additional abdominal pain medication for twenty-four hours. In the recovery room, you may be excessively thirsty; however, you may not be allowed to drink anything because it may lead to vomiting.

After you have stabilized, you are moved to your postpartum room. Although you may be exhausted, you probably do not rest right away. If your baby is asleep in a bassinet beside your bed, you cannot take your eyes off him or her. You also cannot wait to tell the whole world your special news. You place and receive lots of phone calls until you are so tired that you have to nap for at least a little while.

Your postpartum recovery may progress as follows for the next few days:

Vaginal Delivery

DAY ONE

- Perineal and vaginal pain, particularly around an episiotomy. Some women also temporarily experience a numb feeling in the area. Sitting is uncomfortable.
- Getting out of bed, walking to and using the bathroom. Urinating may be uncomfortable.
- Walks to the nursery to get your baby after a nap, or just to look at the baby through the window.
- Fatigue, frequent naps.
- Vaginal bleeding similar to a heavy period.
- Possible hemorrhoids.
- Bloodshot eyes and/or black-and-blue spots on the face, if pushing was difficult or prolonged.
- Constant phone calls coming in and going out. The whole world must know about the most glorious of life experiences.

DAYS TWO TO THREE

- Perineal and vaginal pain continue. Sitz baths may be ordered.
- Crampy uterine afterpains, especially during nursing. These seem to worsen with subsequent children.
- Continued walking in the hallways, to and from the shower.
- Vaginal bleeding continues (for up to four weeks).
- Possible constipation.
- Hemorrhoids may persist.
- More phone calls, excited visitors, flowers and gifts for the baby. A sense that all is well in the world.
- Excessive sweating, chills, hot flashes as a result of sudden drop in hormones.
- Emotional highs and lows. (See chapter 6 for more about postpartum feelings.)

Cesarean Section

DAY ONE

- Abdominal pain that probably is severe enough to require medication.
- Getting out of bed and (painfully) walking to the bathroom, probably with help.
- If you can urinate, removal of the catheter.
- Fatigue, frequent naps.
- Vaginal bleeding, similar to a heavy period.
- Possible hemorrhoids.
- Constant phone calls coming in and going out.
- Diet of clear liquids. If you can hold them down, removal of the IV.

DAYS TWO TO FIVE

- Persistent abdominal pain that gradually disappears after several weeks. The numb feeling around the incision lasts for several months.
- Uterine afterpains, especially during nursing.
- Daily walks in the hallway, to the nursery.
- If your physician permits, you may shower. Take it slow and easy to avoid slipping or hurting yourself.
- Continued fatigue that accompanies major surgery.
- Return to regular diet.
- Possible constipation and gas pains. If constipation persists once you are eating normally, your doctor may prescribe a suppository.
- Excessive sweating, chills, hot flashes as a result of sudden drop in hormones.
- Engorgement (full breasts) on days three to five. (See chapter 6 for more information on breast-feeding.)
- More phone calls. Excited visitors, flowers and gifts for the baby. A sense that all is well in the world.
- Emotional highs and lows. (See chapter 6 for more about postpartum feelings.)

During a woman's recovery from childbirth, fathers have a wonderful opportunity to spend time with mother and child while they remain in the hospital. Of course, you are together when you arrive home, but to be honest, you never have such exciting and joyous days in the first few months as you do during the day or two following delivery.

The reason that this time is so special is that while you are in the hospital, all the daily tasks such as cooking and cleaning are out of your hands. Your meals are brought to you on a tray. You can sit on your behind all day long (or on one cheek, if you had a vaginal delivery), raising and lowering the bed frame so it fits your mood just perfectly. Chances are that you have a television in the room and that it has remote control. You can turn on whatever show you want and keep the volume at whatever level you choose. (Of course, no television scriptwriter can compete with the entertainment snuggled in your arms or sleeping in the bassinet next to your bed.) You can play with your newborn, but you have help caring for it.

Because moms are pampered and probably getting a lot more sleep in the hospital than they do after they are home, they are very happy and quite amenable to a healthy dose of bonding with dad and baby at this time. Savor every minute of this. If you are encouraged to leave the hospital earlier than you feel is comfortable for you, do what you can to extend your stay. Early discharge is a favorite tack of insurance companies and overcrowded hospitals, but it is not always in the best interest of the new family. Sometimes if you stay an added day, you gain a tremendous amount of confidence and information about caring for your baby. You might enjoy the extra care that you receive, too.

I probably do not have to remind you to take pictures or videos of your newborn. Keep a journal. Do whatever you can to capture these special days and bottle your positive emotions. Unfortunately, they do not last, and for a while at least, they may be difficult to identify again. If somehow you can preserve even an inkling of these happy days in the hospital, you may be able to draw from this well of wonderful feelings to survive the more difficult days ahead.

Funny Things that Babies Do

When I had my babies, most women were "put to sleep" for the birth. Afterward, their babies were brought to them for short visits, but most of the time mom stayed in her room and the baby stayed in the nursery. Thankfully, that system has changed. If your baby and you are healthy, you two (three, with dad) will be spending many hours together in your postpartum hospital room.

As you get to know one another, you will probably discover that your baby looks quite different than you had imagined. An infant's look changes almost hourly during the first day or so of life. When babies are born, they often have elongated heads, receding chins, bent ears, and squished and swollen faces from being squeezed through the birth canal. Their color may be bluish until oxygen has enriched their blood. They are wet, so their hair is matted, and they sometimes are coated with a white, creamlike substance called vernix, which is a protective coating from inside the womb.

By the time you have reached your postpartum room, however, your baby probably looks a lot different. He or she has been bathed, so the hair and skin are soft and clean. The color is more robust. The baby may look less swollen, and the eyes may be more open. The molding of the head and chin go away gradually, too.

In these early days you witness many, many newborn behaviors and reflexes. Some of these delight you. Others may surprise you. To ward off any stray thoughts that what your baby is doing is not perfectly normal, here is a list of some of the funny things that tiny babies do.

Hiccups

Babies get hiccups even before they are born. You may have felt these tiny, jerky movements while the baby was inside you. Newborns also get hiccups quite frequently, usually during or immediately after eating. Hiccups are of great concern to new mommies and daddies because baby's tiny body jumps so much it looks like a Mexican jumping bean. Despite the apparent discomfort, most babies do not mind the hiccups as much as their parents do. Hiccups are not dangerous or unhealthy. If hiccups start during a feeding, you may continue. Swallowing may relieve the hiccups, but even if they last for several minutes, do not worry about them. They pass in due time.

Meconium

Meconium is a greenish black, tarlike bowel movement that all newborns have for about three days after they are born. I love watching new daddies trying to change a meconium diaper. Before they are through, the baby's foot is in it, dad has it all over his knuckles, it is sticking to the soiled diaper . . . and the clean one. It's a real mess. Meconium is a naturally occurring phenomenon. All babies have it. Do not be alarmed by its dark color or consistency. Until it runs its course, the best way to handle it is to cover baby's bottom with petroleum jelly at every changing to help you to wipe off the meconium. Otherwise, you may have to remove it with a chisel.

Jaundice

More than 50 percent of newborns have a condition known as physiologic jaundice, in which their skin looks slightly yellow as the result of excess fetal red blood cells needed *in utero* that have been broken down so fast that they cannot be handled by the immature liver. While this type of jaundice is considered normal, babies who are very jaundiced are apt to be lethargic and may not nurse well right away. Some doctors recommend that physiologic jaundice be treated with special sunlamps that are a common sight in hospital nurseries. Others suggest that you give your baby daily sunbaths near a window inside your home. With either treatment, physiologic jaundice usually clears up within a week or two without any lingering side effects.

Sneezing

New parents who are not told in advance that babies do a lot of sneezing ask me all the time if perhaps the sneezes indicate the onset of a cold. Actually, babies carry a good deal of immunity to colds and other germs, and sneezes are nothing more than your baby's method of clearing the nasal passages. My theory is that with so many new blankets always wrapped around your baby, the child is bound to collect lots of little fuzzies in the nose that tickle. Thus, the sneezes.

Noises

If you have your baby room-in with you in the hospital, you hear many unusual snorting and squeaking noises that he or she makes during sleep. These unusual sounds are normal and do not mean that the baby is having trouble breathing. If you are even a bit concerned, do not hesitate to push the nurses' call button. New moms need all the reassurance that they can get.

Stop, Look, and Listen

It is true that while you instinctively love and want to care for your baby, exactly how to do so may take a bit of learning. I hope that your parent training will begin right in the hospital with instruction by and observation of the nurses. During this time, it is useful for you to learn the basics of holding, feeding, and burping your baby. You also can practice changing diapers and get used to handling the baby during both good and fussy times. (See chapter 5 for bottom-line baby basics.)

Hospital routines around the country differ, and new parents have varying opportunities to learn about basic baby care while still under medical supervision. Regardless of whether you are discharged after twenty-four, forty-eight, or more hours, you will not have a better chance than you do while in the hospital to learn basic baby care and to ask questions of the doctors, nurses, and attendants who are there to help you.

This story about two new moms might be useful. Mother A enters the hospital in the early stages of labor, and she is determined to deliver without medication. Her labor is long. By the time the baby comes, she is equally exhausted and excited. After a short nap, she eagerly tries to begin breast-feeding, but her baby also is tired after the long labor and is unable to suck easily. Mother A becomes discouraged and returns to sleep. The next day, feeding is again difficult, and Mother A, angry at her self-perceived failure, asks her husband to feed the baby with formula. She does not learn to burp the baby. At diaper-changing time, when the nurse swabs the umbilical cord stump, Mother A watches with some resentment. The baby has begun to breast-feed by the time the new family is discharged, but Mother A is sent home without ever having changed a diaper or swaddled her baby.

Mother B also delivers after a long labor, and like Mother A, also finds it difficult to breast-feed right away. However, Mother B asks one of the nurses for advice. By their second try, the baby latches on and both mom and baby seem happy with their progress. During her brief hospital stay, Mother B is not shy about talking to her nurses regularly to ask about everything from her baby's hiccups to the best way to hold him to make him feel more secure. Sometimes her questions seem stupid, but when Mother B is discharged, she is certain that her basic baby-care skills have a firm foundation.

The choice is yours whether you feel up to actively participating in your baby's care for the first twenty-four or so hours. The duration and type of your delivery undoubtedly will play a role in your decision; however, I cannot stress enough taking advantage of the nurses' presence to learn and to ask questions. Do not feel intimidated or stupid. It is smart to ask as many questions as you can and put the answers into practical use while you are in the hospital. You will have more than enough time on your own once you leave.

Sharing the Joy

Whether family members live near or far, they probably want to be by your side as soon as possible once your baby is born. I would never say anything to discourage family togetherness, but I must caution you about what you may and may not be able to handle in the first few days postpartum.

Remember that this time is called your recovery period. That is why you stay in the hospital—to rest and recover from the trauma that your body has undergone. If you have a cesarean, your recovery is not that different from that which follows any other type of abdominal surgery.

In order to recover properly, you may want to limit your visits to a specific number of people or to specified hours of the day. I realize that in your excitement, this suggestion may sound ridiculous, but it may save you from wearing yourself out. Some hospitals permit immediate family in the labor and recovery rooms. Whether you wish to have company during these times again is up to you. Do not hesitate to be a bit selfish with your time if you feel that it is necessary for your health or that of your baby.

I often am asked about friends and relatives visiting and whether the baby is at risk to catch colds or other infectious diseases. I have to suggest that you use your best judgment and ask people with runny noses or other signs of infection to stay away, no matter who they are. Children often carry germs, and the less time they spend with your newborn in the first few weeks, the safer the baby is.

Being a "professional grandmother" as well as a "real" grandma myself, I am a big fan of grandparents playing a very active role in their grandchildren's lives, if possible. However, when I hear that both grandmothers are coming to help with the new baby, I try to discourage it. No matter how well the two women get along under normal circumstances, both should not arrive at the same time for an extended stay with the new baby and the young parents. Rivalry almost surely springs up, and the two of you are frustrated and probably apprehensive when you need to be concentrating on being—and becoming—parents.

A Personal Invitation

Many couples tell me that when they are packing their belongings to leave the hospital, it has not quite sunk in that they are bringing their child home with them. When you arrive home, of course, it quickly becomes clear that your baby is with you. Not only is the baby with you, but you are the people to whom he or she looks for care and affection. This child's life literally is in your hands.

When you realize the enormity of your responsibility as parents, you may, as my grandchildren would say, "freak out." It is indeed a huge responsibility. There are a lot of decisions to be made. There are a lot of things to remember.

So before you leave the hospital, I extend a personal invitation to a short lesson in bottom-line baby basics. Upon completion, you will be ready for discharge, to leave your labor and delivery experiences behind you and set off on your own as new parents. Grab your pencils. We have a lot of material to cover, and your babies are waiting.

5

Bottom-Line
Baby Basics

This call came in on my "warm line" from a new mom whom I had never met. Her name was Linda, and she called me when her baby was two months old. Life with baby had been going along fine, she said. She had had a baby nurse to show her how to care for her baby. The nurse had set a strict three-hour feeding schedule. She helped Linda give the baby a bath every day at 10:00 A.M. "After a night's sleep, they are wet and need their bath," the nurse had said. The baby always went down for his nap at exactly 2:00 P.M. and 5:00 P.M. whether he was tired or not.

When Linda called me, she was very frustrated because her nurse had left, and Linda was unable to keep her baby on the schedule that she had come to expect. Linda blamed herself. "I just can't get everything done between eleven and one after the baby's bath and before his two P.M. nap," she said. "Sometimes I have to take him out in the afternoon, and that throws

119

off his schedule." The baby also had difficulty falling asleep, she said. When I suggested that many babies fall asleep more easily after an evening bath, she acted surprised that not every mom gave the bath at 10:00 A.M.!

Baby nurses—or any other help that you can get with a new baby—are a welcome sight in my book, but sometimes new moms like Linda need to be left alone a bit to learn to care for their babies in their own manner. There is more than one way to take care of your baby, and only you can decide what works best for you. You can bathe your baby at any time of the day or evening, once a day or once a week, and he or she will be just as healthy and happy as any other baby.

In the beginning, of course, you may not want to try anything other than what your best friend or favorite books suggest, and that is okay while you are learning. In a few weeks, however, as you get to know your baby, you can respond by doing things that suit the baby—and you—best.

The key is to be flexible enough to try different approaches to caring for your baby. Let your partner experiment carefully, too, so that he can learn his own "style." He may do things very differently than you do, but neither way is necessarily the "right way." Together, you can build a varied repertoire of caretaking skills, which is the critical fifth step in learning to parent.

I'm fond of telling new parents that "a baby is a baby is a baby." Indeed, infants are not much different today than they were hundreds, even thousands, of years ago. What is different is that, unlike your parents and grandparents, many of you did not learn basic baby-care skills when you were growing up. As a result, you may approach every task—from feeding to changing to burping to just holding your baby—with trepidation. You may be afraid of unintentionally harming your baby. You may not want to "do the wrong thing" in front of your partner or family. Your inexperience with babies, combined with an all-too-common prenatal bias toward childbirth rather than child care, can turn you into a bundle of nerves around your baby in the first few weeks.

Certainly, while you are in the hospital, you are learning a great deal about caring for your newborn by observing the nurses and by having them show you techniques for proper swaddling, feeding, and burping. In my hospital, I help this learning process along with a daily baby-care class called "Happy Baby Hour." This chapter reviews the baby-care skills that I teach in this class.

Picking Up Your Baby

In my years of working with parents and babies, I have picked up so many infants that I am initially at a loss to describe what has become for me, and certainly will for you, second-nature. Use your common sense and do about ten jumping jacks to loosen up before you begin, and you should be fine if you are guided by these suggestions.

Understand that as awkward as you may feel, chances are that your baby feels equally so, having spent the last nine months snuggled in a warm place, protected from loud noises, bright lights, and sudden movements. Being bombarded by outside stimuli must be shocking for your baby. It is up to you to comfort the baby and to make him or her feel welcome and secure in this new world.

When you approach your infant, try to do so on the baby's level. Lower the volume of your voice. Slow and compact your movements so as not to startle the baby. Talk quietly and make eye contact for a moment before you lift the baby up. Your child needs to become acclimated to you, as you do to him or her.

Until your baby is about two months old, the head needs constant support to prevent it from falling backward or flopping to the side. (Flopping frontward to the chest is okay.) Always use one hand to cradle the head and neck. With the other hand, reach underneath the baby before you lift, then gently guide the arms and legs if they are not secured in a blanket. As long as your baby does not feel a falling sensation, he or she should respond positively when you do this.

It is a good idea to bend over your baby as you pick him or her up. The more you bend, the less distance between your body and the baby's and the less time your baby is suspended in the air rather than snuggled into a mattress or against your warm body. Minimizing this "air time" reduces the likelihood that your baby will be afraid and begin to cry. Bending with your knees minimizes back strain.

Holding Your Baby

Your swaddled newborn is among the simplest bundles to snuggle against you because he or she is lightweight, compact, soft, and smells so good. You may want to cradle the baby in your arms for hours on end. It is only when babies get a little older and start squirming that you are in for a struggle. Of course, by then you are an expert at dealing with their mischief, so the game is a fair one.

Wrapped in blankets, your infant can be held against your chest or cradled in the crook of either arm with the head propped on your bicep or in a more horizontal position. If you are sitting, you can cross one leg over the other and comfortably lay your swaddled baby down in the triangular lap formed by your bent knee. Swaddled babies can be propped up (reclining, not sitting) against almost anything sturdy, so long as their backs are supported firmly.

Tiny babies can be held safely and comfortably without being swaddled. Some babies prefer to be facing in, in a feeding-type position, while others prefer to be facing out, allowing them a better view of the world. In either case, the head and neck always need support. Your baby's weight should rest squarely in your hands and arms.

There are some positions in which you can hold your baby that may make him or her stop crying. If this sounds hard to believe, give these suggestions a try:

1. From behind your baby, cup the chest with your outstretched palm and hold the baby suspended, facedown, with his or her weight against your forearm and the legs on either side of your arm.

2. While the baby is lying on his or her back in your lap, clasp your baby's hands and arms tightly to the chest. Babies do not feel comfortable with their arms flailing, so pulling their arms onto their chest makes them feel more secure.

Putting Down Your Baby

Now that you are thoroughly exhausted from merely thinking about the contortions required to pick up and hold your baby, you probably are ready to tackle the second half of the sequence—getting rid of the infant, politely called "putting down a baby."

Many pediatricians suggest that babies should not be placed flat on their backs and left unattended in the early months. The reason for this precaution is to make sure that they do not choke if they spit up. Until the stump of their umbilical cord falls off at about two weeks, they are best off not sleeping on their tummies either, as the cord tends to get wet from the diaper, and moisture delays the healing process. In the hospital, most babies are put to sleep on their sides, propped up by small bed rolls that are placed along their spines. The bed roll—which is made from rolled-up receiving blankets—prevents the baby from rolling onto its back. Ask your pediatrician for his or her opinion.

Place your baby in the bed using much of the same support you used to pick him or her up, easing the little body down gently, supporting the neck and head. You may need to adjust the baby some to help the baby find a comfortable position before you put on the covers. Again, bending your knees prevents back strain.

Most of the time, babies are warm enough if they sleep in a diaper, undershirt, nightgown, and one receiving blanket. They should be swaddled in the blanket for the first few weeks of life. (See "Swaddling Your Baby" below for instructions.) Some parents add an extra blanket on top and tuck it tightly under the mattress to help the baby feel snug and warm. Later on, when your baby starts to kick, the blanket may be loosened. In cold weather or in a drafty room, a second blanket may be needed. If you are cold, chances are your baby is, too.

Keep in mind that when you put your newborn down for a nap, it is a good idea to alternate sides, from the left to the right side, after each feeding. Babies' heads are still soft and molding until they are sleeping on their tummies at two to three weeks. Laying them on both sides prevents the head from taking on an unusual shape. A slightly flattened skull does not hurt your baby, but it may take a couple of weeks to become rounded again.

Diapering Your Baby

Of all the tasks that you do for your baby, diapering is the one you do most often, so if you do it poorly the first 100 or so times, don't worry—you have 5,900 more chances to get it right.

Before you begin any diaper change, try to have all the necessities on hand to avoid leaving your baby unattended on the edge of a bed or on a changing table. (Probably the baby would be fine if you did this early on, but it is a terrible habit to get into. Many a baby has surprised its parents with its ability to roll over and has fallen to the floor.) For diapering, you need easy access to the following things.

1. One or two clean diapers, because one might get soiled in the middle of a changing.

2. Diaper wraps or waterproof pants, if you use them.

3. A moist washcloth, if at home, or disposable diaper wipes, if you are out, or both.

4. Clean clothes, in case your baby's clothes have become soiled.

5. Diaper ointment for rashes, if necessary.

6. A waterproof lap pad or some other protective liner to place between your baby and whatever the baby is lying on.

7. Something to distract your baby's attention, such as a mobile hung over the changing table or a mirror mounted on a nearby wall. One of the simplest yet most effective newborn attention-grabbers that I have discovered is a white paper plate with a smiling face drawn on it with a thick black marker. You can hang these little plates all over the house, and babies really respond to and are quieted by them.

Cover the changing surface with a clean liner and lay your baby on his or her back on top of it. If your baby seems particularly uncomfortable about having diapers changed, and the discomfort is making you all thumbs, you might want to change the baby on a pillow (covered by a lap pad, of course). Some babies just hate to lie on their backs on a hard surface; a pillow may make them more secure and cooperative.

Unfasten and remove the pants. If the baby is wearing a one-piece outfit, unsnap it at the crotch and fold the legs out of the way. Next, unfasten the diaper. If you are using cloth, it is helpful to stick the diaper pins in a nearby bar of soap. The soap keeps the pins lubricated so they pierce the diaper more easily. You can stick the pins in the fabric of your shirtsleeve or some other safe place close by as you unfasten the diaper. Keeping track of the pins helps prevent sticking your baby and losing or dropping the pins, which certainly comes back to haunt you when your baby's next bowel movement runs down his or her legs into clean socks. If you use disposables, fold the sticky tabs onto the diaper as you unfasten them. Folding them in this way prevents them from sticking to your baby's delicious thighs.

Survey the scene for damages. If there is a bowel movement, wipe it clean with the top of the diaper as you fold the diaper underneath your baby. If you are changing a boy, drape a clean diaper or cloth over his penis to avoid getting squirted. Then, using a wet washcloth or wipe, wash your baby's front thoroughly, making certain to wipe in all the creases. Girls' labia should be wiped from front to back only to help prevent infection.

Follow the same procedure for your baby's bottom, lifting the legs gently from the ankles to reach the entire backside. It is amazing how a baby can be soiled from the small of the back to the back of the knees. After cleaning off the baby, use a dry cloth to pat dry.

When my children were growing up, powdering a baby was as sacred as saying prayers before bedtime. Today doctors advise that applying any kind of powder or lotion at a regular diaper change is unnecessary unless it is required to help clear up a rash or a healing circumcision.

When your baby is clean and dry, remove the soiled diaper (now folded up in a neat little bundle). Discard the dirty diaper and disposable cloths. If you are using cotton diapers and washcloths, place in a hamper or a plastic bag.

Open the clean diaper. Lift your baby by the ankles and slide the diaper underneath the bottom. Bring the front flap between the legs. If you are using a cloth diaper, place it inside the diaper wrap and fold its sides into the center to properly fit around your newborn's tiny legs. Plastic pants are put on separately. If you are using disposables, the back is the side with the fastening tape. The front may have a design on it.

When the diaper is in place, fasten the sticky tabs or pins securely. Diaper pins should be placed with the sharp point facing away from your baby's belly. A roll of masking tape in your diaper bag is a time-tested solution for emergencies in case you lose a diaper pin or the sticky tabs rip off a disposable diaper. Be sure to overlap the corners of the diaper so you do not stick the pins or tape into or onto your baby's legs. While the umbilical cord is healing, fold the top of the front of the diaper under the cord stump. This helps keep the cord area dry. Long shirts should be folded away from the diaper to keep them dry as well.

Be careful not to put on your baby's diaper too tightly. Sometimes when a diaper looks great, it is really so tight that it pinches much like a belt worn too snugly. I get a lot of calls on the "warm line" from parents who are at their wits' end because they have fed and held and changed their babies, but the little ones refuse to be quieted. When they loosen the diaper, miraculously, it stops the crying.

Dressing Your Baby

There are no strict rules about how to dress your baby provided that the baby is kept warm, clean, and comfortable. If any of these needs are not met, you can be sure the baby will let you know about it.

Most newborns need their sleeves rolled up to permit their hands to be exposed to the environment where they can touch and feel the world around them. Long sleeves are best put on tightly curled arms by reaching through the end of the sleeve, grabbing baby's fist from the inside, and pulling rather than pushing the arm through to the other end.

On the topic of how warm a baby should be, almost all parents seem to be prone to overbundling and overdressing their babies, and I am as guilty as the rest of them. The first time I kept my grandchild overnight, I was certain I could not be too careful with her. I had kept a woolen baby blanket down through the years expressly for this purpose. I was determined that the baby be swaddled securely in it so that no stray draft would chill her. I also made certain that the extra room we had converted into a nursery was warm and cozy. Of course, the baby woke in the middle of the night and was drenched in perspiration from head to toe. Feeling foolish, I changed her, changed the sheets—and the woolen blanket—and learned my lesson for good.

A general rule to follow for babies weighing more than seven pounds is that if you are cold or chilled, they probably are, too. If you are warm enough in a blanket, chances are the same weight cover is suitable for them. Smaller babies who do not yet have the same layer of fat under their skin as we do may need extra bundling.

Swaddling Your Baby

Though not a medical necessity, swaddling your newborn—wrapping the baby tightly in a receiving blanket—seems to offer extra comfort to babies in the first two to three weeks of life. The technique I suggest for swaddling also makes an excellent Mexican burrito if you replace your baby with refried beans.

Lay a receiving blanket on a flat surface with the corners at noon and six on a clock. Fold the "noon" corner down until it reaches the blanket's center. Lay your baby on his or her back on the blanket with the head about halfway over the edge formed by the folded corner. Wrap the right side snugly over your baby and tuck the corner under the back by rolling the baby slightly onto the side. Fold up the bottom corner in a similar fashion, taking care to tuck it under your baby's left shoulder smoothly to avoid any lumps underneath. The third and final side is then easily folded from left to right and tucked under as well.

Some babies do not like to be swaddled. If your baby cries or appears uncomfortable when wrapped tightly, try loosening the blankets and he or she may respond better.

Washing Your Baby

If it seems that, as new parents, you do nothing but dress and undress your baby, you are halfway right, which is why much of this most basic information is going to seem like old hat by the second or third week that your baby is home. By that time, however, you are faced with yet another challenge: giving your baby a bath.

You are not going to give your baby a tub bath until the stump of the umbilical cord falls off at about the second week, when the cord has dried completely. That is the physical cord that has fallen off; the emotional cord never, ever goes away. (If your little boy is circumcised, generally that wound heals in five or six days, well before the umbilical cord drops off, so bathing is safe at this time. If the circumcision is performed on the eighth day, as it is in Jewish families, parents may have to wait a day or two longer until both wounds have healed.)

Until the cord is off, you want to keep the belly button area as dry as possible, giving your baby only a sponge bath. A sponge bath is no more than washing your baby's face and hands with a washcloth and warm water and the bottom with water and mild soap. A sponge bath is sufficient for the first few weeks because, when you think of it, where is your baby going to get dirty?

A quick sponge bath sequence—also called "topping and tailing"—goes as follows. (Have these items at the ready beforehand.)

1. A washcloth.
2. Mild soap.
3. Sterile cotton balls.
4. A towel.
5. The diaper necessities as explained previously.

Before getting your baby undressed, clean the eyes with the cotton balls dipped in warm water. Always wipe from the base of the nose outward, using a new cotton ball for each eye. The face comes next, including the outer ears and the nostrils, which can be cleaned with the corner of the washcloth. Wipe the hands and wrists as well. Cleaning the diaper area is done in much the same way as it is during a diaper changing except that soap is used. Rinse and dry thoroughly before rediapering.

Umbilical Cord Care

While the umbilical cord is still healing, the cord stump needs to be cared for about twice a day. All this means is cleaning the area with a little rubbing alcohol on a cotton swab or cotton ball.

There are no nerve endings in this area, so it doesn't hurt the baby at all.

With alcohol on the cotton, push the healing skin back from the drying cord and aggressively get to the base of the cord, where it is still moist. You may come away with a little yellow discharge. As the cord dries up, that yellow discharge may turn into a little bloody discharge simply because the drying cord is pulling away from the skin. You may find a drop of blood on the front of your baby's diaper around the second week. That, too, is perfectly normal. Just continue with your alcohol until the cord falls completely off. If the cord is taking a long time to heal, your pediatrician may cauterize the area with a drop of silver nitrate.

Circumcision Care

There is very little to do to care for the raw area caused by circumcising your little boy's penis except to protect it from sticking to the diaper. To accomplish this, apply some petroleum jelly or A&D ointment directly to the tip of the penis to protect the area from rubbing. The wound should heal in about a week or so. The gauze patch placed on the penis by the doctor following the surgery falls off in a day or two and need not be replaced.

The debate continues to rage about proper hygiene for a newborn's uncircumcised penis. Your pediatrician may suggest otherwise; however, most of the experts I have consulted prefer leaving an uncircumcised penis alone rather than trying to clean under the foreskin. Just wash the penis with mild soap and water as part of the regular bathing routine.

Bathing Your Baby

When the cord falls off (and the circumcision heals), your baby can be given the first tub bath. It is an exciting time for most parents, who anticipate their tiny, naked infant happily splashing around with a rubber duckie and toy boats. In reality, the first bath usually is a disaster. Most newborns, unlike their parents, do not think being stark naked in the water is much fun, but once babies learn to like their bath, they love it. And once they love it, I cannot think of a more delightful time of day. They are very, very cute. They are alert. They are responsive, and they do adorable things in the tub (keeping a camera on hand is a good idea).

The time of day you bathe your baby does not make any difference with the exception of the fact that it is better not to do so when the baby is very hungry or immediately after the baby has eaten. For this reason, I suggest giving your baby an ounce of formula or perhaps five minutes of breast-feeding before the bath and then finishing up the feeding once the baby is clean, warm, and snuggly afterward.

Room temperature when you bathe your baby should be about 75 to 80 degrees in cold weather. In moderate climates, the bathroom does not have to be much warmer than the rest of the house. In both cases, however, the area should be free of drafts from a window or air vent. The water temperature should be comfortably warm to your wrist or elbow.

How often to tub bathe? When my children were infants, doctors were recommending daily baths. Today, however, even a weekly bathing is considered okay by most pediatricians as long as your baby's hands, face, and diaper area are clean. A common-sense hint: if the baby looks and smells like a wet puppy, he or she needs a bath. Of course, once your baby begins to crawl and eat "by himself," you may opt to hose him down at every convenience.

When you undress your newborn for a bath, you may notice that his or her little feet and the beds of the nails may be purple. That is perfectly normal. Your baby's circulation is not very efficient at first, so purple feet do not mean the baby is cold. This discoloration clears up by the time the baby is about a month old. As for cold hands and feet, babies' extremities are always a little cooler than the rest of their bodies, so mittens or booties are unnecessary. This overenthusiastic response to a normal condition may result in prickly heat or a fussy baby.

When undressing and bathing a newborn, you may be surprised at how much body hair there is, expecially if the baby was born early. Premature infants sometimes have hair on their backs and ears and look a little like baby monkeys. This hair gradually rubs off by the time they are full-term.

As with diapering, bathing your baby goes most smoothly if you have all the essentials on hand. A wet baby who is not quickly dried and wrapped is not only uncomfortable (and very noisy) but also could become chilled.

For your baby's tub bath, you need the following things.

1. A portable tub or large sink. Babies can be bathed in the bathtub, but this method is particularly hard on mom and dad's back. I suggest giving the bath at counter level if at all possible.

2. A mild soap.

3. Shampoo, if you choose to use it; soap works just as well.

4. A washcloth and/or a washing sponge.

5. A towel (receiving blankets work nicely because they are very soft and absorbent). It is best to lay your towel out on the drying surface before you begin the bath so it is all ready when you need it later.

6. A clean diaper, diaper accessories, and fresh clothes.

7. An apron or waterproof coverup to keep you dry. Plastic and terry cloth aprons made expressly for this purpose are sold in many baby stores. Look for one that ties in the back; those that do not tend to slip off easily when you lean forward.

Until you become comfortable handling a wet and possibly slippery baby, start with about two inches or less of warm water in the tub. A sponge insert also may be useful.

When your baby is undressed, slowly lower him or her into the water in a semireclining position, face up, holding the baby securely in the crook of your arm and being careful, as always, to support the head and neck at all times. This is a good time to soothe your baby with a calm and reassuring voice. If the baby's screaming is making you frazzled, fake it.

Once your baby is settled down, use your free hand to wash the face, eyes, ears, and nostrils as you did for the sponge bath. This can be done with a clean, wet, and soap-free washcloth. Then begin on the body, soaping your free hand and using it to wash gently under the chin and neck. As your baby grows, he or she gets more and more chins, so be sure to get under all of them. Soap over the shoulders, the armpits, and down the arms until you reach the wrists. Try to get in all the crevices under the arms and chin. If you miss these spots frequently, your baby may get some smelly white stuff under there. (The same is true for washing behind the ears. It seems to be an accumulation of sweat and dead skin cells.) Do not soap the hands until you are completely finished with the rest of the body, so that your baby cannot put soapy fingers in his or her eyes.

Following the arms, wash the tummy before using the washcloth again to clean the groin area. On boys, wash around the scrotum and penis very gently. As always, girls are washed front to back. Do not be alarmed by bloody discharge from the labia; this is perfectly normal due to the increased level of hormones from the mother. Some babies have enlarged breasts for the same reason; both aftereffects of pregnancy resolve spontaneously within several weeks. Next, soap down the backs and fronts of the legs and down to the feet and toes. Rinse the entire front thoroughly. Turn your baby over now, holding the baby up by the chest in a squatting or semireclining position, facedown but far away from the water. This position mimics one of those described earlier in which your baby should stop crying—if you are lucky. Soap behind the ears and down the back with your hand, and then use the washcloth on the bottom. Now is the time also to soap the hands. Rinse the hands first, then the back.

If this is shampoo day (twice a week is sufficient unless your baby has an oily scalp or gets that annoying puppy-smell, in which case you should wash the hair more frequently), squirt some shampoo (I hope you opened the bottle before the bath; it is very hard to do so with only one free hand) or rub a mild soap on your hand and start rubbing the head in a circular and firm motion from front to back, including the fontanel or soft spot where the four pieces of bone that make up the skull have not yet grown together. Do not be afraid to rub there. Cradle cap may start here because parents are timid. (See chapter 7 for more on cradle cap.) You need not be afraid to touch this area. The soft spot is as firm as a heavy canvas and can withstand shampooing without damage. The soft spot probably will close completely when your baby is between the ages of twelve and twenty-four months. Rinse the scalp by soaking and wringing out a clean washcloth or bath sponge over your baby's head, as far as possible from the eyes. If soap does get in the eyes, flush them with clear water. If this doesn't stop your baby from crying, call your mother.

By this time, certainly you are a nervous (and probably wet) wreck, your heart is pounding out of your chest as you literally run to that waiting towel in the hopes that something—anything—stops your baby's screaming. Wrapping the baby snugly, and holding him or her in your arms, in fact, should do the trick.

Once you both have calmed down a bit, place your baby back on a firm surface and dry thoroughly, making certain to pat between all the folds of skin following the same basic pattern as you used for washing. Any areas that you do not dry well may chap afterward, causing discomfort and irritability. Drying is especially important on the head, under the arms and chin, in the folds of the legs, and behind the ears.

One alternative to bathing that is extremely popular with the parents in my classes is taking their babies in the shower with them. Babies, too, seem to love this time, and it can be a real family experience. Check with your pediatrician if you have any concerns about this suggestion.

Nail Care

Most new parents are surprised to see that their newborns enter the world with long and sharp fingernails. In fact, a fetus begins to grow nails as early as the fifth month of its development, about the same time as it starts to grow eyebrows, lashes, and head hair.

While your baby is in the hospital, the nails may be left long. Even though the nails are quite soft, the hands are covered with a long-sleeved shirt to prevent the baby from scratching its face. After the baby is in your care, however, the nails need to be trimmed. The hands need to be left exposed to encourage the baby to explore the environment by touching and feeling the world within its reach.

The best time to clip the nails is when the baby is asleep and you can uncurl the tiny fingers without waking him or her. Baby nail scissors with rounded edges are interchangeable with nail clippers; both work equally well. In all honesty, the safest way to keep your baby's nails trimmed is to bite them. So if you like to bite your own nails, this is your big opportunity. You get twenty at a time. Do not smooth the nails with an emery board. With the nails so close to the skin and the skin so tender, you can cause a really painful abrasion. If your baby does scratch himself or herself even after the nails are clipped, do not worry. Pediatricians say the scratches are very superficial. A little A&D ointment speeds the healing.

Taking Your Baby's Temperature

Many hospitals provide new parents with a rectal thermometer. This is to be used whenever you think your baby is sick. When you call your pediatrician, he or she will ask for a rectal temperature reading. Most newborns do not mind their temperature being taken. It is only when they get older and see you coming that they scamper away.

To get a rectal reading, lay your baby on his or her back and remove the diaper as you would for changing. As with changing, protect yourself from baby boys. Dab a little petroleum jelly on the end of the thermometer. Lift your baby's legs to expose the rectum and insert the silver tip of the thermometer gently about an inch. There should be no feeling of resistance. That is all there is to it. There is nothing up there but bowel movement, so you do not have to worry that you are going to hurt anything. Leave the thermometer in for two minutes, holding it gently to prevent your baby from squeezing it out. There is no need to apply pressure.

A normal rectal reading is usually a degree higher than an oral reading (98.6), so 99.6 degrees or slightly higher is normal rectally. When you remove the thermometer, be cautioned that a bowel movement may come squirting out with it, so be prepared with a clean cloth or disposable wipe at your side to prevent it from shooting across the room.

Getting Started on a Feeding Routine

Breast-Feeding

If you are like most first-time moms, you may have read a book or an article that helped you make up your mind that nursing is the right alternative for you, but because you cannot "practice" before the baby comes, you have no actual experience with breast-feeding techniques or patterns.

You may have begun breast-feeding in the delivery room as

soon as your baby was born. Sometimes babies are alert enough to latch onto the nipple properly right from the start. This immediate "success" is greatly reassuring to the mom. If you did not nurse immediately, your baby probably was brought to you for feeding some time during the first twenty-four hours after birth. Very often, babies fall into a very deep sleep during this time. If you tried to nurse your baby during this sleepy period, he or she may have had a more difficult time latching on. This difficulty does not necessarily reflect a breast-feeding problem, but it can be frustrating for you. I often suggest to moms facing this situation, "Let's not even give this a try now. The baby is just too tired to even think about eating." And that is the truth!

Cesarean section babies sometimes have some difficulty getting started on the breast because they are sleepy from the transfer of your pain relief medication to them. Also, babies not delivered through the birth canal may have mucus in their lungs that causes them to gag when they suck. Babies born vaginally have the mucus squeezed out during the trip through the birth canal. Cesarean babies usually are better at sucking after six to eight hours.

Whether you began with a rabbit start or not, you should be comforted by the fact that 95 percent of babies learn to latch on quite soon. If your baby still is not too interested, you can try a little glucose water on the baby's tongue and on your nipple. Some babies are tricky and lick the water off the nipple, but usually they get the idea that what was in their mouth also is on your nipple.

Sometimes breast-feeding is inhibited if a mother is very uptight or is putting a lot of pressure on herself to nurse her baby right away. When I see this happening in the hospital and a baby does not latch on, I try to distract the mother by asking her about the flowers in her room or what she thinks of the hospital food. While she is focused on something else, I manipulate the baby onto the breast, and whoosh, the baby starts to suck.

Many hospitals have lactation specialists on staff or available to patients through referral to help new mothers learn to breast-feed. Do not hesitate to ask for help even after you are home. Videotapes also may be helpful.

HOW TO BREAST-FEED

There are several positions in which you can breast-feed your baby. Experiment with them all to find the one(s) most comfortable for you. The most common is the cradle hold. Cradle your baby in one arm so that the infant is facing the breast on which he or she is nursing. Pull the baby toward you so that the head and body are level with your nipple. Place the arms on both sides of your breast so the baby is hugging you.

A second alternative is the football hold, in which your baby lies at your side with the head at your breast and the feet behind you, level with your waist. The baby is face up, propped up by a pillow. The arms hug your breast. With your baby at your side, you have no weight on your abdomen. For this reason, the football hold is a good alternative for mothers who have undergone cesarean sections.

Nursing while lying down is the third position that you can try. Lie on your side with the breast that is ready to be nursed toward the bed. Prop your baby on his or her side facing you so that the baby's belly is against yours. The baby's mouth should be aligned with your nipple. Use the arm closest to the bed to hug your baby and pull him or her to the breast. A rolled-up receiving blanket or pillow under your arm at your baby's back provides additional support.

In all the positions, make sure that your back and arms are well supported. You do not want to be shifting and squirming during the feeding. To begin nursing, hold your breast with your palm underneath and your thumb on top. Compress your breast on the outside of the dark areola and use your nipple to stroke your baby's lips. This causes the baby to open the mouth. When the mouth is open wide, guide your nipple into it at a slight upward angle. Try to get the nipple and areola as far into the mouth as possible. If your baby latches onto the nipple only, he or she does not suck properly and your nipples quickly grow very sore. If your breasts are very large, you may need to press down slightly on the breast just under your baby's nose to give the baby some breathing space while he or she is sucking.

You know when your baby is nursing well when you hear and see swallowing at a regular rate. When your milk "lets down," you also may feel very cozy or sleepy and relaxed; these feelings are caused by the same hormones that cause your milk to flow.

Nurse your baby for about five minutes per side at first, supporting your breast throughout the feeding to help keep it in proper position. To remove your baby from your breast, insert your little finger into the mouth to break the seal the baby has on your nipple. If your baby is sucking well, you will notice that your nipple has taken on a wedgelike shape. This is another sign that nursing is going well.

You need to burp your baby before nursing on the second side. (See "Burping Your Baby" below for instructions.) At the next feeding, begin on the second side first. Switching sides is important because your baby sucks hardest during the first five minutes of nursing, and therefore stimulates and empties the first breast more than the second. Switching starting sides helps keep the milk production even. To help you remember, tie a ribbon or attach a safety pin on your bra on the side that you fed last.

Bottle-Feeding

If you have decided to bottle-feed exclusively or part-time, your baby's pediatrician has recommended what type of formula to use. The choice is between a milk-based formula and a nonmilk substitute made from soybeans. Both are equally nutritious, providing twenty calories per ounce. The soy is used for infants whose family members are prone to allergies, which can be triggered by milk.

In the hospital, you do not have to prepare or heat your baby's formula. It comes in premixed, sterilized four-ounce bottles. (See chapter 6 for instructions on preparing infant formula at home.) Feeding from a bottle is really quite simple. Just cradle your infant in your arms with the head slightly higher than the body. Tip the bottle so that the formula completely fills the nipple. Holding it this way reduces the amount of air that your baby sucks.

To make sure the flow of formula is not too fast or too slow, watch the air bubbles that float to the top of the bottle. They should be quite small and continuous and should bead together like tapioca. If the formula is coming out too fast, the bubbles are large, and your baby may gag. If this happens, screw on the nipple ring more tightly. If the flow is still too fast, you may have to use a different nipple with a smaller hole. If the nipple hole is too small or the ring is screwed on too tightly, your baby may suck very hard, causing the nipple to collapse. Loosening the nipple or replacing it with a new one should remedy the problem.

Most newborns need to be fed every two to three hours and drink about two ounces per feeding for the first three days. After that, the amount increases to nearly four ounces per feeding for a week or so and may go to five ounces per feeding for the first three weeks of life.

Night feedings are necessary whether you breast-feed or bottle-feed. As much as I encourage talking to your babies, one time that socializing is not appropriate is during the middle-of-the-night feedings, which I find go most smoothly if they are done in the quietest, dimmest room possible. Just feed, change, and put your baby back to bed. Your baby has to understand that this is not partytime.

Burping Your Baby

Whether you are nursing or using a bottle, you must burp your baby halfway through and right after feeding. Burping helps bring up the air that your baby has swallowed. Bottle-fed babies tend to swallow more air than breast-fed babies, so their burps tend to be louder.

Sometimes babies' burps bring up breast milk or formula. Do not be alarmed if your baby spits up after feeding. Spitting results because the muscle valve at the top of the stomach doesn't hold the contents down at this age. Until that muscle becomes stronger, some babies spit up after and in between every meal for up to a year! Generally, babies know when they are full and stop eating. Some babies, on the other hand, make little piggies of themselves and continue to feed even when their bellies are full. Babies who overeat are prone to spitting, but again, this is rarely harmful. In fact, the worst thing about spitting is the mess it makes.

Just so you do not think your baby is sick, it is useful to understand that there is a difference between spitting and vomiting. With spitting, milk or formula just spills out of the mouth and dribbles down the chin. With vomiting, however, the vomitus shoots out of the mouth with much more force. Even vomiting is not unusual with a newborn, however, especially if the baby has eaten too fast or too much. If your baby vomits more than twice, or if the vomiting is accompanied by a fever, call your pediatrician.

There are several ways to burp your baby. You can hold the baby on your shoulder with the arms over your shoulder. You can sit the baby on your lap, leaning slightly forward, with your hand against the chest and your thumb and finger under the baby's arms. Or you can lay the baby down across your lap. Gently rub or pat the back to help the baby burp.

Burping is an excellent way that dad can share in baby's care, whether you are bottle-feeding or nursing. In many homes daddy is the CEO of burping. Some mothers may not want to let go of any of the caretaking tasks, but they must in order for dad to be involved. Burping or giving a bottle is something that he can do.

I cannot stress enough how important it is for both parents to come to the scene on equal levels emotionally. Start off that way so that nobody feels they have a so-called edge. It is a fun as well as a frustrating time to be sharing wonderful moments such as trying to put on a diaper and having your baby begin one of those ten-minute bowel movements in the middle of the changing!

Remember, you have equal shares in the child. Each of you wants to do your very best. It is so much better for your marriage and for your family generally to enjoy your baby and not play one-upmanship with the other person. If your schedules permit, try to share equally one day at a time until you both feel competent in your caretaking skills. Let the newborn stage be a time to work closely as a team.

Class Dismissed

There, you've done it! You now know all the skills needed for bottom-line, basic baby care. Take a deep breath and pat yourself and your partner on the back.

Remember that you know what is best for you and for your baby. Do not hesitate to modify my suggestions. As you learn to rely on your own judgment, you become more and more comfortable with making and implementing decisions about your baby. Tempered with advice from your pediatrician, your instincts are there to guide you.

Becoming adept at taking care of a tiny baby does take time, though, especially if you are tentative and a little bit afraid. Be patient with yourself and your mate. Most of the time, your baby will be patient with you, and before you all know it, you are well on your way to becoming a remarkably euphonic trio.

Going Home

As you wind up your stay in the hospital, I hope that you are looking forward to welcoming your baby home. Your baby's car seat is ready and waiting like a chariot in your car. Perhaps dad has washed the car, too, and vacuumed the inside so it looks clean and smells fresh.

You have showered and dressed in the outfit that you packed in your suitcase so long ago. Your baby is bright-eyed and smelling sweet, all spiffed up in that specially selected going-home outfit. Your bouquets and flower arrangements have been loaded onto a cart and are waiting by your bed. Tied together and attached to the requisite wheelchair for your ride to the door are your balloons saying "It's a Boy!" or "It's a Girl!"

With misty eyes, you say good-bye to the nurses and doctors who helped you through this miraculous adventure. You thank them and whisper to yourself how much you will miss them. For your partner, you smile and express your enthusiasm to return home for the first time as a family.

I watch this scene play itself out daily as new moms and dads begin their lives with their new babies. It is such a magical time as you head out the door with your gifts and flowers. You strap your baby into the car seat, carefully adjusting the tiny body so that the baby is comfortable and safe. You may cover the baby with a blanket to keep it warm. You step into the passenger seat, and dad swings the door shut. You wave to the candy striper who wheeled you to the car.

As you drive off, carry with you this one thought: that little bundle in the back seat will bring major changes in your life. You may think that you know what to expect, that you know where Route Parenthood is taking you. Do not be surprised when you find yourself somewhere else.

6

❖

On Your Own: Your First Weeks at Home

I was invited to a beach party with one of my daughters and several of her old schoolmates. Like her, they had families of their own. One of the women was working full-time as an attorney, in practice with her husband. Another had opted for the "mommy track," and spent three days in an office. The only single parent in the group owned her own business, which she ran from her home.

Being the grandmother that I am, I found myself spending the day making sand castles and playing lifeguard. I also had an opportunity to observe the similarities and differences in these young families. What struck me the most was how different the relationships were between the two sets of married parents that were there that day.

"Ellen" and her husband approached child care as a team. With two-year-old twins and an infant, neither parent had the time to patiently apply sunscreen to every nook and cranny, but together, the parents got the lotion on everybody. The twins took their own bottles of juice from the family picnic basket when they were hungry. No one really paid attention when the infant was asleep under the umbrella. This family had a real sense of unity that was inspired by the team spirit of "Ellen" and her husband.

"Sharon," on the other hand, made an issue out of everything that her husband did. She criticized him for letting their ten-month-old eat sand. She argued with him about letting the older child swim in the ocean. Of course, both parents seemed to truly care about their children, but every time that "Sharon's" husband made a move, she found fault. Eventually, he stuck his nose in a book.

The lesson I learned that day was that parents who work as a team seem happier. This lesson is as true on day one as it is when your children are older. Caring for a baby is a classic "feedback loop." The more positive feedback you get from your spouse and your baby, the better you feel about your caretaking skills. When you feel good about what you are doing, you enjoy doing it. The more you do something, the better you become at it.

Moms and dads benefit from supporting each other during the challenging days of early parenthood. Words of praise such as "What a good job you did putting on that diaper" and "How did you get that burp out of the baby?" are not hard to say, yet they communicate powerful and reinforcing messages. I cannot stress enough the importance of nurturing each other as well as your baby, particularly during the next few months. If you lend a hand to one another when you reach step six on the stairway of parenthood, you will not find yourself breathing so hard as you climb.

My children were born in the 1950s, when every family on our block was made up of a mother and a father, a baby, two or three children, a dog or a cat, and maybe some fish. The moms stayed home to care for their babies and dogs and cats and fish. The dads went to work. The children played. We all knew one another's business.

The business of our neighborhood, to be honest, was making babies. It seemed that someone was pregnant all the time. There always were lots of children in our front yards. Along with baby showers and Fourth of July picnics, one of our neighborhood rituals was what I call the "waiting at the windows" dance. Whenever one of us was expected home with a new baby, the other neighbors would stand by their windows, peeking out the curtains, waiting for a first glimpse of the newest arrival.

Although neighborhoods have changed, coming home from the hospital still is a very special time for new parents, especially when you are bringing home your first baby. Even without an entourage of well-wishers, you feel proud and excited to start your new life. Perhaps a friend has made a Welcome Home sign for your front door. Maybe you feel special because the house is spick-and-span in anticipation of your arrival. The air is laced with the sweet aroma of fresh flowers from your congratulatory bouquets.

As you walk proudly into your baby's nursery, your dream is complete. The room is bright and clean, as pristine as virgin snow. The doll that your best friend gave you sits on the dresser next to the lamp that was a shower gift from your co-workers. The bassinet or crib is ready, its clean sheets unwrinkled and perfect. You linger with your baby in your arms, wanting this special moment to last forever.

As you stand there together, you look at your baby in total awe, not quite believing that he or she exists. He or she probably is sleeping, tired from his busy morning. You place the baby in his or her bed so gently that it seems you are handling fine china. The baby might stir a little bit, but chances are he or she settles down nicely. You cover her ever so timidly, carefully wrapping the baby's tiny body in soft blankets. You and your partner may hold hands or gently embrace.

Chances are that you share intimacies in hushed tones, not only because you are afraid to wake the baby, but because it is customary to whisper in sacred places. Maybe you are silent, overcome with joy. You listen to your baby breathing. You stand there by the baby's bed, just watching him or her.

After a minute or two, you tiptoe out of the nursery. You are happy to be home and that your baby is tucked safely in his or her bed. If life were like the movies, the scene would fade out with a close-up shot of mom's and dad's blissful faces. The house lights would come on, and the audience would leave knowing that the new family would live happily ever after. But life is not like the movies.

So what happens to tarnish the perfect homecoming? First, you are totally responsible for your baby, who can do absolutely nothing for himself or herself. You try to anticipate his or her needs, but you do not know what his or her signals mean. Is the baby warm enough? Is the room warm enough? The phone is ringing; will that disturb the baby? If the baby doesn't wake up when you expect, you wonder if you should wake him or her. If he or she cries, you wonder when you should pick him or her up. You are on your own making these important decisions. You no longer have a nurse to ask if it is time for a nap or a feeding. (Of course, you can call your mother. The telephone company loves new parents.)

The realization that "this is for real" can be a bit frightening. I know how you feel. I was a first-time mom myself once (in the Stone Age), and I was scared, too. Chances are good that even your pediatrician would admit to some anxiety the first time he or she was alone with his or her baby! Temporary apprehension is normal, and it does not mean that you will never learn to be a good parent, but it is reason to nourish each other as much as possible every day. Praise each other. Hug each other. Pat each other on the back. Your adjustment to your new baby is as important to the health of your family as your baby's adjustment to you.

This chapter recognizes that life with a new baby often is stressful, particularly when you have to juggle your home life with two careers. It is frustrating and exhausting and filled with situations that you never faced before. Millions of new parents around the world feel this way. My job is to reassure you that, like the rest of us, you will prevail. Take it one step at a time as you encounter the situations I discuss in this chapter. Learn as you go. A few months from now, parenting will come so naturally, you'll feel as if you've been doing it forever.

Someone Tugging at Your Heart

The first universal attribute of parenthood is exhaustion, especially for new moms. It starts when you are preparing to leave the hospital. For the first time in several days, you shower and dress in street clothes and shoes, both of which may be tight and uncomfortable. You pack your suitcase. You diaper and dress your baby, talk with the doctors, gather your cards and flowers, undergo discharge procedures, and finally say good-bye. Admit it; you are exhausted, and you haven't even left yet!

Of course, when you arrive home and get your baby settled, you cannot sleep. You cannot relax, either, when you are listening for your baby and worrying about whether or not you can take good care of the baby when he or she wakes. Any little squeak has you running into the nursery. Even if your baby does not squeak, you are running. There is a whole different feeling in the house than there was before the baby. Something always is tugging at you.

This feeling that you are never alone is something that stays with you as long as you are a parent, even as your children grow and you are apart from them for increasingly longer periods of time. For now, all you know is that there is no turning back. There are no refunds and no exchanges, even if the baby does squeak and leak. And the little one didn't even come with instructions!

All Hands on Deck

Generally your first day home is a jumble of excitement, celebration, fear, fatigue, panic, and love. By nighttime, the combination of all these emotions leaves you exhausted. A cozy bed beckons you about 7:00 P.M., but there is a catch: you are a mommy or a daddy now, and that is a full-time, 'round-the-clock job. Rarely do you get a weekend—or even a day—off. You realize it was a lot easier caring for your baby when he or she was inside.

At least 80 percent of parents with whom I speak after they leave the hospital say that the first night home with baby is very difficult. They report sleepless nights spent trying to get their babies to stop crying (or worrying why they are not crying!). Are these parents inept? Of course not. The baby is merely reacting to changes in the environment. When the baby wakes up, he or she is aware of the new bassinet or crib, of the different smells in the house, of the quiet and empty nursery, of the darkness. The baby realizes that this is a strange and different place.

Even after the baby is fed and settled into mom's loving arms, he or she may not be comfortable enough in these new surroundings to return to sleep. The more the baby resists, the more the baby becomes overtired and the more he or she cries. Crying breeds fear and tension in you. Your baby feels your tension and reacts by becoming tense. The cycle can continue all night.

For the most part, neither prenatal classes nor hospital maternity programs address this very frustrating although harmless pattern that typically persists for the first two to four nights after you come home from the hospital. It would be so helpful if all new parents were aware of this possibility. Most babies settle down within a week.

However, no matter how well prepared you are, the first thought that comes to your mind during your baby's hysterics is: What are we doing wrong? "Our baby didn't cry in the hospital," you might say. "We must have forgotten something." Your insecurities and guilt feelings gush to the surface like freshly tapped oil. To make you feel better, it helps to return to basics.

- Warmth: Is the baby dressed appropriately in a relatively clean diaper, undershirt, and clothing suited for the room temperature (most likely a lightweight nightgown)? Remember, if the baby is over seven pounds, he or she needs to be dressed only as warmly as you are.
- Security: Is the baby swaddled in a soft receiving blanket? Is the blanket too tight? Check also for scratchy labels. Perhaps sucking will provide additional comfort; you may want to offer a pacifier.
- Hunger: Has the baby eaten recently? Has the baby been burped? It is hard to know if your baby's belly is full because babies who do not get a "full" feeding can be hungry an hour later. You can always offer the breast and/or a bottle of formula or water to double-check.

If you check these fundamental needs and your baby still is crying, chances are that he or she just feels uncomfortable in the new environment. All you can do is hold and comfort the baby. Take turns trying to sleep. You will need your rest in the morning.

Whatever Gets You Through the Night

The picture I paint may seem gruesome, but you can consider yourself lucky if you experience none of this crying cycle. I happily report that about 10 percent of babies make the transition easily and continue on the hospital schedule. If you have one of these babies, count your blessings and enjoy him or her! Only one is allotted per family.

Having a grandma to help during the day or night is wonderful, but a dad with a delicate touch who is caring and understands the whole picture is a real godsend. In fact, I think that dads are the most important people in the household in the first weeks at home.

Some couples may not appreciate the emphasis on dads in my child-care classes. The primary reason surfaces during these first few days and nights at home with your baby. Of course, single mothers and women whose partners cannot be with them manage to care for their infants alone, but it is so much harder this way. Couples who share caring for their babies during these long days and nights find the job not only easier but more rewarding, as well. In addition, babies who get to know their dads early in their lives generally are closer to them later, as well.

If there is one comment that I hear most often from new moms, it is that sharing these special days together adds a new dimension to their relationship with their partners. "I felt a real partnership with my husband," one young woman told me. "We needed each other to survive that time. I felt like we were a family because we did it together."

Dads, of course, can help care for their babies in many ways: burping them, feeding them from the bottle, changing diapers, changing clothes, soothing and rocking them. I am sure that all new moms appreciate whatever help dad provides. Most of all, dad's help is needed at night. If your baby does not settle down at 2:00 or 3:00 A.M., dad has the perfect arms in which to rock baby. If your house is cold or if you just cannot stay awake one more minute, dad can bring baby into bed with you. Lay the baby between you, where he or she can feel your body heat all around. The warmth of your bodies is like a magic sleeping pill for your baby. Do not fear that you will roll over onto your infant; I have never heard of that happening. To be sure, you may want to ask your pediatrician about sleeping with your baby.

I always tell the new parents to prepare themselves for baby's nighttime routine by assembling the feeding and changing equipment beside their beds (some bassinets have utility shelves underneath them that are perfect for holding these items). With the essentials on hand, the entire late-night feeding/burping/changing routine can be accomplished without stirring from the comfort of your bed.

Another late-night trick is to warm your baby's bassinet with a hot water bottle or a heating pad. While mom is nursing or giving the bottle, dad can fill a water bottle or plug in a heating pad and place it on the baby's bed under a receiving blanket. Some dads have found that warming the receiving blankets in the clothes dryer works well, too. Then, when feeding time is over, remove the heating pad or water bottle and snuggle your baby into a nice, warm bed.

"Waa Waa"

When new dads call me in the middle of the night, they usually begin the conversation by saying, "Help! My baby is crying, my wife is crying. What do I do?" Indeed, it is hard enough to hear your baby cry; but when mom is crying, too, you have to wonder which end is up.

Many dads find it helpful to know that typically new moms cry a lot, and this is normal. All a new mom has to do is hear her baby cry for the umpteenth time to make her feel totally inadequate. She questions her competence. She wonders if she should have read a different book or paid more attention in the hospital. If she questions whether having a baby was the right decision entirely, she may feel guilty. The baby may not be eating well, or may get diaper rash, or the umbilical cord may ooze some blood. Within a few days, a new mom can feel like a one-armed boxer in the ring with Muhammad Ali. (See the section on postpartum emotions below for more information on mom's feelings.)

Nothing tears at a parent's heart as strongly as listening to his or her baby cry. Some of what you are feeling is instinctive. Studies have shown that even young children experience increases in blood pressure and heart rate when hearing a baby cry. Just imagine how Mother Nature intends for parents to react!

Whether you are motivated by instinct or love or something else, when you hear crying, you have to run to your baby. In the first few weeks, trying to wait even five or ten minutes is out of the question. You cannot do it. For that reason, when your baby cries in this first month or so, I do not see any reason why you should not go right away. In this way, you can learn to comfort the baby while at the same time learn more about yourself as a nurturing person.

Sometimes, however, even when you run quickly, your baby will not be comforted and will continue to cry. Some parents try to wait it out and give their infant five to seven minutes of crying alone. I have heard it enough times that I believe that babies have a seven-minute clock inside them, and if you let them cry for seven minutes, they usually stop on their own. If, however, you find that you are uncomfortable with listening to your baby cry, you can in the early weeks pick up a fussing baby. If the baby still does not stop, and the crying is making you feel like crying, try to realize that, like boot camp, this testing ground does end. When it does, the next stage is a lot easier compared with what you have endured.

To help you survive when every minute lasts an hour, try to look around the house and find something to make you smile. Maybe the dog has dragged a dirty diaper from the trash can and ripped it to shreds under the coffee table. Maybe the baby's dirty clothes that you changed during the night are piled in a heap and on top of that heap lies an especially contented kitty cat. The darling nursery that was so perfect twenty-four hours before looks a shambles. You look worse.

Before you get out of control, try to lighten up. Remember, you are in the midst of one of the most difficult parts of parenthood. You are there together, and you can laugh at yourselves together. All of your uncertainties and the crazy, mixed-up days and nights are only temporary.

Really.

1,001 Answers to Your Breast-Feeding Questions

One of the most common concerns that parents have in the first few days—and often later on, too—is whether the baby is eating enough. One third to one half of the phone calls that I receive from brand-new parents are about breast-feeding.

At first, you may think that your pre-milk, or colostrum, is not sufficient nourishment. This is not so. Colostrum is an excellent source of nutrients and antibodies. On the other hand, the amount of colostrum produced is small, so your baby may lose 10 to 12 percent of his birth weight in the first few days. This is perfectly normal. Bottle-fed babies also may drop a few ounces before they go home from the hospital. If you think your baby needs more than you are producing, ask your pediatrician about supplementing with glucose water.

When the milk comes in on the third day postpartum, breast-feeding—which may have gone smoothly in the hospital—may become temporarily difficult as a result of engorgement, or swelling caused by rapid filling of the breasts with milk. The areolas may become so full that the nipples flatten out, making it hard for your baby to latch on. A baby who does well in the hospital when the breasts are supple may not repeat this performance at home. Both mother and baby may find this situation frustrating.

Engorgement can be quite painful for moms until the milk is released. Some women tell me that engorgement feels like the swelling that occurs in the area of an injury, such as a sprained ankle. The breasts become hot and tight. They may ache from the nipples to the armpits. In fact, because milk fills the ducts throughout the chest area, some women feel that they have huge Arnold Schwarzenegger–like pectoral muscles under their arms.

There are several remedies for engorgement. Try taking a warm shower and gently massaging the breasts so that some of the milk is let out. If a shower is inconvenient, place some warm compresses on the breasts, then manipulate around the nipple and express (squeeze out) some breast milk for a minute or two until the areola is soft.

If you prefer to express with a breast pump, as many doctors recommend, you can be taught to do this as well. (See the section on expressing breast milk for details.) Sometimes a plastic cup (called a Swedish milk cup) worn over the nipples and under the bra can help the nipples protrude until the engorgement subsides, but I find that this is not a quick enough remedy when your baby is hungry and crying. True engorgement lasts about forty-eight hours, after which your breasts become softer. If your baby does not nurse regularly, however, the breasts may become engorged again.

When your milk comes in, you may be surprised at its consistency, which varies from yellowish, creamlike droplets called hindmilk to watery liquid called foremilk that resembles skim cow's milk. Both of these kinds of milk can come from the breast at the same time. For a woman who has never known the feeling of her breasts full of milk, it is an experience that is wonderful, occasionally painful, strange, and unlike anything you have experienced before. At first, you may be surprised by the milk coming out of you, even though you expected it intellectually.

At the same time, you may be bothered by the milk that drips between feedings. You can wear cloth or disposable paper breast pads to absorb the milk, but like diapers, pads need to be changed often to be effective and to avoid chafing. When you hear your baby cry and the milk really begins to flow, there is not much you can do to keep dry.

Your milk supply increases to accommodate your baby's needs. The more the baby suckles, the more milk you produce. Sometimes your baby needs to eat more often than normal to cause your body to make more milk. These "growth spurts" seem to occur when your baby is six to ten days, three weeks, six weeks, three months, and six months old.

Many new moms are troubled by sore or cracked nipples when they begin nursing, especially if they have fair hair and skin. Proper breast-feeding technique lessens the chance of nipple pain, but for most women it takes three or four weeks for the nipples to get used to the constant sucking. Until that time, try the following helpful practices.

• Dry your baby's saliva off the nipple after each feeding.
• Dry your nipple thoroughly. Some women suggest that a hair dryer on a low setting works well for this purpose.

- Rub a little breast milk or lanolin into the nipple.
- If possible, continue to air dry the breasts by going without a bra or blouse.
- Change your breast pads regularly to keep the nipple as dry as possible between feedings.

If nipple soreness is very uncomfortable, you can ask your doctor about a nipple shield, which temporarily protects the nipple during feeding. Any milk residue from the feeding should be washed off the shield with soap and water after each feeding. Some lactation specialists suggest using lanolin to lubricate the nipple. I find that lanolin is helpful in preventing cracked nipples, but it is not as effective as A&D ointment in healing the nipples once they are cracked.

You may find that you are unprepared for the duration and frequency of your baby's feedings. Many women are. A newborn generally suckles about ten to fifteen minutes per side (after a few days of building up to that) and wants to eat every two to three hours. My theory is that once engorgement is gone, it takes a woman's body about three hours to replenish the milk supply, and takes a baby's tummy about three hours to empty. Although a three-hour schedule is ideal, most moms find it impossible to stick to a schedule for at least a week or two. Newborns eat and sleep erratically in the beginning, and trying to get them to eat by the clock usually turns out to be more trouble than it is worth. See what your baby is doing and follow its lead. The baby may establish his or her own schedule quite nicely.

If within three weeks you are trying to get your life back in order (if you can remember what that is) and you need your baby to eat fairly regularly, try to work toward a schedule in which the baby eats about every three hours. If your baby is napping during a regularly scheduled feeding during the day, I suggest waking him or her up. Over the years I have found that babies who eat regularly during the daytime wake less frequently at night. If your newborn weighs more than seven pounds, you do not need to wake the baby at night to eat. Rather you can let the baby wake you up. In this way, the baby is encouraged to go as long as possible between nighttime feedings.

Your pediatrician is the most important person with whom

to discuss a feeding schedule. Some pediatricians want small babies to be awakened for feedings every two to three hours, around the clock, for example; others do not. Sometimes babies want to suck for longer periods of time or more frequently than every three hours. It is helpful to have some guidelines from your baby's doctor.

Sometimes your baby may sleep three or four hours at a time at night for several nights and then revert back to waking every two hours. Parents frequently call me to ask what they are doing wrong. If there is one constant that I have found to be true over the many years that I have loved babies, it is that they are totally unpredictable. What happens today does not happen tomorrow, especially for the first six weeks. Inconsistency is normal and expected.

Whether your baby is a good sucker or not, breast-feeding goes much more smoothly if you and your partner lend essential emotional support to each other as you and your baby become accustomed to a routine. Support is critical in the first month or so after the baby comes home. For example, a mom who has chosen to breast-feed may find that her baby is not gaining enough weight to satisfy the pediatrician. If the doctor suggests that she supplement with a bottle, she may feel incompetent. If someone whom she loves also tells her to stop nursing—as one grandma that I know told her daughter—this suggestion is all the more disparaging. If her partner stands by her, is willing to help with bottle-feedings, and reminds her that the bottom line is the health of the baby, then the new mom may have an easier time making the emotional adjustment.

What to Eat and Not to Eat While Breast-Feeding

To help your body maintain an adequate milk supply, doctors recommend that you increase your fluid intake by as much as two to three quarts (eight to ten glasses) per day. A good habit is to drink a glass of liquid at every feeding. An increase of about five hundred calories per day to your diet and a supplement of vitamins are also suggested.

Some lactation specialists say that it does not matter what you eat while you are nursing. I disagree. I have talked to so many moms over the years whose normally good babies had very bad days, and almost always we traced the behavior back to something mom ate. Some new moms can eat anything they want. Others can have one slice of pizza or one chocolate chip cookie and their babies are gassy for hours.

For this reason, I suggest that nursing moms watch what they are eating, especially in the early weeks. You are dealing with so many other issues that adding gas to an already gassy baby (all newborns pass a lot of gas) does not make sense. What foods may cause problems? The biggest culprits often are the same foods that may cause gas in mom: spicy foods, onions, garlic, tomato, cauliflower, cabbage, broccoli, chocolate, and drinks and foods containing caffeine. Not only are these things problematic in their raw state, they also cause trouble when used in recipes such as pizza, chocolate milk, and cole slaw. Wine and beer in moderation are okay in my book, but check with your pediatrician before partaking.

Some foods are absorbed into your blood and make their way into your milk supply quite quickly. Alcohol and chocolate can affect your baby within one hour of consumption. The other foods that I mentioned affect your breast milk about four to six hours after they are eaten.

If your new situation is causing you some stress, you may feel it first in your stomach. New moms often do not have an appetite during the first few days at home. If you are not eating well, let me assure you that as long as you are taking your vitamins and drinking fluids, a temporary change in appetite does not affect your milk at all.

Expressing Breast Milk

Expressing milk is useful to relieve engorgement, as a method of collecting milk for a supplement bottle, and to maintain your milk supply if you cannot nurse your infant because of illness or separation. You can express milk manually or by using a breast pump.

To start, make sure your hands are clean and that you have a sterile container into which you can pump your milk. Sit comfortably in a quiet room where you can relax and think pleasant thoughts about your baby. Try to have someone on hand to respond to your baby's needs and to answer the telephone so you are not interrupted.

Begin by placing warm towels on your breast (one at a

time) for about five minutes. The warmth helps promote the letdown of the milk. When using a breast pump, follow the manufacturer's instructions. Make sure that your nipple is in the center of the suction and all parts are sterile.

I have found from talking to nursing moms that the best time of day to express milk is in the morning or midday when the supply has yet to be depleted by a day's nursing. By 3:00 or 4:00 P.M., most moms have less milk, and any milk that they express is not available to the baby later in the day. Some moms find that they are most successful expressing milk immediately after a morning feeding when the letdown reflex is still working.

Storing Breast Milk

Breast milk is a breeding ground for bacteria if it is not stored in sterile containers and refrigerated immediately. Use a separate storage container each time you express your milk. Warm milk should not be added to that which is already refrigerated. If you refrigerate the milk in separate containers, you can combine several small, cold amounts into one bottle for feeding. Write the date and time you expressed the milk on the storage container. Breast milk can be stored in the refrigerator for thirty-six hours.

You can freeze your breast milk if you do so in a sterile container as soon as it is expressed. It will stay good for up to six months in a deep freezer (0°F) or about three weeks in a standard refrigerator freezer. To thaw frozen breast milk, let the container stand in a bowl of tap water until it reaches room temperature. Never heat milk or formula in a microwave. It may heat unevenly, and hot spots could scald your baby. For additional details about how to store expressed milk safely, check with your pediatrician, La Leche League, or local lactation specialist, who are most familiar with current thinking on the topic.

Feeding from a Bottle: A Man's Job?

Once mom's milk is in and well established after two to three weeks, a supplement bottle can be introduced without affecting the milk supply. This bottle is best given by dad. I have several reasons for reaching this conclusion.

Very often when a bottle is introduced to a nursing baby by the mother, the infant balks at it. Babies can smell their mother's milk and may wonder why she is giving a bottle when she is so close and can feed with milk. Ideally, dad should give the bottle with mom not even in the room. If it has been at least three hours since your baby has eaten, he or she should be hungry enough to latch onto a rubber nipple. The evening is a good time for dad to give a supplement bottle because breast milk tends to be not as plentiful at this time. A supplement bottle allows the milk supply to build up again for the 9:00 or 10:00 P.M. feeding.

Even if you are bottle-feeding exclusively, I have found it is helpful for dads to take over the early evening feeding. Babies need extra care and attention during this sometimes fussy period of the day, and dads offer a nice change of pace. On a regular basis, dads call me saying, "I'm not sure if my wife is normal. I walk in the door at night, and she practically shoves the baby in my arms." Yes! This is normal. By the end of the day, mom has had it. Dads literally can save the day!

The early evening before you settle down to dinner can be a special time for mom, too, during which she can take a bath or return phone calls or read the newspaper. It is important that she leaves dad alone with the baby. Hovering over him and making sure he is "doing it right" is counterproductive for everyone. There are many ways of doing things. You cannot expect dad to hold the baby or bottle like you do. It does not matter. The end result is that the baby is fed, dad and baby spend time together, mom gets a break, and everybody is happy.

On the other hand, mom has to remember that although she may be feeling stir-crazy, dad is not playing golf all day either. He may be tired, too. In my house it worked out best if my husband could sit down for fifteen or twenty minutes with a drink or a cup of coffee and look at the sports page when he came home from work. After a short break, he was refreshed and asked, "What can I do to help you with the kids?" Just the idea of "dad taking over" was music to my ears. It made the end of the day a happy time I looked forward to.

Finally, I must add that I do not believe in what some lactation experts call "nipple confusion." Babies who are hungry will suck on anything. As long as your baby is introduced to a nipple before a few months of age, he or she should do just fine. If you nurse exclusively for longer than three months, you may have more difficulty with the transition to a bottle, which is best introduced at two to three weeks.

Preparing Infant Formula

When my children were young, we used to mix our own baby formula from evaporated milk, water, and Karo syrup. In addition to mixing the ingredients as precisely as a chemist, I remember how careful I was to keep everything sterile. In fact, my kitchen probably was as sterile as an operating room! God forbid if I sneezed at the moment I was making bottles. I had to start all over again!

Today, infant formula is premixed and comes in three different forms. The first is ready-to-feed, which is packaged in thirty-two-ounce cans. Its advantage is that it is easy to prepare. However, the cans are heavy to carry home from the grocery and take up a lot of space in your pantry. Ready-to-feed also cost more than the alternatives.

Another option is formula concentrate that is mixed with equal parts water. The concentrate also comes in cans, and one can makes about twenty-six ounces. While requiring a little more pouring than the ready-to-feed, concentrate still is an easy, quick choice. The cans are about half the size of the ready-to-feed cans and may cost slightly less per ounce.

If you do not object to mixing formula, you may want to try the third option: powder. Powder comes in small cans that make up to one hundred and two ounces (or approximately twelve eight-ounce bottles). The powder is not difficult to dilute according to the manufacturer's instructions except when your baby is drinking eight ounces (a full bottle) at one sitting. If you choose to prepare the formula directly in the bottle, you cannot fit eight ounces of water plus the powder. You must mix the formula in a larger, sterile container and then pour it into the bottle. Powder is the best alternative for traveling because, until it is mixed, it does not need refrigeration.

When using powder or concentrate, you need a fresh water source. Check with your pediatrician for his or her advice on using your local tap water or bottled water. You also must make sure that all items that come into contact with the formula are clean. For example, it is important to wash the top of the formula can with soap and hot water. The can opener and the scoop used for the powder also must be washed before use. Find out what your pediatrician thinks about sterilization before getting started. He or she will be helpful in suggesting proper methods for preparing bottles.

When you buy formula, be sure to check the expiration date on the can. Once formula is opened or mixed, refrigerate it immediately in a clean container or in clean, covered bottles. Refrigerated formula is good for forty-eight hours; powder should be used within three weeks.

While all the attention to germs may seem overwhelming at first, once you go through the procedure several times, you will not think twice about what to do. It may be helpful to set aside a portion of your kitchen counter space as your "clean area" and to always prepare your baby's bottles there. That way, you have everything you need on hand (as you do by the changing table), and you do not have to worry that the preparation area is contaminated with other food.

Refrigerate bottles immediately after preparation and until use within forty-eight hours. Babies may be given cold formula, or you can heat the bottle under a warm tap or in a pot of water on the stove. Once taken from the refrigerator, formula generally is safe to use until it reaches room temperature or shortly thereafter.

Until your baby establishes a regular schedule and is consuming the same amount of formula at each feeding, you may be tempted to save some of the formula that is left over in the bottle. This formula is no longer sterile, and bacteria from the baby's mouth can quickly grow on the bottle and in the milk. Would you drink a half-empty glass of milk that had warmed to room temperature and had been sitting around for an hour or more? The milk in either case may have begun to sour. Even though it may be wasteful, throw away leftover formula. It is not worth the risk of giving your baby a stomach illness.

DOES MY BABY NEED WATER?
Most pediatricians tell parents that once a mother's milk is in, her baby does not need to drink water. Basically, I agree, but I have observed a trend over the years that makes me wonder whether water has more merit than we think.

I have found when I talk to mothers who have very few problems with their babies, a great many tell me that they give their babies water after each nursing. These women started doing this because their mothers had helped them in the early weeks, and the mothers had told them to try the water when the baby was through at the breast and still seemed fussy. Only a half ounce to an ounce of water seems to prevent the baby from depending on a pacifier for extra sucking, and it seems to help the baby settle down, too.

A bottle of warm water after a feeding also sometimes helps soothe babies with colic. (See chapter 7 for a full discussion of colic.) After taking water from a bottle, a baby usually will give a larger burp than normal. Perhaps the burp brings up air that might otherwise have caused stomach upset. Besides, water has no calories and no sugar (do not add any), so it really cannot hurt.

The one time that I always suggest giving babies water is in warm weather. One of the phone calls that I get all summer long is, "My baby is so fussy. We were outside all day, so I thought he would be tired, but he won't go to sleep." The truth be told, the baby is really parched; generally, parents do not think about that possibility. Because they are small, young babies also become dehydrated easily. Signs of dehydration include cracked and parched lips, an acetone smell on the breath, sunken fontanel, concentrated urine, and too few wet diapers. If you think your baby is dehydrated, call your pediatrician immediately.

Pacifiers and Thumbs: How Babies Relax

Some pediatricians do not permit babies in their care to have any synthetic nipples—on pacifier or bottle—insisting that the babies be fed only from the breast or an eyedropper. I do not agree. At the hospital in which I work, we give infants pacifiers from day one. Newborns need to suck more than they have a chance to, either on the bottle or the breast. Those who are allowed a pacifier seem to improve their sucking skills.

Sucking instinctively helps babies relax, too. In my day, of course, we did not know this, and pacifiers were considered unsanitary and detrimental to proper jaw development. Today, however, we know that these concerns are unwarranted. Most babies love to suck, and if denied a pacifier, they find something else to put in their mouths.

Of course, there are two sides to every story. Some babies become so attached to their pacifiers that every time the plug falls out they scream. I knew a mother whose three-month-old lost his pacifier every ten minutes all night long and screamed until mom retrieved it. My suggestion in this case: go cold turkey. The baby had two terrible nights, I admit, but after that, he—and mom—slept a lot better. If you choose to use a pacifier, please do not attach it to your baby or to the crib with a long cord in which the baby could become entangled.

As for thumb sucking, some parents say that the day that their babies discovered their thumbs was a great one in the family's short history. The thumb never falls on the floor, it is always close by for comfort, it never goes in another kid's mouth (not usually), and it is easy to wash. The downside: you cannot take it away, and you do not want your six-year-old sitting in school with that thumb still in his or her mouth. If you are concerned about long-term dental problems, raise the issue with your pediatrician or dentist.

Bowel Movements: A Favorite Topic of New Parents

Bowel movements change during the first three or four days after birth while the meconium in your baby's intestines is evacuated, going from a tarlike, black substance to a waste product that looks like green cottage cheese (lovely thought, isn't it?). Breast-fed babies have frequent very loose bowel movements that sometimes look like yellow cottage cheese. These bowel movements come quite frequently and with force, as often as six to eight times per day. On many occasions, a breast-fed baby who has several regular bowel movements per day for weeks does not have any for three to five days. Of course, parents panic when this happens, but they need not. Irregularity is perfectly normal in infants. Most doctors do not worry as long as the baby is not disturbed by it. However, when your baby finally does have a BM, be prepared for the biggest mess you ever saw in your life. If the "silence" lasts more than five days, check with your pediatrician.

Bottle-fed babies generally have well-formed, pasty stools

two to three times a day. They vary in color from tan to greenish to yellow even though the diet remains the same. It does not matter what color the bowel movement is, although I must admit that color is of major concern to new parents. I get many calls from moms saying, "My baby's stool is green. I hear green is bad." Green is not bad unless the stool is watery, comes many times per day, and is accompanied by cramping. Neither black nor yellow are necessarily "bad" either. What is of concern? Hard, pelletlike stools and signs of blood should be reported to the pediatrician.

Babies often make big productions out of bowel movements, pushing and straining, holding their breath and turning red. Do not mistake this production for real constipation. It is a normal and typical thing to see in infants until they learn to relax their anal muscles without using the rest of their bodies.

Diapers: The More the Merrier?

Needless to say, you are going to be changing diapers constantly when your baby comes home. At first, diaper changing feels like juggling as you try to get your baby clean and get the new diaper on without the baby's getting hysterical. Most newborns hate being naked and/or cold, so until you become more adept, you might have a struggle on your hands. (Battle scars often include bowel movement everywhere—and urine on the ceiling if your little boy's fountain spouts. Be sure to wash your hands afterward.)

Despite the fuss, your baby needs to have the diaper changed frequently, especially in the first month or so when baby's skin is so delicate. Remember that the baby's tiny bottom was not diapered in the last place he or she called home, and now baby has to get used to the irritation of fabric and urine being rubbed on his or her bottom twenty-four hours a day. If your baby has a red bottom, try removing the diaper and laying the baby on his or her tummy (on a waterproof sheet, of course) near a sunny window. This is a home remedy for diaper rash, and it feels good for baby to be warm and naked, too. After a few weeks, your baby's bottom toughens up a bit after all that has gone on inside the diaper. If your baby's skin is sensitive in the meantime or if a rash begins, airing out should help. While the diaper is on, keep the sensitive area covered with A&D ointment or petroleum jelly.

You do not need to change diapers while the baby is asleep, even if the baby has been wearing the same diaper for several hours. You may watch baby starting to stir in the bassinet, think the diaper must be wet, and wake baby. Give yourself a break. Once your baby is awake, you have plenty of time to change diapers. Wet diapers are ten times more disturbing to parents than babies.

. . . And You Thought Only Teenagers Got Acne

One constant about new parents is that they love to inspect every inch of their newborns. Consequently, they often find themselves calling the pediatrician to ask about this rash or that bump that just appeared on their flawless babes. If you examined yourselves with such meticulous detail, you would find a lot to concern you, too.

To make you feel better, you should know that most newborns have many harmless skin irritations. First, a newborn's skin usually is quite dry after birth. For this reason, it often peels, particularly on the hands and feet. Peeling is more likely on babies that are born after their due date because their skin is drier. Peely skin is not problematic from a health standpoint, and there really is not much you can do about it. In most cases, a mild lotion is not harmful, but all it does is stick down the dead skin cells so they are less noticeable.

Another skin condition that you may notice on your baby is what is called a milk blister in the middle of the upper lip. Formed from sucking, this blister does not break or pop; it is just loose skin that heals without treatment.

Lots of babies suffer from poor complexions as a result of active glands. By the time they are three weeks old and for about three months, they may get a condition known as newborn acne. It is very common, and predictably, many new mothers who come to my postpartum classes bring their infants with blankets over their heads. When the blankets come off, all the moms are thrilled to see so many rashes and pimples that you might think they were at a high school prom. The only way that I have found to clear up newborn acne—and this solution is only temporary—is to wash your baby's face two times a day with a mild soap that is mixed with cold cream. Sometimes a thin layer of medicated powder rubbed on the affected area helps. Your pediatrician may have some other solutions if the rash fails to clear up. Many babies have a skin rash that looks like flea bites. Quite upsetting to parents with pets in the home, this rash, called erythema toxicum, is not caused by fleas. It does not need treatment and goes away on its own.

Naptime (or, Thank Heaven, the Baby's Asleep)

Sleeping is second only to feeding as new parents' biggest concern. The truth is that your baby sleeps when it is tired. He or she may sleep better in the day than in the night, or vice versa. He or she may change his or her sleeping pattern daily. He or she may fall asleep while being fed. Or the baby may stay awake between feedings so that you are without a moment's peace.

In the beginning, nothing you do, short of banging cymbals in your baby's ear, disturbs its desire to sleep according to its own, incomprehensible timetable. Some people feel that they have to tiptoe around with a newborn in the house. In fact, the opposite is true. If you think about the chaos in the hospital nursery, you realize that a dim and quiet room is not what your baby is used to. Babies sleep in the nursery with other infants screaming all around them day and night, nurses pushing their bassinets from one corner of the room to the other, frequent conversation, and phones ringing. Loud sounds might startle them but not wake them. It makes sense for babies to get used to household noises so that they can nap while you are doing your thing. (Yes, one day you *will* get back to doing your thing!)

As to where your baby sleeps, it is safest in its bassinet or crib, rather than on your bed or a couch. It may not be able to roll off yet, but it will be mobile before you know it, and it is better not to begin bad habits. If your baby is sleeping in a bassinet, I suggest introducing it to its crib by the time it is three or four weeks old. Place him or her in the crib for nap-time. Once he or she feels comfortable sleeping in the larger area during the day, it will be easy for him or her to make the adjustment to a crib full-time.

You Mean We Are Supposed to Play with Our Baby, Too?

Sometimes it seems as if all you ever do is take care of your baby. Who has time to think about playing with him? Until babies are two to three months old, they really cannot appreciate your efforts to play with them. They do, however, love to be held and talked to. Tactile and verbal communication are the beginnings of play.

In the hospital, I always talk to the new babies. Actually I make quite a fool of myself, but that's my job! Just about any morning, you can find me in the nursery or in a postpartum room talking in a high, squeaky voice. "You're sucha cutey bay-bee," I say as I hold these tiny bundles in my arms. "I will wuv you for ever and ever." I talk to the babies because I love them, of course. I also think that watching me makes new parents feel more comfortable doing the same. Talking to your baby can be as therapeutic for you as it is a wonderful, loving experience for the baby. Babies never talk back, and they listen when you are complaining. No matter what you say, they love you unconditionally.

All of us love to sing, but most of us are embarrassed to do so outside of the shower. Well, your baby is the perfect audience before which to audition your deepest singing fantasies. Your baby loves for you to sing to him, day and night, even if you have a terrible voice.

Don't Forget to Take Care of Mom

If singing is the furthest thing from your mind right now, do not despair that you are the only parent in the world who feels this way. Moms, in particular, may have a hard time recovering from childbirth, particularly if delivery was difficult or if postpartum depression is severe. Your recovery also depends in large part upon the type of baby you have. If your baby is good and sleeps well, then your life is less stressful and topsy-turvy than most. If your baby is fussy, it is harder for the entire family to find an even keel.

New moms sometimes find that adjusting to life with a baby is a bit of a letdown. Society treats pregnant women better on the whole than it treats people at any other time in life. When you are pregnant, friends lavish attention on you. People ask how you are feeling. Strangers smile at you, open doors, carry packages, query about the baby. You are the star, and you feel important. While you remain in the hospital, the staff there looks out for you and cares for you. Friends call and ask about your labor and delivery. Relatives send flowers and gifts. Then you find yourself at home, isolated, overwhelmed, and tired. People still are calling and writing, but the attention is no longer focused upon you. Everyone only asks about the baby. People who come to visit dash right past you to the baby. "He's so cute. He's so wonderful, so tiny, so bald . . ." Sound familiar?

This shift in attention and concern can be a big letdown. Of course, I know—and the other mothers out there know—that you are working fifteen times harder now than before! Remind yourself of that. Praise yourself. Look to your partner for reassurance. Hang in there. Before you know it, you will be meeting other new moms who share your feelings, and you will not be alone for long. (See chapter 8 on parents' support groups.)

Singing the Blues

Even while you are in the hospital and "high" from having your baby, the roller coaster of your emotions starts chugging down the track. By your third or fourth day postpartum, it begins to pick up speed, and you may be carried off on a wild ride of unexplained crying and mood swings. Called "baby blues," this emotional roller coaster is something many women ride for a few days or a few weeks until their bodies adjust to the sudden and drastic plunge in hormonal activity following childbirth.

Fatigue adds to these up-and-down feelings. When you are tired, everything grows out of proportion. If your baby does not sleep well, your symptoms may be more severe than those of a new mom who has an easier baby. You may cry easily. You may not know why you are crying. You may snap at people for the most harmless trifles. In fact, it does not surprise me that the topic of concern to many of my "warm line" callers is postpartum emotions. Even though I have told the women in my classes many times about the baby blues, nobody really believes me. "It is not going to happen to me," everybody thinks. You are not crazy if you suffer from baby blues. Almost all postpartum women do to some degree.

Of course, there are varying degrees of baby blues, as there are varying theories as to the cause. Some women suffer debilitating feelings that are more serious than the typical baby blues. Termed "postpartum depression," this disorder tends to begin several weeks—rather than days—after childbirth. If not treated by a doctor, it lasts longer than baby blues, too, sometimes well into the first year of the newborn's life. Postpartum depression can be mixed with psychotic behavior such as hallucinations and fantasies about harming one's baby. If your depression is severe or persists for longer than a month, you may need professional help. Consult your obstetrician or a local women's health resource center. (See Resource List for a telephone number you can call for help.)

In the emotions department there is something else that causes many new moms to lose track of what they are doing. Because I never heard of a name for it, I call this syndrome "milk brain" because it begins when your milk comes in a few days after delivery. Rather than define milk brain, let me share some of the things that it makes new moms do: call a phone number, and then forget whom they are calling; lock the keys, and the baby, in the car; put the wash in the machine without any soap; leave a cup of tea somewhere in the house and not be able to find it. . . .

Clearly new moms have a lot on their minds, and it is easy to lose track of things. If you are not sleeping, there may be times that you fear you do not have a mind at all. Do not despair! You will feel like a competent person again soon . . . maybe when your baby goes to college.

Laundry: Getting Out from Under

When it comes to your household routine, I always tell parents to be flexible. Being flexible is the key in all aspects of baby care, and it is helpful in managing your household, too. Of all the demands that have been thrust upon you, keeping your house picture-perfect may be one that has to take a back seat until you get your life in order. Your house will wait for you to get around to cleaning it. Your baby will not wait for anything.

Of course, if you can afford it, this is a great time to hire cleaning help. Perhaps you and your partner can divide the chores between you. Not only does this result in two people sharing the load, but it may foster an understanding between you as to how work gets done and an appreciation for tasks that cannot get done. (In dividing the work, some couples fall into the trap of wanting to make everything a fifty-fifty proposition. Many men resent this suggestion if they are working outside the home all day. Try to approach the issue with flexibility and understanding on both sides.)

Sometimes it is easier said than done, but if you can share baby-care tasks between you—as well as routine vacuuming and dusting—you will be better parents for doing so. Dads deserve to share in the fun things, too. It is very easy for new moms to fall into the trap of saying "I am feeding the baby, and I am with the baby more than dad, so I know best how to care for baby." This feeling may stem from insecurity about your ability, not superior skills. Talk to your partner about how you are feeling, and share your concerns with him. Then, try to share feeding time or bath time together, and see how it goes. Gradually, both parents will feel more competent in doing and sharing.

I have to add that most dads do very well with their children. All they need is to be given the opportunity. They may need a little more time to adjust to their new role, but with support and help dads are an invaluable part of the new family.

Regardless of who is in charge of the laundry, you'll find that there is always a load waiting to be washed. Babies need to be changed often, and they go through sheets and towels faster than a cheap motel. Baby laundry also has a special flair to it because it seems always to be stained with various things going in and coming out of your little one. Some of these stains have world-class staying power. To help you fight back, the following list of cleaning tips may be useful.

Getting Rid of Stains and Spills

- Diaper creams and similar baby products: Pretreat with heavy-duty laundry detergent or spray-on pretreatment before laundering as usual.

- Breast milk: Pretreat or soak using an enzyme-based laundry soap or bleach, and launder as usual. Because of the fat in breast milk, a dry-cleaning solvent may be required for stubborn stains.
- Infant formula: Rinse fresh stains in warm water, then soak for one to two hours in nonchlorine bleach and warm water before laundering. Old stains may have to be removed with a rust remover (because of iron in the formula) or by rubbing the stain with undiluted bleach and rinsing immediately. Bleach may remove color from some fabrics.
- Food stains: Soak in a solution of warm water, detergent, and nonchlorine bleach for at least thirty minutes before washing. Wash in hottest water possible.
- Feces, urine, blood, vomit: Rinse immediately in cold water. Soak in a solution of warm water and enzyme-containing product. Wash in hottest water possible. For laundering cloth diapers at home: Always remove feces from diapers immediately. While accumulating a laundry load, soak soiled diapers in a solution of water and detergent (one half cup per gallon). For heavy stains, soak overnight in a solution of water and bleach (one half cup per gallon). Wash in hot water using detergent and bleach. Rinse in cold water.
- Adding a small amount of bleach to every laundry load brightens whites and helps clean messy clothing. Dry all baby items on low heat to lessen shrinkage.

When to Say Yes, and When to Say No

Just because you are home from the hospital does not mean that you are up to entertaining day and night. In fact, with all the demands of a new baby, you probably are less willing and/or able to play hostess than before. You may think that you want all your friends and relatives to come over to "ooh" and "aah" over your baby. As nice as it sounds, these visits can be very stressful. Even if people come for only fifteen or twenty minutes, they need to be entertained. You need to learn to sort through the offers and preserve some "alone time" for yourself and your new family.

If you are not up to handling company or phone calls, one way to protect yourself is to buy and use an answering machine. An answering machine can be a real life-saver when people are calling every minute. A cute message gives callers all the information they wanted to know, and they can share the news with family and friends.

"Hello, this is Sandy. Tom and I are busy taking care of little Lisa, who was born on Friday. We think she's a lot of fun, but we're not sure yet. Call back in a week and we'll let you know more."

"You've reached the Smiley family. George and I are trying to get five minutes sleep because we've been up for the past three nights. We'll call you back."

Very often a voice on the machine just says "It's a boy!" or "It's a girl!" with all the pertinent information. It is so much fun to make these tapes and share the news with everyone. (I must admit that some parents whose babies are less than perfect have admitted to wanting to leave a message saying "No, our baby is not cute, and we really do not like him at all yet. If you would like to borrow him for a month or so, please leave your name and phone number after the beep . . .")

Sometimes callers ask in advance if there is anything they can bring you. You might want to ask for a harem of servants, but that might sound too forward. There are some very helpful gifts, however, that someone might be willing to buy or make. Some require only a quick trip to the store or a phone call. If you feel comfortable making your needs known, you might consider the following suggested gifts that I have found invaluable with a new baby at home.

- Home-cooked meals all ready to pop into the oven.
- A reading pillow (provides great support when nursing in bed); it is helpful to have a lot of pillows in your bed for the same reason.
- A coupon for a manicure or massage.
- Prearranged baby-sitting service.
- Coupons for photo developing.
- Photo albums, photo frames, and baby memory books (can be personalized).
- House-cleaning service.

As baby gifts arrive, it is fun to keep a list of what you receive. You may want to add the list to your baby's record book, in which you can keep a diary of special moments. Another thing that I love to do whenever I receive flowers is to take a Polaroid photo of the bouquet and send it along with my thank-you note. You can do the same with your baby gifts, taking photos of your newborn wearing the little outfits people sent or lying near the beautiful bouquets of flowers that arrive daily.

When relatives visit, you may find that they are full of advice, if not criticism, for your parenting style. When you are new at it, it is very easy to fall prey to harsh words and to become overwhelmed by the fear that you are doing everything wrong. When you are young and insecure, the intimidation of someone giving advice, even if they are right and you are wrong . . . well, you are not ready to hear it. You start to feel inadequate, and your confidence plummets. I cannot tell you how many phone calls I get from new parents who find themselves in this situation and feel that they cannot resolve it.

As a grandma, I have to fall back on my experience and common sense and suggest that some things are worth fighting for, while others are best let go. When your mom or mother-in-law comes to visit, most of the things she tells you really are harmless, and probably none is worth an argument. Remember that whatever she says is well intentioned, so no matter what your reaction, it helps to be kind. She will not be staying long, and you can survive.

If you feel that you must defend your way of doing things to a critical relative or friend, the ideal way of doing so is to say, "My pediatrician said . . ." and then make up whatever you want. As long as you say "My pediatrician said . . ." you can justify whatever decision you make, and no one can question you.

It Only Seems Like the World Stopped

A very common question from new parents is "When is a good time to take baby outside?" The answer, of course, depends on where you live and the time of year. For example, I would not suggest taking baby for a walk in January in Chicago and with a windchill factor of ten below zero. You know that already. On the other hand, on a sunny Chicago day when the temperature is above normal, a short walk with a well-protected baby is a good idea.

If at all possible, getting out of the house after the first few days at home can be a wonderful mood elevator for the new mom. When you are home all day, it may seem as if the world outside has stopped. You may feel quite isolated. I received a call from a new grandma who reported that her daughter was very depressed. After I suggested that the daughter simply take a walk around the block, the grandmother called me back. "That walk changed her whole outlook," she said. "I cannot believe it. She even looks different. Her cheeks are rosy, and her eyes really lit up when she saw the baby."

When you are depressed from being at home with the baby and are not feeling well enough to exercise, the best therapy is to get out on a walk, at the mall or in a nearby park. You can take the baby or leave him or her with a sitter; either way you have an improved perspective when you return.

There is nothing more exciting than that first stroll you and your partner take with your new baby. Everyone loves a newborn, and people want to peek in your carriage, no matter where you go. It is a very cozy, warm time when you start to share your baby with the world. Sometimes, though, parents are not comfortable with everyone and his brother peering into their baby's face. Some parents fear that this public showing may infect their babies with germs, and I certainly agree that you should not let strangers get too close to your baby. Try to use your best judgment about taking your baby to public places.

Most pediatricians suggest that you keep your baby away from crowded, enclosed places such as department stores during the first month of life, when the immune system is immature. This is especially true in the winter, when cold viruses run rampant in warm, stuffy buildings. Enclosed places where there are children—such as indoor ice skating rinks or schools—are the worst offenders. If you are uncertain about taking your baby somewhere, check with your pediatrician first.

Packing Your Baby's Diaper Bag (or, Life Was Simpler When I Carried Only a Purse)

Most moms find that keeping their baby's diaper bag packed and ready to go makes getting out of the house with baby a

little easier. Depending on where you are going and how long
you will be there, you need to bring different things. Here are
the basics.

- Diapers (disposables are the easiest; if you bring cloth,
  make sure you have room to carry them home).
- Diaper wipes (many brands have convenient travel sizes).
- Ointment for diaper rash, if necessary.
- Powder (to dry wet areas if you run out of cloth).
- A changing pad.
- Moist towelettes (like those you get in a restaurant) to
  wash your hands with after a messy changing.
- Several plastic bags for dirty diapers (if a garbage can is
  not available or if you use cloth) and for used bottles and
  dropped toys and pacifiers.
- Clean pacifiers, if used.
- Plastic comb and brush (if your baby has hair).
- Enough premixed bottles for all anticipated feedings, plus
  one. If you are going on an extensive trip, you need an
  insulated bag to keep bottles cold. The other option is to
  carry bottles of clean water and powdered formula and
  mix it fresh.
- A few extra nipples and rings, in case yours are clogged
  or fall on the floor.
- A four-ounce bottle of water that can be used to feed
  baby or to wash things.
- A hat for warmth and another with a brim for sun
  shading.
- An extra pair of socks or booties.
- A sweater.
- A blanket.
- A bib.
- A few small toys or rattles.
- One or two cloth diapers for burp cloths.
- A travel-size package of tissues.
- An extra set of car keys (many new moms have locked
  both their keys and their babies in the car!).
- And last, a porter to help you carry the bag!

Doesn't Anyone Have All the Answers?

Before you left the hospital, your pediatrician probably advised you to call his office to schedule your baby's first visit. Typically, this appointment falls within three weeks, unless your baby is ill or jaundiced. Personally, I think three weeks is fine for second-timers, but parents with first babies are best bringing them to the doctor within a week to ten days of birth. This visit is as much for your reassurance as it is for your baby's health. Three weeks is a long time to wait for that critical pat on the back from a medical expert.

The first visit is an exciting time. It may be the first time since your trip home from the hospital that you are out and about. As you sit in the waiting room with your little bundle, you may reflect upon your new status as somebody's mom or dad. The other parents look at you as their equal, even though you may feel like a kid. You should have a list of questions, even if you called the office twelve times since you left the hospital. Do not worry that you are overly concerned; this is quite normal in new parents.

If your baby's first appointment comes within ten days of birth, that is adequate time for him or her to have made strides in the weight department. The first weigh-in is a major milestone for all parents. New moms often measure their mothering skills by their baby's weight gain. If I happen to talk to my new moms on the day of baby's first visit, they almost always say proudly, "Guess what, Lanie? My baby gained three and a half ounces and grew a whole inch. Can you believe it? I never thought she would be so big so fast!" It is a very reassuring time when you get that report.

If, on the other hand, your baby has lost weight, this news can be discouraging. Breast-feeding moms take it the worst because they assume it is their fault; after all, they are the ones providing the milk. If your baby has not gained weight, or if the umbilical cord is infected, or if baby has a yeast infection, this news can be devastating. Pediatricians generally are very warm and caring people, but no matter how reassuring your doctor is, sometimes you still need someone else to tell you it's okay. In many ways, that is what my job is all about. That is what a grandmother's role is generally. You just need that one more person to say, "Yes, I have heard that happens frequently. I'm sure by the time you go back for your next visit, it will all be resolved." (And it usually is.)

The Light at the End of the Tunnel

Life with a baby probably is nothing like you had imagined. I will never forget the comment one new dad made. "My day seems to have shrunk," he said. "The books all say, 'A baby eats every three hours.' My wife and I figured we would have three hours in between feedings to do all these wonderful things while I was off work—play gin rummy, have a nice quiet lunch or dinner. No way."

Perhaps not all of you are so naïve, but I am sure that like most new parents you have found parenting different than you expected. First, almost all the young parents that I meet are amazed at how much time it takes. There is very little time during the day when you can do anything but take care of the baby, if you are doing so on your own. Between changing diapers, feeding your baby, making your baby's bottles or expressing breast milk, doing load upon load of baby laundry, catching a few minutes of sleep, taking a shower . . . It is a full-time job. Anyone who thinks differently clearly has not done it.

Second, many new moms come across unexpected nursing problems. You, too, may have thought you would just breeze through the learning period. Perhaps you did not even realize that breast-feeding is a learned skill for you and your baby. Life can be very frustrating until you get it right.

Third, I am sorry to say that so many new parents find that the stresses thrust upon them by a baby cause them to stop talking honestly to one another. Many fail to support and nurture each other as perhaps they did before the baby came. Moms feel overwhelmed and find inadequate support from dads. Dads often feel left out of the relationship with baby and are angry at their partners. These feelings serve only to compound a difficult situation.

While you are in the middle of this maelstrom, it may seem as if your life is forever going to be a constant battle to survive. You may feel as if you are giving, giving, giving, and getting nothing in return, but I promise you that you will not feel this way for long. The first few weeks of adjusting to your baby are such a short time in the overall picture. Try to enjoy them. When you look back on them, you will remember the good parts and forget the bad. There are wonderful, exciting, and life-changing things happening all around you. You are witnessing a miracle every minute.

There always will be difficult aspects of parenthood, even when your children are grown up, but as you head into a more settled phase of parenthood in the upcoming months, you find that life with baby gets easier and more fun. Not only have you learned to trust your caretaking skills, but you soon are sleeping more. Your baby is becoming more responsive every day, smiling and laughing before you know it. You cannot believe that you were once awake half the night or that you once did not know how to change a diaper. Soon you will look back on these difficult times and smile!

7

The Budding Family: Your First Three Months Together

A hospital would not be a hospital without a bunch of silly jokes always making the rounds among the doctors and nurses. Being so close to the miracle of life on a daily basis makes us all awestruck sometimes. Laughing is our way of easing the tension.

One of the quips that has been around a long time, but one of my favorites nonetheless, goes like this: How can you tell the difference between a first-time mom or dad and a veteran parent?

When the baby drops his pacifier, the first-timer washes it with soap and water before gently placing it back in the baby's mouth.

The dad with two children wipes the pacifier off on the leg of his pants and hands it back to his baby.

The mom who has three little ones picks up the dirty pacifier and tosses it within her baby's reach.

The parent with four kids just hopes that one of the older ones will find the pacifier before the dog eats it.

Jokes are, of course, exaggerations of the truth, but the lesson of this little tale is not. New parents would be so much more relaxed if they could start out with their second child. You can get a bit crazy with the fussing and fretting that you do over your first one as you learn your way around parenthood. By the second child, you can laugh at your mistakes. You know that most little slip-ups are inconsequential. You know that your baby will be fine even if a diaper is on backward or he or she is not bathed every day.

This more relaxed feeling starts to surface in most parents when their first baby is three months old. By this time, you have lived through many days and nights of decision making and of carrying out your decisions to the nth degree. You are starting to sense that your instincts about your baby are good ones. You are learning to trust your judgment. Your self-consciousness is replaced with self-confidence.

Making this leap of faith in your feelings and abilities is a sign of your growth as a parent. It also is a prerequisite to learning to enjoy your baby. When you worry less, you have more energy to expend on having fun. When you reach the seventh step on the parenting stairway (and you all will sooner or later), you will find that having a baby is as uplifting as falling in love.

The first three months with your baby are a time of great ups and downs not unlike the first three months of pregnancy (can you even remember back that far?). As the days and weeks go by, you may find that you have very mixed feelings about the changes taking place in your life.

Remember when you were trying to get pregnant and nothing thrilled you more than hearing your obstetrician confirm the good news? You could barely contain your excitement. Bringing your baby home from the hospital probably made you feel much the same way. It was a very special day.

As your pregnancy progressed, you might have suffered from morning sickness. You might have been tired from dawn to dusk or felt just plain old rotten for several weeks in a row.

Some days you might have wondered whether having a baby would be worth all your suffering. It's déjà vu all over again! There are plenty of days in the first three months at home with a new baby when you may not feel sick, but you sure feel tired. You may be granted sainthood if you never long for the way things used to be.

I make the comparison between pregnancy and the postpartum period because hopefully it leads you to an obvious conclusion: that the physical and emotional intensity of the first few months with a newborn—like that of the first trimester of pregnancy—exists for a finite (and short) period of time. While you were nauseous, you were afraid it would never end. Likewise, while you are awake all night listening to your baby cry, you worry that it will last forever. Soon you find, of course, that the craziness stops. Your difficulties become fewer, and times that are fun and exciting become more frequent.

I see the difference that a few weeks makes in the new moms and dads in my "Adjusting to Parenthood" class. In almost all cases, the first time I see them, two to three weeks after their babies are born, they are smack in the middle of the cyclone that follows going home from the hospital. When I see them again two weeks later, close to 80 percent are sleeping five to seven hours at night, and they are starting to feel like themselves again.

In this chapter, I answer many of the questions that new parents ask in my "Adjusting to Parenthood" class. I also recognize that the first three months with your baby continues to be a time of great change, and change can be unsettling. As I tell my "students," enjoy your baby as much as you can anyway. Try not to feel overwhelmed every minute. This time truly slips away too fast.

Finding a Common Ground

One of the most frequent questions that new parents ask me in the fourth to sixth week postpartum is how to get their baby on a schedule. Of course, all babies are not on the same schedule for feeding or sleeping. Some babies eat often and catnap between feedings. Some are less interested in their stomachs and are satisfied playing or napping for long stretches of time.

Others are erratic and vary their schedules to some degree every day. There are as many variations on schedules as there are babies.

As a generalization, most babies can be urged to eat at three- or four-hour intervals during the day. When babies eat this often during the twelve to fourteen hours that they are awake, they usually do not need to be fed more than once during the night. Although most babies fall into this pattern on their own, some parents have to encourage their infants to wait a decent interval between feedings.

Some breast-feeding babies suck for five minutes or less and then fall asleep, only to awaken in an hour and want to eat again. Called "snacking," this routine gets old after a while, and it is really hard on mom. (First your baby was a permanent fixture in your belly; now, he or she seems forever attached to your breast.)

There are two reasons for snacking. The first is a natural product of your baby's growth spurts, during which baby nurses more often for a few days about every three weeks or so. This additional nursing causes your milk supply to increase to meet the baby's needs. If you think your baby is nursing more often than every three hours for this reason, then there is no reason to stop. The behavior should let up in a day or two and baby will return to the old schedule.

The second reason for snacking is just plain old bad habit, and moms are well within their rights to try to wean their babies from this routine. Increasing the time between feeding has to be done gradually, perhaps by only ten to fifteen minutes per day. You can do this by using various tactics to postpone eating such as distracting your baby with a toy or going for a walk or giving water.

If you can distract your baby for a short time, I urge you to do so. Eventually, you can increase your baby's ability to wait between meals, provided he or she is physically ready to do so. If, on the other hand, delaying tactics do not work, there is no need to torture yourself. If your baby is crying and you believe that baby is hungry and you want to feed before the clock says it is time, go ahead. Perhaps the baby is not ready to go so long between meals. Perhaps he or she will make up the time on the next feeding, or will stay on track better another day. Remember that for some babies, it takes time and patience to establish a schedule. The most important rule is to be flexible. Try to follow your baby's lead. Look for patterns in behavior and build the schedule around them.

Like feeding, sleeping becomes more regular about the second or third month, when your baby begins to respect established nap and bed times. Babies' sleeping schedules develop gradually during the first few months of life. At about four to six weeks, they generally sleep four to six hours at night. During the day, some babies catnap on and off. Others may take two long naps, one in the morning and one in the afternoon.

Each series of two or three weeks generally adds another hour or two of nighttime sleep for the average baby and the parents. What you do or do not do has little effect on your baby's evolving sleeping pattern, which is regulated more by increasing stomach capacity than anything else. The more milk or formula that the baby can hold in its little belly, the longer the baby is able to sleep at night. It is really very simple. Larger babies tend to eat more and sleep for longer periods of time. Smaller babies, on the other hand, may wake to nurse as often as every hour and a half. Expect your infant to sleep nine to ten hours at night at three to four months old or when weight reaches at least thirteen to fifteen pounds.

Because your baby's ability to sleep is directly affected by when and how much he or she eats, you may find it helpful, if your baby falls asleep at 7:00 or 8:00 at night, to wake the baby for a feeding just before you go to bed around 10:00 or 11:00 P.M. By the time your baby is a month old, the 10:00 P.M. feeding probably can sustain him until 6:00 or 7:00 A.M. Dads frequently report to me that they have taken responsibility for the 10:00 P.M. feeding, using a bottle of formula or expressed breast milk. This routine seems to work quite well. Once your baby is three months old, the late-night feeding likely can be omitted.

Your baby may have been sleeping on his or her side until now, if your pediatrician suggested that you put the baby to bed this way. Once the umbilical cord stump falls off, however, your baby may be put to bed on the tummy, and you may find that baby prefers this. Some parents are afraid that their babies may not get enough air when their faces are down on the mattress. Babies, like adults, have very keen survival instincts; they turn their heads from side to side so that they can breathe easily.

Just be sure baby is on a firm mattress and not a pillow or beanbag. If your baby seems to prefer lying on its back, it is no longer worrisome for an infant to fall asleep that way, either. Babies who are more than a month old have the natural ability to cough up any mucus or spitup that may drip into their throat during the night.

There may be times, of course, when your baby is particularly fussy and you may want to rock the baby to sleep or hold the baby in your arms until he or she nods off. Babies love to fall asleep this way. Very often gently patting or rubbing your baby's back while baby is lying in the crib will help. However, I caution you not to rock your baby to sleep at each bedtime. Putting baby to bed while awake encourages him or her to learn to fall asleep alone.

Babies can learn to comfort themselves even if they are tired. Some babies turn to thumb sucking or the use of a pacifier. Others pull on their ears or have a "blankie" that they rub against their faces (many older babies have security objects). When settling down, most babies wriggle around, bend and stiffen their legs repeatedly, and turn their heads from side to side until they find a comfortable position. Sometimes this routine is accompanied by noises similar to those that precede crying spells. Some babies do cry, but this fussing is not necessarily a signal to run in and pick up your infant. Generally the noise and squirming ends within seven minutes when your baby falls asleep. Parents who allow their babies to learn these self-comforting techniques find that their children are better sleepers when they get older.

"Happy Hour" Redefined

I would bet that from about 4:00 P.M. until bedtime is your baby's most fussy time of the day. This is an almost universal truism that I hear from the parents in my classes. Honestly, that the hours around dinnertime are the most difficult does not surprise me. Like many of us who need a coffee break at this time, many babies run out of steam in the late afternoon. They are tired, but cannot seem to nap. They are cranky and out of sorts. They give new meaning to the time of day you once called "Happy Hour."

When your baby's blues start, it is a good time to try a

swing. For some reason, many babies find the rocking motion comforting, and they settle down or even fall asleep while swinging. Some babies calm down after a warm tub bath. Bathtime is soothing because mommy (or whoever is giving the bath) has her total attention on the baby. The warm water feels good, as does the gentle washing. Afterward, babies feel cozy in their nightclothes, and can be given a feeding and a few minutes in the rocking chair before going to bed.

If you are not ready to end your day when your baby is fussing, you might try carrying baby with you in the front pack. This way, baby can feel warm and secure, and your movements may be additional comfort. One word of caution: please do not carry your baby in your arms or in a front pack while you fix dinner. There are too many hazards in the kitchen, such as sharp knives and the hot stove. It is much safer to put your baby in a swing or infant seat on an empty countertop than to risk hurting him or her with the slip of a hand.

If nothing seems to work at home, you may be able to break your baby's fussy pattern by going out, particularly in the car. Usually babies fall asleep or at least are quieted by the motion and sounds of the engine. Car rides seem to work even better than walks in the stroller.

If your baby seems particularly fussy, to the point at which he or she is inconsolable for all or part of the day, you soon will realize that there are differing degrees of unsettled behavior. Your baby may go beyond mere fussiness, and may suffer from a condition known as colic. As with all aspects of baby care, I recommend flexibility in your response to your baby. Try to realize that the baby's problem times are neither purposeful nor necessarily a reflection of your parenting skills. If you believe this, then you may be less concerned while trying to figure out what is wrong. All of the techniques for soothing colicky babies may be tried with fussy babies, as well.

Colic: Every Parent's Nightmare

Typically, a baby shows signs of colic around the third week of life. Why it does not appear in the first two weeks, we do not know. (Personally, I think it is because grandma never puts baby down during this time, but perhaps I am biased.) The first sign is irritability, generally around the dinner hour. This is a fussy time for most babies, but colicky babies may continue this irritability and crying throughout the night and into the next day.

There are two types of colic: the baby that is colicky consistently all day long, and the baby that is colicky consistently for part of the day. It is as important to distinguish between these types as it is to make certain that you are not mistaking fussiness for colic. The reason for the distinction is more for your sake than for your baby's. Most parents can handle four hours of evening colic but those whose children suffer all day long really need help.

Colic (sharp intestinal pain)

- Baby screams, rather than cries.
- Draws legs up to belly, arches back.
- Turns red in the face.
- Passes gas.
- Inconsolable.
- Wakes after short nap and screams immediately.
- Even when baby stops screaming, shakes and sobs continue until screaming begins again.
- Colic occurs a good part of the day and evening.

Fussiness

- Baby has trouble settling down at times, but eventually falls asleep, usually within the hour.
- Occasional bouts of screaming or crying, but not at any particular time of day or night.
- Does not draw legs to belly, even during hard crying.
- You can calm your baby to some degree.
- Fussiness does not follow a pattern related to eating.

The general consensus among pediatricians is that colic is caused by an immature digestive system, in which the baby's milk or formula causes pain as it is digested. Why some babies have colic and others do not, we do not know. It is not because the colicky baby is smaller or premature; this has not proven to be the case. Big and postterm babies can be colicky, too.

I have found that colic seems to occur most often in firstborn babies. For this reason, colic may be related to some degree to the circle of concern that parents have with their first babies. Perhaps babies pick this up, and they become fussy. So if we do not know the cause, and we do not have a cure, what can you do about colic?

The first thing to consider in dealing with colic is mom's diet if she is breast-feeding. Very often pediatricians recommend taking mom off certain foods. Some physicians suggest eliminating all milk products from mom's diet for up to a week trial period. In some cases, colicky babies have an intolerance to dairy foods in the mom's diet. Sometimes other foods are forbidden in the hope of finding the culprit.

Truly colicky babies do not do well in noisy places or being handled by a lot of people. They seem least disturbed by quiet and scheduled life-styles. This is important for parents to understand because often when a baby is fussy, parents think, "If we just get out, perhaps go for a ride in the car, the baby will settle down." That is usually not the case when the baby has colic. (Some colicky babies like the car, however.)

A technique that I tried on my grandson—and it worked— was to give him some very mild chamomile tea immediately after a feeding. Maybe a half ounce to an ounce with a pinch of sugar was all that he needed. (We also had poi imported from Hawaii because we heard that helps the digestion. He seemed to like the taste, but it did not make his colic go away.)

Some moms say that putting their babies on top of the clothes dryer while it is on seems to work. The combination of the heat and the motion seems to be very soothing (like the car ride). Of course, you have to stand there and hold your baby or he or she may jiggle right off! If that seems like a silly way to spend your evening, one dad told me that when his baby was colicky, he held him and gently bounced up and down while standing on the bed.

Some colicky babies respond to white noise, such as radio static, a hair dryer, a ticking clock, a fan, or a vacuum cleaner. Others show improvement when sleeping on sheepskin or lying on their tummies on blankets that have been warmed by a hot water bottle or a heating pad (never lay baby directly on a hot water bottle or a heating pad, which can cause burns). Keeping the colicky baby tightly wrapped in a blanket sometimes helps.

There are medical remedies for colic that you may want to discuss with your pediatrician as well.

Along the way one or two of these home remedies may work, so we continue to suggest them, but generally the colicky baby needs to outgrow the condition. There is not much anyone can do to help.

What about your suffering through this reign of terror? Parents of colicky babies are at much higher risk for child abuse than other new parents. They might be the most wonderful people in the world, but all of us have a limit, and without a very good support system, anyone can be pushed to the edge. As difficult as this suggestion may sound, you must get away from your colicky baby as often as possible. Parents feel terrible about leaving the baby to torture someone else, but a stranger does not have the same concerns as parents, and the baby may even respond better to a sitter.

Above all, try not to feel guilty and blame yourselves. For moms, in particular, let me reassure you that there are an equal number of colicky babies on the breast as on the bottle. Neither feeding method seems to make a baby more prone to colic.

There is, in the end, a bit of good news about colic, which may seem hard to believe after reading the last few pages. First, some pediatricians feel that colicky babies have higher IQs. Remember that fact as you are pacing the floor night after night with your screaming infant. You can console yourself knowing that you may be nurturing a little Einstein or Madame Curie. Second, I believe that colicky babies turn into the most delightful three-month-olds who seem to do especially well developmentally. Perhaps this is a result of all the love and attention they require—at your expense—during the first three months. Third, one phenomenon that I have found in working with families of fraternal twins is that only one baby seems to be the fussy one and one the quiet one. Clearly colic has little or nothing to do with one's parenting skills.

It Is Going to Hurt You More Than It Hurts Them

When you were young, did your parents ever tell you "This is going to hurt me a lot more than it will hurt you"? When your baby gets the first immunizations, you will know exactly what that old saying means.

Parents always cringe when the nurse sticks their infant in the thigh and the baby lets out a long wail, followed by unfettered sobs. With a little comforting, babies calm down quickly, however. Only the parents feel bad for hours.

Immunization Schedule

Diphtheria/Pertussis (whooping cough)/Tetanus (DPT): 2, 4, 6 mos., 1½ yrs., 4–6 yrs.

Polio: 2, 4, 6 mos., 1½ yrs., 4–6 yrs.

Hemophilus influenza type b: 2, 4, 6, 15 mos.

Measles (rubeola)/Mumps/Rubella (MMR): 15 mos., 5 yrs.

(If there is an epidemic, vaccines may be given earlier. With rapid medical advances, immunization schedule may change. Consult your pediatrician.)

You may be concerned about the side effects of immunizations. In rare instances, a baby may have a negative reaction to a particular shot and may develop a severe reaction to it. Most babies suffer only mild reactions, such as fussiness, sleepiness, or a low-grade fever. It is wise to ask your doctor about all of the risks; however, you can rest assured that the benefits far outweigh the risks in almost all cases.

As you grow to love your baby more and more each day, you find that you want to protect this child from even the slightest harm. The most inconsequential fall or the mildest illness causes your protective feelings to surface. For example, when your baby gets that first cold, and you hear the snorting and wheezing, you wish you could breathe for baby. The first little bump on the head is a major catastrophe for all parents. Babies are pretty good about bouncing back, though, and luckily a kiss makes it better most of the time.

The hard part is accepting that there are some things from which you cannot protect your child, no matter how hard you try. Frequently, parents ask me about Sudden Infant Death Syndrome (SIDS), which has received so much media attention. Commonly accepted statistics indicate that one in every five hundred babies will be a victim of SIDS, an unexplained condition that causes apparently healthy babies to stop breathing and die in their sleep.

Unfortunately, SIDS is one of life's tragedies that we cannot ward off, but parents do not have to stand around helpless in the face of many other things that cause babies harm. For example, using a car seat religiously can save your baby's life in case of an accident. Never leaving your baby unattended except in a safe, enclosed area can insure that he or she does not fall.

Preventative measures can help avoid tragedy. Just as a preventative approach during pregnancy helps avoid having an unhealthy newborn, so pediatric emergency-care experts suggest—and I concur—that the best way to reduce childhood injuries and deaths is to reduce hazards in children's environments and promote safe practices in everyday living.

You may think that your baby is too young to swallow a penny or get into a cupboard. That may be true at this minute, but baby will be mobile soon enough. Now is the time to begin adopting smart habits so that you always stay ahead of your baby's motor development in safeguarding him or her. The following information is adapted from literature available from the American Heart Association and the American Academy of Pediatrics:

- Always use a properly fitted car seat for your child.
- Place an easy-to-spot emergency sticker on your telephone with numbers for the local police, fire department, rescue squad, hospital, poison control center, and your child's pediatrician.
- Prevent falls by never leaving your baby unattended. Once babies can roll over, they can easily propel themselves to the edge of even the largest bed.
- Help prevent burns by cooking with the pot handles turned in toward the stove. This precaution may seem silly with only an infant in the house, but it is a good habit to acquire in preparation for the toddler stage. To help prevent scalding, lower the temperature on your water heater to 120 to 130 degrees. Water at 120 degrees takes five minutes to burn; water at 140 degrees takes only six seconds.
- Do not drink hot liquid such as coffee while holding your infant in your arms. A sudden movement could knock your arm, spilling the hot drink on the baby.
- Install babyproof latches on all cabinets that hold poisonous products, medications, soaps, glue, liquor, toiletries

such as nail polish or hair spray, paint, mothballs, and gasoline. Keep poisonous plants from child's reach. A good way to recognize potential hazards is to literally crawl around your home. Seeing the world from a child's perspective helps identify problem areas.

- Inspect your baby's toys for small parts that your child could pull off and swallow. Do not leave a baby or child to play unsupervised.

- Choking and suffocation are the most common causes of preventable death in children under one year old, according to the AAP. Do not prop your infant's bottle or feed baby lying flat on the back. Do not hang a pacifier by a string; it could get wrapped around the baby's neck. As baby begins to crawl, keep a watchful eye for small items on the floor such as pennies, buttons, pins, and other things that almost certainly will end up in the baby's mouth.

- Never lay your infant on his or her tummy on a pillow, beanbag, or other cushiony surface in which he or she could suffocate.

- Learn cardiopulmonary resuscitation (CPR). Call your local American Red Cross for classes in your area.

Keeping Your Perspective

As many things as new parents worry about, there are some worries of which you can let go, particularly when your baby is a little older and more used to this great big world. For example, older babies no longer need to be swaddled for comfort. Similarly, most are content and safe sleeping on their tummies or backs, rather than on their sides as they did for the first two or three weeks.

When your baby was brand new, you were very careful about the skin. By the time baby is a month old, unless his or her skin is extremely sensitive, you probably do not have to be as cautious. Most pediatricians suggest that it is no longer necessary to wipe your baby's bottom with only water. Baby wipes are just fine for the average infant. The third month is a good time also to try to switch over to your regular laundry detergent, if you wish. Wash one of your baby's shirts with your own. When baby wears it, check to see if a reaction to the stronger soap develops. If not, then that is one less thing to worry about.

One very common condition that babies get that you do not have to worry about is cradle cap. Although harmless, cradle cap can look pretty yucky, and it may bother parents who think that their babies look unclean. To make you feel better, you can rub off cradle cap to some degree. To do so, massage a little baby oil into the affected area and leave it on your baby's scalp for several hours. Before shampooing, rub the cradle cap with a soft-bristled toothbrush or fine-toothed comb. Then shampoo using a mild soap, shampoo, or dandruff shampoo. Cradle cap rarely persists beyond the first year.

The Tiniest Best Friend You Will Ever Have

Learning to enjoy your baby is one of the most important aspects of this stage of development as a family. For the first three or four weeks, you can be so concerned and overcome with responsibility that you forget to enjoy the baby! Caring for a baby is still a big responsibility, but now you are starting to get some of the rewards.

It is important to do little things to enjoy your baby. Looking at babies while they are asleep is wonderful. Picking them up and holding them and smelling them and cuddling them are the best. One activity that almost all babies seem to love is observing their moms or dads around the house. Babies need to get out of their cribs during the day, and one of the best ways for your baby to interact with you is to put him or her in a portable infant seat or infant car seat that you can move from room to room.

If you are working in the kitchen, you can put your baby on the counter while he or she still is tiny and relatively immobile. Tell the baby what you are doing and why. Although babies don't understand, they appreciate hearing your voice. New moms often laughingly tell me that they expect their children to take over the household chores by the time they can walk because as infants the children were subjected to a constant banter of "This is the way Mommy does the dishes" and "Now Mommy is folding the laundry." Always keep in mind that no matter where you have baby in the infant seat, the surface must be sturdy so the seat does not topple.

Having your baby in an infant seat is an excellent way for you to take a shower while your baby is awake. Put baby in the seat on the bathroom floor. Shower noise is very soothing to babies. They can watch you, and you can talk or sing to them.

Another good place to put them is the stroller, which you can wheel around your house so you can be together. New babies can play on a blanket on the floor if your house is not drafty and there are no pets around. Putting your baby on a blanket is a good way of getting an infant used to having his or her own space and not being held all the time.

If you plan to use a playpen, it is helpful to get your baby used to it around the second or third month. (See chapter 8 for a list of items to buy for the older baby.) If your baby thinks of the playpen as a happy place early on, he or she will adjust easily when you must use it for safety reasons later on.

The End of the Beginning

When your obstetrician gave you the A-okay to leave the hospital, you might have wondered how you could go six weeks without seeing this special person who was your mentor and comforter during your pregnancy and whose hands were the first to hold your baby in this world.

Now you can see that those six weeks fly by. It is time for the final cut of the umbilical cord and on to the rest of your life. Because the six-week postpartum check is a special time, you may begin anticipating it several weeks before it is scheduled. You may try to shed a few pounds before going back to the office or may think about what you want to wear so that you make a good impression. Most new moms bring their babies to show them off for the same reason. These feelings are healthy because they indicate your readiness for that important breaking-away step.

In your doctor's office, you are examined to see whether you have healed completely. You are weighed, and unlike your reaction in the pediatrician's office, the weigh-in may discourage you. Moms who nurse may carry about ten extra pounds of weight until they wean. Even moms who are bottle-feeding probably have not regained their prepregnancy figures by this time either. Your obstetrician may ask how you are feeling emotionally. Any postpartum depression that you may have suffered usually should have ended by this time. If not, it is appropriate to raise the issue during your exam.

Provided that you receive a clean bill of health, your obstetrician probably will permit you to resume your previous level of activity. Getting back into shape seems to be a priority with most new mothers. On a daily basis, I see new moms in my neighborhood walking along the street with their partners by their sides and their babies in front or back packs. Sometimes she has the baby attached to her, and sometimes he is carrying the load. They are walking briskly, and they are talking and laughing. As I see them, I think to myself what a wonderful time they are spending together. They are both getting their exercise, and they are sharing good times together as a family.

As I am a fan of special exercise classes during pregnancy, I like to see new moms participate in mother-and-baby exercise classes, if not for the physical benefits then for the emotional well-being. Held at various community and women's centers, these classes are geared for postpartum women; everyone is big-breasted and flabby, so you do not feel self-conscious as you might if joining a regular gym. Moms are expected to bring their babies and cater to them when necessary. Whatever contact you can have with other parents with children around the same ages will give you the best outlook on life that you will find anywhere.

If you are breast-feeding, your obstetrician may already have suggested that you continue to take your prenatal vitamins. Discuss with him or her your nursing plans and how they might affect your diet and your menstrual cycle. Finally, this is the time to ask your doctor about the resumption of birth control, if appropriate. Most couples resume sexual relations around this time.

Sex and Marriage: Keeping Them Intact

When I decided to call this book *The Miracle Year*, I was referring to the miracle of starting a family. If you are like many new parents, you might think it is a bigger miracle that you and your partner are still together after the turmoil your baby has brought into your relationship.

It comes as a surprise to many couples that babies can wreak havoc on grown-up relationships. Babies demand a huge amount of physical and emotional energy that once went into the marriage. (I use the term "marriage," but clearly what I have to say applies to all long-term relationships between moms and dads.) The result is that new parents often are tired, and their relationship gets shoved to the back burner. Neglect eventually may lead to resentment and anger.

Not only are babies energy-sappers, but they force both partners to make new demands on the other. Women expect their partners to act like fathers, and men have the same expectations of "mom." Yet neither of you really knows what you are doing, so you both fail to meet all of the other's expectations. Not only does a baby cause your partner to be less available to you, but you may observe that he or she is not doing a perfect job in his or her new role.

Alongside the psychological implications of parenthood, there are the physical side effects of pregnancy with which to contend, including changing feelings about your body during and after pregnancy and birth. Breast-feeding adds yet another dimension to the way your body has changed. In turn, your sex life is different, and that change takes some getting used to. In some ways, you have to get to know each other all over again, because truly, you have become different people than you were when you met.

Expectant couples often ask me how to be good parents. Of course, I cannot describe specifically what must come from one's heart. However, I can share some of the insights that I have discovered. The first is to nurture your relationship as you do your baby. If you do not do it for yourselves, do it for your baby. The greatest gift you can give your child is to love each other.

I am reminded of a conversation that I had with a group of new moms who expressed to me great concerns about their relationships with their husbands after their babies were born. Fathers are so much more involved today than ever before, yet no one teaches men how to become dads. "All my husband was taught was how to count 'One-and, two-and . . . breath and relax,'" one mom said. "I had an epidural, so for us all his counting seemed pretty useless." Another mom was feeling pressure to resume work soon after her baby was born, and she was unprepared for how difficult it would be to leave him in day care. She said her husband did not understand her mixed emotions.

All of the women agreed that despite the popularity of childbirth education classes, there is not enough information available to young couples to prepare them emotionally to become a family. Childbirth classes are just that—lessons on how to give birth. Some teachers also include what to buy for baby's layette or how to choose a car seat, as if these are the most critical decisions of the coming months! The focus is mainly on the pregnancy, the birth, and the baby. No one mentions the hardest part: becoming a family.

No matter how strong your relationship is as a couple, it changes tremendously when you have a child. You face an enormous adjustment, probably as big as any adjustment could be. What keeps throwing parents off in meeting this challenge is that when they realize they are having a baby, the excitement of having a child becomes their focus. They may forget about each other and about the relationship. This is a mistake because, like a baby, a marriage needs nurturing to flourish. Love withers when it does not receive any care.

True, the baby dominates a lot of your conversations and your shared experiences, but couples need to get to know each other again once the baby is settled into their lives. Share some happy times without the baby, if you can. Bringing the focus back to the marriage is a sign of growth. You can do this by taking time out of each day to be together without the baby to talk or just hold each other until you feel comfortable again. Sex may or may not follow, depending upon how you both are feeling.

Sex may be a sore point for new parents, both literally and figuratively. I urge you to discuss your concerns with your obstetrician and with each other.

If you worry that because of your baby you do not have the time to work on your relationship, I must say to you that *it is essential to make time*. Perhaps you cannot do so for the first month or two until you feel more comfortable with your baby, but by the time three months have passed, strengthening your relationship needs to become a priority.

I have had the pleasure of meeting so many interesting young couples in my parenting classes. One that stands out was a sportswriter and his wife. This young man asked so many questions and took so many notes, one would think he was conducting an exclusive interview with Babe Ruth. He said that he wanted to "do the right thing" when his baby came. As luck would have it, the baby arrived in June, just three weeks before the Wimbledon tennis matches that he was assigned to cover. It was an annual trip that he and his wife usually extended into a vacation. When the baby arrived, the couple decided to bring him to Wimbledon, too.

When I spoke to the sportswriter several weeks later, he told me that the trip had been a great success. His baby was healthy, and his wife had little trouble taking care of the infant while staying in a hotel near London. After the tennis matches, the family stayed on for a few days. They even saw the musical *Cats*, and his wife nursed the baby throughout the performance!

I share this story to illustrate the importance of fitting your baby into your family, not the other way around. At first when the baby is very young, this is difficult to do. Extra precautions have to be taken if the infant is ill or needs special care. In the beginning, there is so much learning going on and so much interference from other people that it is nearly impossible to live normally.

Once you are more used to the rigors of parenthood, however, you can begin to integrate the baby into your routine. Your life-style need not change that drastically. If you want to go for a stroll or a weekend camping trip, there is no reason why your baby should not be part of it. So many things in life are more enjoyable if you can just tuck your baby in your arms and do your thing.

Weaning: Finding the Best Path for You and Your Baby

When the time comes that you are getting out of the house regularly, you may want to begin the process of weaning your baby from the breast to a bottle. There is no perfect time for weaning. In fact, weaning can be done gradually and partially over several months, if that suits your needs. I have known many working moms who weaned their babies to bottle-feeding quite early, but who continued to nurse in the mornings before work and in the evenings after they returned home. Your body can accommodate whatever schedule you choose.

Weaning is most comfortable for you and your baby if it is done gradually over several weeks and if you continue to give your baby lots of love and attention when he or she is not on the breast. The easiest feeding to give up first is the one during the middle of the day. At that time, offer a bottle instead of the breast. Hold your baby as you would during nursing so that baby feels the security that he or she is used to. If you introduced a supplement bottle when your baby was younger (three weeks is a good age), you should have no difficulty making the transition.

If your breasts fill up at feeding time, express just enough milk so that you are comfortable. If you pump too much or let the baby suck, your body may become confused and produce more milk. Cold compresses on the breasts offer temporary relief, and cutting back on your fluid intake will serve you well in the long run.

After your baby is used to one feeding from a bottle, you can begin to eliminate the other breast-feedings, one at a time. The schedule that I recommend is to make the switch first during midday, followed by the early evening and the morning. Last to go is the late-night feeding. This schedule is only a suggestion, however. Many moms like to nurse before they head to work in the morning. If you feel this way, there is nothing wrong with continuing to do so.

Some moms delay weaning because it makes them feel sad. They feel that they are giving up the last vestige of their baby's early infancy. These feelings may be compounded by hormonal changes in the mother's body following weaning, which can cause some mild depression similar to that which occurs postpartum. Try to remember that weaning is a natural stage of your baby's development and of your growth as a parent.

Going Solo

Along with getting more sleep and starting to see some positive feedback from your baby, getting out of the house seems to make most new parents feel human again. Whether you go with your baby or just the two of you, it is refreshing to be a part of the world again. When you are walking as a new family in the local shopping mall and you catch the eyes of other moms and dads out with their children, you can smile at each other knowingly and share the silent language that only parents understand.

Once you are confident going out as a family, you are ready for the next major milestone in your development as parents. Usually four to five weeks after the baby is born, it is time for mom to take off an entire day from the baby. Dad's job that day is to stay at home.

New dads almost always call me on their first "dad's day home." "I didn't have a clue what it was like being home all day until my wife went out and left me with the baby," they say. "Boy, she really has a full-time job here."

This one day can have more impact on a new dad than any other experience he has with his baby until this time. It is a very special, often frustrating time, but when the day is over, dad feels good to have survived, more confident about his parenting skills. Of course, mom feels better after a day going solo or with friends, too. It is amazing how good it feels not to have both arms full with your baby and the diaper bag and everything else you seem to need.

As your baby gets older—and perhaps you continue "dad's day home" at least once a month or so—you find that you gradually rise above the confusion that surrounds you after you bring your baby home. The tremendous burden of caring for a newborn starts to ease as you are sleeping more and feeling better physically and emotionally. The first time you do something together that reminds you of the good old days—such as bringing home flowers or sharing a bottle of wine in bed at night—it feels wonderful.

These special times that you share as a couple need to be preserved and encouraged to make you both feel that you are someone special in your own right, and not just your baby's mom or dad. My husband used to bring me flowers once or twice a month with a note saying simply "I love you" or "You mean so much to me." Moms can send flowers to dads, too. When flowers arrive at the office, dad may be embarrassed, but he almost always is secretly thrilled. Leaving notes under the pillow or in each other's briefcases or lunch bags is another special and inexpensive way to rekindle your romance.

On the Road Again

Getting out eventually means getting away, and there is no better time to travel with a child than before the five-month birthday, when baby starts to jiggle and wiggle. Road trips are ideal because most little babies cannot stay awake in the car, no matter how bumpy the road or how loud the radio. The motion rocks them to sleep, and they have been known to stay that way for hundreds of miles.

The only concession you have to make to your baby is to stop regularly for feeding time. As much as I hate to say never, never take your baby out of the car seat to feed while you are on the road. This is an invitation to tragedy and it is illegal, to boot. Trips in the car—and the feeding stops—can be so much fun that there is no reason to flirt with disaster. When you stop, all of you can take a break. Perhaps you can arrange to stop at a scenic lookout or a quaint roadside café and use the time that you have together to find your new identity as a family. When on the road again, buckle up!

On occasion, new moms have complained to me that having the infant seat properly installed—facing backward in the center of the back seat—means that they cannot see their babies to make sure that they are all right. If this bothers you, try taping a compact mirror to the rear window or ceiling so you can see your baby's reflection in your rearview mirror.

One If by Air . . .

Until your baby is five or six months old and eager to move around, traveling by airplane is fairly simple with proper preparation and planning (and a pack mule for all your baby's stuff). There are several things you can do to make your trip go smoothly. First, it is reassuring to have the name of a pediatrician at your destination. Your pediatrician may know someone or may be able to put you in touch with a hospital for a recommendation.

Second, when traveling by air, alert the airline that you are traveling with an infant. Sometimes airlines can make special arrangements if you need extra help with your luggage, for example. Airlines offer preboarding for families with infants, as well. When talking with the reservations agent, request bulkhead seating. This gives you extra room for the diaper bag and other equipment.

The Federal Aviation Administration is looking into requiring a safety device similar to a car seat for infants on airplanes, but as of July 1990, no regulations have been approved. Nevertheless, some experts believe that using an infant car seat during the flight is the safest way for baby to travel. (Overseas flights may offer on-board bassinets; ask your ticket agent if a bassinet is available.)

While in the airport, you might find that you are less encumbered if you are carrying your baby in a front pack. A diaper bag with a built-in changing pad also is useful at times such as these, particularly during long layovers and flight delays. A portable umbrella-type stroller may be your best bet for traveling and is useful during long treks through airports. Generally, small foldable items such as these can be carried on board, but check with the airline first.

Once you are on board, keep a small bag at your side in which you can keep a small toy, a bottle of water or formula, facial tissues, or a burp cloth, changing necessities, and a warm blanket. Babies generally do best on flights if they are sucking on either a bottle or the breast during takeoff and landing. The sucking and swallowing movements do the same thing for babies that you do to "pop" your ears. If your baby is asleep or does not want to suck, having a bottle on hand is a good idea in case baby wakes during the departure. Your pediatrician also may suggest a dose of acetaminophen prior to takeoff and landing.

What to Bring on a Long Trip (and what to leave at home)

- Diapers: Enough for the trip plus one extra day, in case you get stuck in an airport. You can buy the rest of the diapers you need almost anywhere in the world. If you use cloth diapers, many diaper services have reciprocal service or what they call "vacation packages" for temporary service. Call your local diaper service for more information.
- Diaper bag with all its goodies (ointment, wipes, moist towelettes, plastic disposal bags, lap pads, burp cloths, etc.).

- Front pack or baby carrier, which is especially helpful for trekking through airports and at other times when you need your hands free.
- A few small toys: musical ones do double duty for playtime and sleeptime.
- Formula: A day's supply of formula, bottles, nipples, etc. if you use them. Powdered formula is ideal as long as you also bring bottled water. Also convenient are disposable bottles, but try them first because your baby may not take to a different nipple. If you use a formula that may not be easily available, ask your pediatrician about using a substitute. If you must stick to that particular brand, you may need to bring it along.
- Baby acetaminophen: In case of travel discomfort, falls, emergencies. Consult with pediatrician first.
- Pacifiers, if used.
- Receiving blanket: In case you are in air conditioning, and for use as pillows or padding when your baby needs to sleep.
- Lap pads.
- Car seat, unless you can rent one at your destination: Also bring a locking clip to secure the seat to the car's seat belt (see car seat instructions); you may need it even if you are borrowing or renting a car seat. The American Red Cross runs an inexpensive, short-term car seat rental program through which car seats are available nation-wide. See Resource List for more information.
- Nipple and bottle brushes and dish soap, or you can buy at your destination. Check with your pediatrician about sterilization. Dishwasher box for nipples and rings may be useful.
- Mild baby soap, or you can purchase at destination.
- Crib or bassinet, usually can be rented at a hotel or rental service.
- Crib bumpers: these are bulky and should stay at home. Weave towels in and out of crib slats as a substitute.
- Familiar blanket, doll, sheepskin, etc. to make your baby feel at home.
- Clothing: Depends on climate and length of stay; a hat is a necessity if you plan to be outside at all. Take a change of clothes for baby in the diaper bag. You would not want

grandma to see baby for the first time with vomit down the front of his or her shirt.
• Baby sunscreen.
• Nursery needs: Aspirator, rectal thermometer, baby scissors, petroleum jelly.

On a regular basis, parents ask about traveling to different time zones. Unfortunately, babies do not understand time changes and generally are thrown entirely off schedule by long-distance travel. Not only do they have to contend with the time change, but if you are visiting the baby's grandparents, for example, you have got to be very generous in letting the grandparents enjoy the baby. All the fuss contributes to the disruption of the baby's eating and sleeping habits, but because of the tremendously important role of the grandparents, I think it is worth it.

The good news is that it only takes about three days to get babies straightened out once they get back home. It is worth it to have had a special time while you were gone.

Vacation Precautions

Whether sallow or fair, babies' skin is extremely sensitive to the sun and must be protected at all times to prevent sunburn now and skin cancer later. In the summer or in warm climates, use a baby sunscreen all over the body and face. Make sure your baby wears loose-fitting, light, long-sleeved clothing or is covered by a lightweight blanket. A hat is a must at all times during the day. Try to keep your baby out of the sun altogether during the hottest times of the day (about 10:00 A.M. to 2:00 P.M.).

Unless you suspect that your infant may be allergic to bee stings or other bug bites, you probably do not need to protect baby with netting. If the baby is bitten, however, expect the area to swell, turn red, and itch. Wash the area with soap and water and apply calamine lotion. (However, check with your pediatrician before applying any lotions to your baby.)

A common skin condition in the warm summer months (and in winter when baby is bundled too warmly) is prickly heat. Caused by clogged sweat glands, prickly heat can be very itchy, although it is not considered a serious condition from a medical perspective. To make your baby feel more comfortable if he or she does have prickly heat, try patting the affected area (usually on the neck or chest) with cornstarch or a solution of bicarbonate of soda mixed with water.

Young babies can be taken into swimming pools for brief dips, but they should never be submerged. While some parents believe that babies can and should learn to swim at an early age, the American Academy of Pediatrics recommends that children under the age of three years stay out of swimming classes. Lessons tend to give parents a false sense of security when their children are in the pool. Of course, never leave an infant unattended in or near a pool. Infants and children can drown in as little as two inches of water.

If you are traveling with your infant to a cold climate, try to anticipate any special arrangements that you may have to make to keep the baby warm and dry. Extra hats and blankets always seem to come in handy.

The Trials and Triumph of Returning to Work

"I just cannot imagine what it is going to be like turning my baby over to a stranger." I hear that comment so often from new moms, yet more than one half of all mothers with children under the age of three are working outside of the home.

It is hard returning to work and leaving your baby, there is no doubt about that. Even the most dedicated career woman may find that she is drawn to staying at home with her baby in ways that she never imagined. She may feel this way some or all of the time, temporarily or on an ongoing basis. Truly, it is hard to predict how you will feel about your career and your sense of motherhood once your baby comes.

Some mothers find that they are so attached to their infants that they take them to work with them (if their employers permit). This solution may be fine while the baby is very young, but do not expect to do so long-term. By the time babies are six or seven months old and start crawling, it is hard to confine them and keep them amused. In addition, placing children into day care for the first time at six or seven months of age often causes great difficulties for the children. Children at this age experience great separation anxiety and are extremely attached to their mommies. If possible, start day care before your baby is five months old; he or she will adjust better at a younger age. The when and wheres of day care are appropriate matters to discuss with your pediatrician.

Some moms who return to work may find the transition doubly hard to make if they are not satisfied with their baby's day care. In fact, if you cannot find a caretaker with whom you feel comfortable, returning to work can be intolerable. Think of the time that you invest in finding good day care as an asset to your career: If you are confident about your baby's care, you are freed up to be more productive and creative on the job. The mother who is satisfied with her baby's sitter often says, "It is still hard for me to leave my baby, but at least he is well cared for." That feeling of confidence can make or break you.

When the workday is done, some moms find that they have a hard time making the transition from career woman back to mommy. The switch in mentality and priorities from professional to wife is hard enough, but when you have to come home and relate to an infant, it is not unusual to feel awkward. I have spoken to many working moms about this problem, and I have found as many solutions. Each person and each baby has different needs and different ways of meeting them. In general, it seems helpful to ease into your role as "mommy" by taking twenty to thirty minutes of quiet time with your baby at the end of each work day.

A second credo that I have heard is that working moms have to come to terms with a house that often is messy. The hamper is full and the carpet may need vacuuming, but unless you can afford a housekeeper, you cannot sustain your former level of tidiness once the baby comes and you return to work. By the same token, I hope that you and your partner are not disappointed when you realize that on some nights, the best you can do for dinner is to order a pizza. During this busy time of your life, something has to give. This is perfectly normal, and the sooner you accept your new reality, the happier you are.

Finally, remember that there are times when both of you have nothing left to give, and your best intentions to provide your baby with "quality time" after work are thrown out the window. Perhaps it is a reaction to the "super-mom" concept, but I find it unfair to place additional performance pressure on a mom who is eight weeks postpartum, whose baby may not be sleeping through the night, and who has to return to a nine-to-five job.

One mom called me to share the story of her return to work at eight weeks postpartum. After a long first week, she found herself totally exhausted. After picking up her baby from day care and returning to her messy house, it was all she could do to sit on the couch with her baby in her arms. Then like a sudden storm she began to sob. The more she cried, the more guilty she felt for subjecting her baby to her sadness instead of playing with him and giving him all that "quality time" she had heard about.

She said that she cried for about ten minutes until she finally felt relieved. When she looked at her baby and smiled at him, she was astonished to find that he smiled back. "It was the best lesson. I learned that it is okay for kids to know that we can be sad and that we can be happy after being sad," she said. This lesson is so true. Children can understand happiness and sadness, and we do not need to protect them from our feelings. If they can see their parents in up and down moods, it teaches them that it is okay to show emotion and talk about their feelings.

Coming Into Your Own

As you head into the next stage of your development with your baby, I hope you are satisfied with your metamorphosis into motherhood or fatherhood and only occasionally yearn for the carefree days of youth. Life is, and will continue to be, very, very different from now on. It is the life about which you used to dream.

New parents often ask me, "Lanie, when will life get back to normal?" This *is* normal! This is the new definition of "normal." As the months go by, you will be more comfortable and enjoy your new "normal" status. As hard as it may be to believe, you may even enjoy each and every month better than the last. Soon you may not even remember what the old "normal" was.

8

❖

The Miracle Revealed: Living with Baby from Three to Six Months

When I reflect upon the great changes that young people experience during the miracle year, I am reminded of a (true) story about a woman with three magazines on her coffee table: *Cosmopolitan, Better Homes and Gardens*, and *Parents*. There was a time in this woman's life, she told me, when she could not wait until the latest issue of *Cosmopolitan* arrived in her mailbox. She defined herself then in terms of her personal achievements and her relationships with men. Then the woman married, and not long afterward, *Better Homes and Gardens* became her "priority mail." It catered to her needs as she and her husband fixed up a new home. *Cosmopolitan* found its way from the coffee table to her nightstand. With the arrival of a baby several years later, *Parents* took the place of the other two magazines as the most-coveted piece of reading material in the house.

The story does not end here, however. This woman told me that by the time her baby was five months old, she looked forward to reading all three magazines each month. "They all are important to me again because now that I am settled in my role as a mom, I can turn my focus back to my husband and myself. I am not thinking only about the baby anymore," she said. "I am interested in my house again. My husband and I have our romance back on track. Having a baby revealed more sides of myself than I have ever known. The better I feel about myself, the more I can offer my family."

The transition from new mom or dad to a more mature, family-oriented parent is an important one. It is healthy for you to "find yourself" once again after you and your baby have settled into a routine. By the same token, couples have to put their relationship on the front burner again, not selfishly, but because it is critical to the health of the family. Couples who maintain a loving relationship with one another make better parents.

Step eight to becoming good parents is to re-create yourself based on your new definition of "normal." Who have you become over the course of the miracle year? How does the "new you" fit into your family and vice versa? As you become comfortable with the answers to these questions, you can reestablish your emotional and physical ties to your partner while at the same time recognizing the importance of your family. Your relationship and your family have lives of their own, but they are integrally linked. Finding a balance is essential for the long-term survival of both.

When you reach this stage of your development as a family, both you and your baby are well on your way to a relationship that grows more wonderful and multidimensional every day. I have to admit that of all the babies that I have known and loved over the years, I have not found any to be cuter than the three-to-six-month-olds. To me, at this age, they are more lovable than at any other time.

I am sure that you are aware of how wonderful your babies are as you observe them achieving new and exciting things each day. You probably are so crazy about your baby that you almost cannot fathom that this is the same stranger whom you brought home only a few months ago. You have learned to care for this child, to recognize its likes and dislikes, and to comfort it. You know the baby's personality, what games he or she enjoys, and whether the baby prefers roughhousing or quiet, thoughtful play. You see your child as a "real person."

At the same time, your perspective is sure to have improved now that you are sleeping more and that you likely have returned to some of the pursuits of your "former life." Your body has recovered from the trauma of pregnancy and childbirth. You look good again. You feel good, too, because you are settled and confident about your new status.

By this time, working moms are used to their hectic routines. Chances are that any kinks in your day-care situation have been ironed out, and the family is functioning smoothly. The routine has to leave you feeling content at the end of the day. Moms who are not working may have joined mom-and-baby exercise classes or play groups in which you have met other women who are experiencing motherhood for the first time. Dads, too, find that fatherhood gives them more in common with many of their co-workers and acquaintances at the gym, church, or temple. New parents seem to find each other with a special radar. They love to talk about the trials and trivialities of having a newborn and the triumph that they feel at having survived the first three months.

Most of all, though, it is your baby who makes you feel so special and joyful. Each day brings new developments as baby learns to swat at a crib gym, reach for a rattle, and wrap those little fingers together like a tiny knot of rope. A few weeks later, the whole body gets into the act as baby learns to "swim" on land, roll over, and laugh out loud with so much enthusiasm that he or she wriggles all over with excitement. Your baby is a constant source of amusement.

As parents, you are so proud each time your baby does something new. Never mind that he or she is four or five months old; your baby seems so grown-up to you and so different from that helpless, sleepy little infant of only a short time ago. There is not a parent on earth who does not interpret his or her baby's progress as a sign of genius.

This chapter looks at some of the developments of the final months of the miracle year and how those developments contribute to your becoming parents. Growth is rapid and exciting for baby and for parents during this time. If the depth of your relationship can keep pace with the development of your baby, you will have built the solid foundation necessary for a healthy and happy family.

A Major Milestone

If there is one development of your baby's first six months that is an especially proud milestone for both parent and baby, it is when baby can sit up on his or her own. It is the greatest thing in the world—until you see baby's first step or hear the first word or see your "baby" handed a high school diploma or walk down the aisle at his or her wedding. . . .

Sitting up is a significant development for your baby because it encourages social interaction. Being upright changes a baby's perspective, and it changes the way parents and others react to the baby, too. Babies really become part of the world when they can see so much more than they could while they were reclining. It is a great leap forward in many ways.

Very often parents of babies who are between three and six months of age ask me what new equipment they may need once the baby is sitting up (or close to it). Here is what I suggest.

Jumper

Your baby probably is starting to outgrow the swing by now and will enjoy playing in a jumper, which is a slinglike seat that hangs on an interior door frame. The baby can bounce up and down in the jumper, which most babies love to do. Baby can look around from a safe vertical position, and will love for you to applaud this acrobatic prowess. Most jumpers are good until baby reaches about twenty-five pounds.

Playpen

If you plan to use a playpen in which your baby can entertain herself or himself in relative safety, it is advisable to get your baby used to it from a young age. Four-to-six-month-old babies usually can play with their toys in a playpen for at least fifteen to twenty minutes at a time. The most popular playpens on the market are made of nylon mesh. Most models fold up easily and are light enough to carry.

Full-size Car Seat

Depending on size, your baby may be ready to move into a large car seat by six months or so. There are many car seats available, and all of them sold in stores meet federal safety standards. You can check if any seats have been recalled by contacting the Auto Safety Hotline operated by the National Highway Safety Administration. They will send you a list of seats that are unsafe. (See Resource List for hotline number.)

Walker, High Chair, Back Pack, Bicycle Seat

To use all of this equipment properly and safely, your baby should be able to sit up quite well on his or her own, which most babies cannot do until they are about seven months old. You do not need to purchase this equipment until that time.

While it is fine to encourage your baby to play alone in a playpen or jumper, I feel it is equally important to play and to interact with the baby. This is an age at which you can begin real play and exploration. For example, six-month-olds are old enough to learn to play catch with dad. You can roll a small ball toward the baby and encourage baby to roll it back. Some babies like rougher games, such as "flying" in the air or wrestling on the carpet.

This is a time for exploring, too. I advise all parents to help their babies touch and taste and smell a variety of things around the house. Show babies their faces in the mirror, let them feel the smoothness of the mirror, the soft carpet, daddy's scratchy face. One of my favorite games is to sit a baby on my lap and blow soap bubbles above the baby's head. Babies love to try to grab the bubbles as they float down, and they delight in popping them.

Take cues from your baby and tailor your play to the baby's moods and development. Peek-a-boo, for example, is an excellent game to teach your baby at this age. Try covering your face with a towel or bending down beside your baby's crib while he or she is in it. When you reappear and smile and shout "Peek-a-boo," your baby will delight in your trickery. The child also is learning that you exist even when you cannot be seen. When this cognitive leap of understanding is made, you will have taught the baby a very important concept and reinforced lessons about trust.

Food: A Whole New Way to Play

Sometime between four and six months, when your baby is beginning to sit more erect, your pediatrician probably will suggest that you begin to supplement your baby's diet with solid foods. You may see this milestone as a personal triumph—that your baby is growing up and starting to eat like a "real person." In fact, most new parents are very proud when their babies learn to eat solids. That feeling lasts a few months until you discover how much simpler and neater it was just to give the bottle or breast. By the time your baby is a bit older, you probably will spend the better part of the day cleaning up after mealtimes, scraping puréed carrots from the floor and the ceiling, not to mention trying to wipe the meal from all the crevices in your baby's ears, under the chin, between the fingers . . .

Despite the mess, feeding time can be fun, especially if your baby likes to eat from a spoon. (This is a great occasion for the video camera, by the way.) Most pediatricians suggest that you start your baby on rice cereal mixed with breast milk, formula, or water. Begin with one to two tablespoons of very soupy cereal that is at room temperature or slightly warmed. Place a small amount on the tip of a baby spoon and hold the spoon to your baby's mouth so that baby can lick the cereal. Most babies seem to push out more cereal than they take in when they are learning to eat. This reaction does not mean that they do not like the cereal; they just have to learn to accept food from a spoon and likely will do so quite well after a few weeks of practice.

Some moms like to use a baby spoon covered with a soft plastic. I think this is a good idea to help soften the feeling on your baby's gums, particularly when teething begins. These spoons are dishwasher safe.

Most babies like solids, but if your baby does not, do not force things. If baby fusses or balks at solid food, try feeding again at another time or on another day. Establishing good eating habits and attitudes is extremely important.

Once your baby is accustomed to cereal and has shown no adverse reaction to it, your pediatrician will advise you on what foods to give next. Diet for the first six months generally consists only of rice cereal, fruits, and yellow vegetables. It is advisable to give your baby only one new food at a time for at least three to four days. That way, if a reaction to it develops (a rash, nausea, or vomiting), it is easier for you to trace the cause of the reaction than if you had a variety of new foods from which to choose. Of course, some babies are allergy-prone, so always check with your pediatrician for dietary guidelines tailored to your baby's specific needs.

Honey should be avoided during the first year because it may contain bacteria that causes botulism in infants. Teething cookies and biscuits also should not be given until the baby is older than six months because bits can break off and cause choking. If your baby seems to have some early teething discomfort, offering a wet, frozen washcloth may soothe the gums. The baby is probably always quite wet from drooling so he or she will not mind the washcloth melting. Some moms rub their baby's sore gums with an ice cube, liquor, or a teething gel. Consult your pediatrician for his or her opinion.

Your baby can begin to learn to drink from a cup at about five months of age. Begin with water or diluted juice in a small cup with or without a lid. The lids are useful in teaching babies to accept liquid from a vessel similar to a bottle (or breast). They suck on the lid as they do a nipple. It is a good idea to try the cup right before bathtime so your baby will not need an extra changing when he or she becomes a sticky mess.

There is one "side effect" of feeding that I must mention, and that is changes in bowel movements. Fresh mashed bananas was one of the foods that I fed my first baby. When I changed her diaper later that day I noticed tiny "worms" in her bowel movement. I rushed her to the pediatrician only to find that these were not worms at all, but residue from the banana! Because of their immature digestive system, babies often have feces that come out looking similar to what went in. Do not be surprised if when you feed your baby carrots or beets the bowel movement is orange. As long as there are no traces of blood or persistent diarrhea, everything probably is proceeding normally.

Teach Your Children Well

Many moms with whom I keep in contact after they leave the hospital report that they notice a different kind of behavior in their babies somewhere between the third and sixth month. During these months, you, too, may notice that your baby becomes more alert and aware of the environment. This awareness is what motivates the baby to reach for things, to touch and taste whatever is within reach, and, eventually, to crawl and walk so that he or she can expand this environment.

Along with showing a burgeoning sense of self, your baby may behave in ways that you do not understand and that may worry you, as many parents do. For example, some babies quickly feel comfortable in their expanding world and can play for twenty or thirty minutes or even longer without giving a thought to what is going on around them. Others are frightened by their new awareness at times and may cry suddenly in the midst of play. They may need to know that their caretaker is there with them. They may cry until they are picked up or comforted.

Some babies are more at ease in a familiar place than they are with strangers. Many pediatricians tell me that when they see babies who are between five and six months old, the babies often look at them suspiciously. Pediatricians are very careful in dealing with this reaction, which they deem "separation or stranger anxiety." This very common emotional passage of infancy starts at around this time and may continue well into the first year as your baby learns to distinguish familiar faces from unfamiliar ones.

It is useful for parents to observe their babies' behavior patterns and to talk about how they want to handle bouts of fear or crying, for example. Is it acceptable in your home for your baby to screech just because he or she likes to hear the sound of his or her own voice? Is it acceptable in other people's homes? How long do you let the baby cry if you know that he or she is fed and dry? Should you make a distinction between what you consider legitimate crying and what you fear may be the precursor to a temper tantrum? By the time your baby is crawling, you have other important decisions to make, so setting up the ground rules now (even if they are in your mind only) helps establish a pattern for the future. For example, do you remove fragile objects from the coffee table, or do you teach your child to respond to "No" and redirection? Either approach is okay, so long as you are consistent.

Consistency is particularly important when you are trying to break bad habits, such as using a pacifier. When baby starts solid food is the ideal time to remove the pacifier because the instinctive need to suck has diminished. When parents ask me, I advise them to remove the pacifier entirely. Your baby may fuss for a day or two, but will soon learn to comfort himself or herself by some other means. If you do not take measures to remove the pacifier now, you may find yourself crawling on the floor in the middle of the night in search of a lost pacifier for months to come.

From three to four months of age, most babies are sleeping through the night for about ten to twelve hours and are taking two naps during the day. That is how it probably will be for most of baby's first two years. However, babies sometimes fall into their old habit of waking up at night, particularly after they have been ill.

On a regular basis moms tell me that their babies are suffering through their first cold or flu, and that they have begun waking during the night. When a baby is sick, this disruption cannot be avoided. However, the moms tell me that after the illness has subsided, the babies continue to wake. This is the start of a bad habit that should be discouraged as quickly as possible. You may have to listen to your baby fuss and cry for a few nights, but the baby will soon relearn to comfort himself or herself, and your schedule will return to normal.

Baby-sitter Basics

In addition to finding regular day care, most parents by this time have the names of at least one or two baby-sitters who can watch the baby for a few hours at a time in the day or evening. Although you may feel like an ogre giving your neighbor's teenaged child the third degree, baby-sitters should be screened to the degree that you feel comfortable leaving them in charge. Ask about their experience with infants, if they have had any training in CPR, and if they have an adult whom they can call in case of an emergency or if they need help or advice.

Once you find someone, it is useful for them to spend some time with your baby while you are at home, particularly if your baby has shown signs of stranger anxiety. After a couple of brief visits, your baby may learn to recognize the sitter and feel less frightened when you leave.

When you are planning an outing, be sure you leave your baby-sitter the following information:

- A phone number where you can be reached.
- The phone numbers of your pediatrician, local hospital, paramedics, and poison control hotline.
- Your address, phone, and nearest cross streets, all of which the sitter will need to report to 911 during an emergency.
- Feeding instructions, including where to find bottles and food, how to prepare them, and when your baby is expected to eat.
- Baby's schedule for naptime, bedtime, etc.
- Where you keep diapers, extra blankets, change of clothes, special toys, and fire extinguisher.

In case an emergency does occur, your baby-sitter must have written permission to obtain medical treatment for your baby. The following form can be copied and left in a prominent place.

Authorization for Treatment of Minors

(I) (We), the undersigned, parent(s) of (insert name of your baby here), a minor, do hereby authorize (name of baby-sitter here) as agent for the undersigned to consent, in advance of any specific diagnosis, to be treated by a physician, to submit to any X-ray examinations, anesthetic, medical or surgical diagnosis or treatment and hospital care that is deemed advisable by, and is rendered under the general or special supervision of any licensed physician or surgeon.

The authorization should be signed by both parents and notarized. To cover all your bases, make sure that copies are available at your day-care center, at home, at grandma's house, and anyplace else where your baby may be without you. While you are thinking about legal matters, I urge you to take the time to prepare a will, with the help of an attorney, and to obtain a birth certificate and Social Security number for your baby, as well.

Mommy Friends and Baby Friends

When you have a baby, your relationships with your friends are bound to change. Sometimes this change is for the better when, for example, your best friend has children of her own and the two of you share an additional common interest. Fathers, in particular, find that they relate to other fathers quite differently than they do to childless men.

Too often, however, I hear about new moms whose relationships with those closest to them have soured. More often than not, a former friend without children of her own has difficulty being sympathetic to the plight of the new mom. "I am sick of hearing about what color *it* is or how hard or soft *it* is," I was told by a woman whose older sister had just had her first baby. "All she talks about is the baby."

So many of us live far from our families that it is a shame to let a child ruin a good adult relationship. The key is for new parents to understand what their friends are feeling and to be sensitive to the changing dynamics of the friendship. Old friends may want to see your baby and may be amused by the baby's antics, but regardless of who they are, they are not as interested in every detail about your baby as you are. Remember to ask about their lives, to talk about the topics that attracted you to each other before the baby came. Nurturing a friendship is almost as important as nurturing a marriage.

On the other hand, there is no reason you should not indulge your overwhelming interest in your baby once in a while. The perfect way to do this is to join a parents' support group, or what we call in my community a "play group" for your baby. A play group is a group of parents and their babies who meet on a regular, ongoing basis to get to know each other and enjoy activities together. Some towns have established play groups through the local community or religious center. If not, it is very easy to form your own group among the new parents in your neighborhood or whom you may have met in your prenatal classes.

The groups seem to work best if they meet at least weekly with the moms and babies, and then perhaps monthly with the dads, as well. These groups offer invaluable friendships, advice on baby care from more experienced moms, and an excellent network for baby-sitters and good buys on diapers and infant clothing. Once your babies are older, you can plan many fun outings, invite local child-care experts to speak, or even meet without your babies once in a while.

To help your play group to function smoothly and to avoid spreading illnesses, I recommend not bringing your baby to a group meeting if the baby has a fever or has had a fever the night before, has diarrhea or has had it in the last twenty-four hours, has a rash (unless it has been diagnosed as noncontagious), has been vomiting in the last twenty-four hours, has a congested cough or yellow/green runny nose, or has been diagnosed or is acting sick in any other way.

Keeping the Home Fires Burning

Your baby play groups may be the first place that your infant learns to socialize with other "little people." This experience is a healthy one, and the baby will learn by leaps and bounds as he or she heads into the second half of the first year.

Children need two basic ingredients to grow up to become productive and happy adults. First, they need roots. Roots are nourished by loving and nurturing parents and by interaction with grandparents and members of the extended family. Roots grow even stronger when a child has a sense of community awareness and commitment, and religious and cultural education. Those roots are the foundation upon which we build our lives.

Second, children need wings to help them strike out on their own and become independent human beings. Parents can help children find their wings by teaching them to believe in their own abilities, to nurture and care for others, and to love and trust themselves and their world.

When your baby was really tiny, you began to teach about self-worth when you held the baby close and looked into his or her eyes. You spoke to the baby gently. You smiled, and soon the baby learned to smile back. You made goo-goo eyes like you did when you first fell in love. Without even knowing it, you kept your baby's "emotion tank" full.

As your baby grows and begins to become more interested

in the world, he or she may seem less interested in you. The baby may wiggle and squirm when you hold him or her, anxious to explore on the floor or in the grass. Even so, hugging and touching and eye contact remain important, and parents need to make time for them every day. Physical closeness is a magical gift that children need all their lives.

The bottom line is that your parenting determines how your children feel about themselves and their world. What you teach your children and what you show them about relationships within your family is what they take with them as they grow.

"The family is our brain baker, the place for a leavening of our spirit, and the creator of how we will see our world, how we will interpret it, and what we will choose to do about it. . . ." writes Dr. Paul Pearsall, author of *The Power of the Family*. "Being placed in charge of God's unfinished product and assuming the sacred and awesome responsibility of providing a place for spiritual development is a task that requires more human, physical, and emotional energy than any other human or animal activity. Babies emphasize in the most sobering and awesome way that we ourselves are far from 'finished' in our own development, that we still need raising, and that family is a necessity."

I cannot agree more with Dr. Pearsall's eloquent words. Nor can I overestimate the importance of the road upon which you embarked more than a year ago when you decided to have a baby. You created a human being, and that human being is entirely dependent upon you and your family to help him or her become an adult. Your child will grow in your image. Your child's future is both your burden and your gift.

9

❖

The Miracle,
the Gift

When I close my eyes and envision the perfect family, I see a mommy and a daddy sitting on a hand-stitched quilt on the floor of their living room. Their six-month-old baby is between them, trying his best to sit up on his own. His balance not yet perfected, he tilts sideways, then forward, wobbling back and forth as much for the fun of it as to learn how to do it right. Sometimes he catches himself and proudly sits erect as if master of all he surveys. Other times, he falls over, only to roll quickly onto his belly, furiously kick his legs, and eagerly look to his parents to sit him upright again.

Eager for their child to communicate with them, mommy and daddy play peek-a-boo, covering their faces with a small blanket and asking baby, "Where's Mommy? Where's Daddy?" Each time they remove the blanket and shout "Peek-a-boo," their little baby beams with delight, displaying his toothless gums and laughing out loud. He is learning to trust, to communicate, and to have fun.

"The Miracle Year" comes to a close when your baby reaches the six-month birthday. In a sense, it is a sad time because never again will you witness the miracle of life with virgin eyes. At the same time, I urge you to celebrate this milestone as a beginning, a beginning of a lifetime of happiness together.

Maybe you can prepare a cupcake or a muffin with half of a candle on it. Sing happy half-birthday to your baby and to yourselves. Rejoice in how far you have come! So much has happened in such a short time!

You might wish that I would congratulate you on reaching the final step on what I have called the parenthood stairway, but I cannot honestly do that because, as your family grows, there will be many more steps to climb. Learning to be a good mom or dad is a lifelong process. It is a process that places different demands on you at different times in your child's life.

That said, the ninth step is to accept that as much as you have learned, there is much more to know. Parenting is a challenge every day. It is reason to laugh and to weep, to rejoice and to despair, to learn and to grow. You have a solid foundation with which to meet the challenge. I applaud each and every one of you for having come so far and having the conviction to go even further.

It is late, and your baby is asleep in his or her bed. The baby is breathing steadily and contentedly, a few specks of frosting from the half-birthday cupcake dotting those porcelain cheeks. You, too, are in bed, listening to the quietness in your home and reflecting upon the changes that have occurred in the past twelve months. The changes are so wondrous that you might not have believed them if you had not lived through them yourself. Your memories are many and varied.

Do you remember how you felt the day you could no longer zip up your favorite jeans? Did you feel special, instead of fat, even though you ate an extra scoop of ice cream that day because you were "eating for two"?

Do you remember when you announced that you were going to have a baby? To your parents? At the office? To your best friend? To anyone who would listen? Did you feel as if you could just take off like a rocket, you felt so great?

Do you remember how strangers used to make a fuss over you when you started to show? Do you remember your friends who have children wanting to tell you all the details about childbirth? Are you amazed that the rigors of labor and delivery were so important?

Do you remember shopping for maternity clothes and thinking everything was so huge? Do you remember outgrowing your maternity clothes? If that did not make you want to get it all over with, nothing did!

Do you remember planning your baby's nursery? Selecting wallpaper? Trying to choose a crib and a stroller, and not having a clue where to begin? Do you remember worrying how expensive this whole year was going to be? Were you right?

Do you remember wondering if you were going to have a boy or a girl? Do you remember how hard it was to select a name for a baby you did not know?

Do you remember receiving your baby's layette at a baby shower or from your favorite aunt who lives far away? Did you fold each garment and place it gently in your baby's dresser? I will bet that you do not have time to be so careful now!

Do you remember the first time that you heard your baby's heartbeat and the first time you felt the baby kick? Do you remember placing your partner's hand on your tummy when the "three" of you lie in bed? What did it feel like to know that you were carrying a life inside you? Is it not a miracle that the life that was inside you is sleeping in the room next door right now?

Do you remember the apprehensive giggles in your childbirth classes? When the man in the back fainted during the birth video, and you hoped you would not be next?

Do you remember visiting the hospital, looking in the nursery window, and imagining that someday your baby would be sleeping in there? Were you envious of the new moms in their postpartum rooms? Were you nervous?

Do you remember how you "fell in love" with your obstetrician? Did you memorize the office phone number? What did you tell him or her when you felt your first contraction? Was it as you had imagined? Did you laugh on your way to the hospital?

Was it fun, scary, chilling, exciting? Does it seem as if it happened forever ago?

Do you remember your labor bed? Holding hands with your coach and your labor nurse? What was it like in the delivery room? Will you ever forget that day, every moment of that hour when your baby was born? When you first heard the baby cry? When you felt the baby's skin against yours? Are you amazed that holding the baby is more wonderful every day?

Do you remember the sweet aroma of your hospital room, filled with flowers from well-wishers? Wasn't your baby so tiny then? Didn't the baby seem utterly frail and helpless? How did it feel to accept the responsibility for the baby's care? Do you still stare at your baby in total amazement that he or she is yours and that he or she loves you so much?

Do you remember your first night home alone with your baby? What was it like to feel so insecure, so overwhelmed, so afraid? Did you want to return to the hospital? Did you wonder what you had gotten yourself into?

Do you remember being in a daze, when one morning blended into another and you never had a chance to change from your pajamas? Did you ever want it all to go away and wish for the security you once knew? Are you amazed to find that your "new normal" is just as good as the life you used to live? Is it better?

Do you remember your first visit to the pediatrician? Who were all those parents in the waiting room? Were you one of them? Did the nurse call you to the office as "so-and-so's mom or dad"? Were you surprised when she spoke to you about your son or daughter?

Do you remember the first night that your baby slept for five hours? How did it feel to wake up and not be totally exhausted?

Do you remember your baby's first smile? Was that one smile worth all the time and energy you had put into your baby thus far? Did you fall madly in love?

Do you remember the concern you felt about leaving your baby with a sitter? What crazy things did you imagine might happen? How was your first day back at work? Do you feel better about it now?

Do you remember realizing that you still are yourself, that you are part of a couple and a community and that your baby need not be your sole focus in life? Are you surprised at who you have become?

All of those milestones led to the birth of your baby and a brand-new human being. As important, they signify the creation of three people who can change the world by changing the way the world sees the family.

You have the power to effect change in the next generation by teaching your child the importance of family. You can show your child that parents can work out their differences rather than toss in the towel right after a fight. You can show your child what real love and friendship mean in a family and how they can sustain you through hardship. You can be role models so that your child can grow up in a nurturing family in which the parents' relationship is strong and sustaining.

Parenting is an endless process that begins with the steps that you have learned:

- Practice honest and respectful communication.
- Appreciate each other as friends, recognizing strengths and weaknesses.
- Work together to make decisions that serve the family and implement your decisions with consistency and team-work.
- Reconnect with your own parents and families and invite them to share in teaching your child about his or her past and the world.
- Be flexible, and let each other grow into the role of mommy or daddy as you learn a varied repertoire of baby-care skills.
- Nurture each other and lend a hand to one another as you face the challenges of parenthood.
- Believe in yourself and each other so that you may enjoy each other and your baby.
- Do not forget the importance of finding a balance between the needs of your relationship and those of your family.
- Enjoy each challenge and recognize that not only are you learning new parenting skills, but ultimately you are giving your child the gift of family.

Although it is not an easy job, parenting is, in the long run, quite straightforward. Love each other and your child. Trust each other and your child. Rely on your instincts, on common sense, and on the moral underpinnings of your faith to help you make the best decisions for your child. The bottom line is not to be afraid to give up some of yourself for the good of your family. You give up some of yourself when you fall in love and when you marry, but when you give to your family and to your child, your return lasts a lifetime. Your miracle year may be over, but the true rewards of parenthood are just beginning.

RESOURCE LIST

American Academy of Pediatrics (AAP)
141 Northwest Pointe Boulevard
Elk Grove Village, IL 60007
800-433-9016

American College of Nurse-Midwives
1522 K Street, NW
Suite 1120
Washington, DC 20005
202-289-0171

American College of Obstetricians and Gynecologists
Resource Center
409 12th Street, SW
Washington, DC 20024
202-638-5577

American Red Cross
National Headquarters
17th and D streets, NW
Washington, DC 20006
202-737-8300
or check phone book for local chapter

Center for Auto Safety
2001 S Street, NW
Suite 410
Washington, DC 20009
202-328-7700

Department of Health and Human Services
Social Security Administration
800-234-5772
800-325-0778 (TDD)
or check phone book for local office

Depression After Delivery
Postpartum Support, International
P.O. Box 1282
Morrisville, PA 19067
215-295-3994

International Childbirth Education Association (ICEA)
P.O. Box 20048
Minneapolis, MN 55420-0048
612-854-8660
800-624-4934 (Book Center)

La Leche League International
9616 Minneapolis Avenue
Box 1209
Franklin Park, IL 60131-8209
708-455-7730

National Highway Safety Administration
400 Seventh Street, SW
Washington, DC 20590
Auto Safety Hotline (for car seat recall information)
800-424-9393

National Sudden Infant Death Syndrome Foundation
10500 Little Patuxent Parkway
Suite 420
Columbia, MD 21044
800-221-SIDS

National Women's Health Network
1325 G Street, NW
Washington, DC 20005
202-347-1140

U.S. Consumer Product Safety Commission
1750 K Street, NW
Washington, DC 20207
800-638-CPSC

INDEX